WELLBEING, EDUCATION AND CONTEMPORARY SCHOOLING

Wellbeing, Education and Contemporary Schooling examines the role of wellbeing in schools and argues that it should be integral to core policy objectives in health and education. The whole school focus chosen is conducive to the review of wellbeing in schools, and assists in better understanding the complex relationships between learners and teachers in policy contexts, where every teacher has a responsibility for learners' wellbeing.

By exploring a range of debates about the nature of wellbeing, the book shows how children's wellbeing is inseparable from their overall capacity to learn and achieve, and to become confident, self-assured and active citizens. Drawing on international curriculum developments, it considers the ways in which wellbeing could reshape educational aims in areas such as outdoor learning and aesthetic imagination, helping to inform programmes of professional learning for teachers.

Separated into six parts, the book covers:

- philosophical perspectives on wellbeing
- policy perspectives on wellbeing
- professional perspectives on wellbeing
- practice perspectives on wellbeing
- future prospects for wellbeing
- a personal perspective on wellbeing.

Examining ways in which wellbeing can become a central component of the ethos, culture and environment of contemporary schools, *Wellbeing, Education and Contemporary Schooling* is an invaluable guide for all students, teachers, researchers and policy makers with an interest in learning, teaching and children's wellbeing.

Malcolm Thorburn is Lecturer in Physical Education at the Moray House School of Education, University of Edinburgh, UK.

WELLBEING, EDUCATION AND CONTEMPORARY SCHOOLING

Edited by Malcolm Thorburn

Routledge
Taylor & Francis Group

LONDON AND NEW YORK

First published 2018
by Routledge
2 Park Square, Milton Park, Abingdon, Oxon OX14 4RN

and by Routledge
711 Third Avenue, New York, NY 10017

Routledge is an imprint of the Taylor & Francis Group, an informa business

British Library Cataloguing in Publication Data
A catalogue record for this book is available from the British Library

Library of Congress Cataloging in Publication Data
A catalog record for this book has been requested

ISBN: 978-1-138-66848-5 (hbk)
ISBN: 978-1-138-66849-2 (pbk)
ISBN: 978-1-315-61859-3 (ebk)

Typeset in Bembo
by Deanta Global Publishing Services, Chennai, India

MIX
Paper from
responsible sources
FSC
www.fsc.org
FSC™ C013985

Printed in the United Kingdom
by Henry Ling Limited

CONTENTS

PART VI
A personal perspective on wellbeing 203

ACKNOWLEDGEMENTS

Collectively, as authors we would like to thank a number of people for their help, encouragement and support during the preparation of this book; in particular, the many students and teachers in schools who have shaped and informed the development of our respective views and who have been so generous with their time. We are also extremely grateful to the educators, academics and policy makers who we have shared dialogue with us over many years and who have offered us constructive feedback on our various writings and presentations. Likewise, we thank the student teachers at our respective universities with whom we have been able to discuss various ideas over many years. Lastly, we would like to thank Annamarie Kino from Routledge for her editorial assistance throughout.

LIST OF EDITORS AND CONTRIBUTORS

Editor

Malcolm Thorburn is a Lecturer in Education and Physical Education at the Moray House School of Education, University of Edinburgh. He joined the University of Edinburgh after teaching for twenty years in Scottish secondary schools during which time he held a number of curriculum development roles at local authority and national level. His main research interests are on professional change issues for teachers, especially in terms of conceptualising educational values, curriculum planning and pedagogical practices. Malcolm has published widely on aims and values, policy and professionalism and planning and practice issues in education and wellbeing specifically.

Contributors

Claire Cassidy is a Senior Lecturer in Education in the School of Education at the University of Strathclyde. Claire's research interests are closely aligned and lie in Philosophy with Children; children's human rights; and concepts of child/childhood. She is the course leader of the Postgraduate Certificate in Philosophy with Children. She is interested in how facilitating children to think well might support them to live well.

Donna Dey is a Lecturer in Education at the University of Dundee. Donna is interested in the implementation of health and wellbeing and child-centred policies in secondary education and the impact they have for learners and teachers. Prior to joining the University of Dundee, Donna spent thirteen years as a Principal Teacher of Guidance and Pupil Support in Scottish secondary schools.

Christine Doddington is a Senior Lecturer in Education at Cambridge University working within the discipline of philosophy of education with specific interest in the arts. Christine's research has a theoretical focus with a strong emphasis on exploring theory's direct significance for educational practice and policy. Her recent writing focuses on aesthetics and the ethical nature of teaching and learning, drawing on Deweyan and Aristotelian notions such as phronesis and somaesthetics.

Sue Ellis is a Professor of Education at the University of Strathclyde. Sue is interested in how literacy research, policy development, knowledge exchange and implementation interact with, and impact on, teacher development. Sue has a strong commitment to research that directly supports improved literacy outcomes for disadvantaged pupils. Recent projects include developing the Strathclyde Literacy Clinic approach to initial teacher education and researching initiatives to close the gap in attainment between children from high-income and low-income households. Sue is co-Director of the Centre for Education and Social Policy, which is located in the International Public Policy Institute of Strathclyde University.

Christine Forde is a Professor of Leadership and Professional Learning in the School of Education in the College of Social Sciences at the University of Glasgow. Christine's research focuses on two areas in education; first, leadership and professional development and second, gender and equality. Christine works regularly with national bodies and organisations in education on issues related to leadership and teacher development. Christine was part of the General Teaching of Scotland working group for the revision of the professional standards for teaching research.

James MacAllister is a Lecturer in Education at the University of Edinburgh. James's research is primarily concerned with how philosophy informs and influences education policy and practice. James's publications to date include philosophical explorations of the following areas: school discipline, teacher authority, ethical issues in educational research, the Scottish curriculum, the role and importance of the body and emotions in education, physical education, epistemology and education and education and human agency. James is also interested in conducting empirical investigations that explore teacher philosophies and innovative school discipline practices.

George MacBride is an Honorary Senior Research Fellow in the School of Education at the University of Glasgow. Before this George taught in Glasgow secondary schools for thirty years in support for learning. George was long-serving Convener of the Education Committee of the Educational Institute of Scotland (teacher union). He was a council member of national curriculum agencies and a member of government working groups on curriculum, assessment and school qualifications. More recently, George has carried out commissions for the Scottish Government and Education Scotland related to assessment and curriculum development and contributed to research projects in the School of Education on sustainable innovation in school curriculum and assessment.

Maeve O'Brien is Senior Lecturer in Sociology and Head of the School of Human Development at Dublin City University. Maeve's research interests are in the areas of care and relationality and their significance in education today. Maeve worked in Dublin's inner city as a primary school teacher and home school liaison co-ordinator for almost twenty years and issues around equality and social justice remain to the fore in her research and teaching. Maeve is currently working with a Human Development colleague on the NCCA (National Council for Curriculum and Assessment) conceptual framework document for the new post-primary, junior cycle wellbeing curriculum.

Monica Porciani is an Associate Lecturer in Health Promotion at the University of Strathclyde. She has also contributed two chapters on Health and Wellbeing in Primary Education and Secondary Education for a best-selling guide to Scottish Education.

Vivienne Smith is a Lecturer in Primary Education at the University of Strathclyde. Vivienne's interests are in language, literacy and literature and she has published both on the development of children as readers and on children's literature. She is particularly interested in positioning reading as a creative and social practice and in the role of texts in this process: how texts encourage readers to think, to reflect and to moderate their understanding of reading itself. Recent projects have included a Creative Reading project with Inverclyde Council and Reading Fictions, a series of seminars funded by the British Academy.

Ina Stan is a Senior Lecturer in the Learning Development Unit at Buckinghamshire New University. Ina is currently conducting research on the impact of group work on the learning experience of learners in higher education. Her previous research has centred on 'The Well-being and Outdoor Pedagogies Project', which involved an in-depth examination of teaching and learning focused largely around the outdoor 'classroom'. The study examined a variety of issues including concepts of risk at primary school level: body image, wellbeing and participation in outdoor activities and the impact of the messages that children and teachers received from government policies and media.

LIST OF ABBREVIATIONS

ACARA	Australian Curriculum, Assessment and Reporting Authority
ASN	Additional Support Needs
CEO	Chief Executive Officer
CFE	Curriculum for Excellence
CLPL	Career Long Professional Learning
CoPI	Community of Philosophical Learning
CYPCS	Children and Young People's Commissioner Scotland
GDP	Gross Domestic Product
GIRFEC	Getting it Right for Every Child
GNH	Gross National Happiness
GTCS	General Teaching Council of Scotland
HWB	Health and Wellbeing
ITE	Initial Teacher Education
LLPA	Lifelong Physical Activity
LTS	Learning and Teaching Scotland
NAPLAN	National Assessment Programme – Literacy and Numeracy Programme
NHS	National Health Service
NSPCC	National Society of Protection to Cruelty of Children
OECD	Organisation for Economic Cooperation and Development
PISA	Programme for International Student Assessment
PIRLS	Progress in International Reading Literacy Study
PSD	Personal and Social Development
PSHE	Personal, Social, Health and Economic (education)
PwC	Philosophy with Children
P4C	Philosophy for Children

SCCC	Scottish Consultative Committee on the Curriculum
SHANARRI	Safe, Healthy, Achieving, Nurtured, Active, Respected, Responsible and Included
SHRE	Scottish Health and Relationship Education
SNCT	Scottish Negotiating Committee for Teachers
SPEN	Scottish Peer Education Network
TIMMS	Trends in International Maths and Science Study
UNCRC	United Nations Convention on the Rights of the Child

INTRODUCTION

Malcolm Thorburn

The rise of wellbeing in contemporary schooling

In recent years there has been a heightened interest in educating for personal wellbeing; the belief that even when beset by troubled economic times schools can be a civilising force for good and can help make young people's lives more fulfilling and meaningful (Layard and Dunn, 2009). However, in this comparatively new area of curriculum priority, there remains a relative lack of analysis of wellbeing values; of how learners can flourish in schools and of how wellbeing aspirations can articulate with realising wider societal ambitions (Coleman, 2009). Furthermore, evaluations of practice have often privileged easily measurable constructions of wellbeing (e.g. levels of academic attainment or attendance) in ways which make it difficult for policy makers and teachers to review the extent to which learners' wellbeing is thriving in schools (Eccelestone, 2012). What we often have therefore is a situation where school and curriculum mission statements cite the educational centrality of learners' wellbeing but where the extent to which learners are *well* remains insufficiently explored and understood (Soutter, Gilmore, and O'Steen, 2011). These claims are consistent with recent United Kingdom Government reporting from the All-Party Parliamentary Group on Wellbeing Economics (2014) where one of four key recommendations was that wellbeing needs to be seen as integral to core policy objectives in health and education, and where a child's mental health and wellbeing is inseparable from their physical health and from their overall capacity to learn and achieve. In this light, we consider wellbeing within *Wellbeing, Education and Contemporary Schooling* to be a feature of individual happiness and welfare as well as a feature of community connectedness. This whole school focus is designed to be helpful when reviewing wellbeing within mainstream schooling contexts, with all that this entails for analysing the often complex relationships between learners and teachers and between contemporary schools and the communities they serve.

Wellbeing and contemporary schooling contexts

Due to the focus on wellbeing in current schooling contexts, we try to note rather than become overtaken by wider societal concerns which span various fields of study e.g. economics, psychology, sociology, the health sciences (Soutter *et al.*, 2011; White, 2011). Therefore, issues such as the rise of consumerism, the decline of the nuclear family, changing leisure interests, changes in patterns of employment and the demise of religious beliefs are not considered in detail, important as all these influences are. Nor do we become overly drawn towards specific public health targets such as improving diet and increasing physical activity rates. We also resist the temptation to argue for a radical restructuring of schooling and instead recognise and appreciate the constraints which often impact on how schools function. By noting these matters in advance, we consider greater insights can be gained into learners' wellbeing within the context of everyday school life: in short, capturing in more vivid detail the range of factors which help and hinder personal progress (Thorburn, 2014). This focus also supports the notion that providing increased opportunities for wellbeing can help schools thrive as human places where activist-inclined teachers proactively engage with the full range of responsibilities they have.

The book: Structure and context

Through its overall focus on *Wellbeing, Education and Contemporary Schooling*, the book invites student teachers as well as academics, teachers and policy makers to critically consider ways in which wellbeing can become a more central component of the ethos, culture and environment of contemporary schools and a more prominent concern of learning and teaching. It pursues these aims through a six-fold focus on:

- *a philosophical perspective on wellbeing*, which focuses on theoretical constructs of wellbeing and learner-centred perspectives on wellbeing;
- *a policy focus on wellbeing*, which focuses on the global rise in prominence for wellbeing as well as attempts to evaluate health and wellbeing progress in schools;
- *a professional perspective on wellbeing*, including a focus on professional implications for school leaders, subject teachers, teachers in training and teachers with an enhanced pastoral remit for wellbeing;
- *a practice perspective on wellbeing*, focusing on the relationship between cognitive and emotional aspects of learning and their possible impact on learners' wider achievements;
- *a future prospects focus on wellbeing*, which considers the part wellbeing might play in reshaping educational aims, especially with regard to outdoor learning and aesthetic imagination;
- *a personal perspective on wellbeing,* which adopts a longitudinal perspective on wellbeing, where reflection and review are used to recall professional experience.

The perspectives unpacked

Wellbeing, Education and Contemporary Schooling seeks to engage with on-going *philosophical, policy, professional* and *practice* debates about the nature of wellbeing and of how wellbeing intentions and aspirations can become a more central part of schooling. Thus, the aim of the various perspectives is to focus specifically on school-based attempts to emphasise how wellbeing could become a more visible feature of everyday learning and teaching and a more vibrant part of the ethos and culture in schools. This focus is important due to current variations in how well schools are achieving these aspirations (Formby and Wolstenholme, 2012; Thorburn, 2014), plus as Dewhirst *et al.* (2014) note, teachers-in-training are often poorly prepared for their role in supporting wider public health priorities.

Philosophical perspectives on wellbeing

If personal wellbeing is to be a foundational cornerstone of children's education, then what are some of the main conceptual issues which professional educators would benefit from reviewing? The first two chapters in the book aim to help in this respect by introducing, reviewing and discussing key issues associated with the promotion of wellbeing and how wellbeing can coherently articulate with whole school aims and in so doing become a more unifying component of education and schooling.

- Chapter 1 by *Claire Cassidy* focuses on 'Wellbeing, being well or well becoming: Who or what is it for and how might we get there?' The chapter calls for an emphasis on 'being' as well as 'wellness', as there is often a disconnection between the aims of education, preparing children for their adult lives and the notion of well*being* at a time when many teachers are working under increasingly performative cultures, where little account is taken of their wellbeing. What is proposed is that, in order to address the deficit model of child as becoming that impinges upon wellbeing, a philosophical approach should be adopted by children and teachers which moves beyond the rhetoric of desiring children's wellbeing to an exploration of what this might mean in terms of wellbeing and living well. The chapter asserts that treating children as in a state of becoming is disempowering for children and proposes that *being* well and living *well* are facilitated through critical reflection and philosophical dialogue.
- Chapter 2 by *Malcolm Thorburn* reviews 'Contrasting concepts of wellbeing and their implications for educational planning'. The chapter argues that even though wellbeing has become more prominent as an explicit educational aim it has rarely been clearly defined or investigated. Subjective constructs of wellbeing (e.g. hedonism, desire fulfilment and life satisfaction theories) which value reflections on personal experiences are contrasted with objective theories (e.g. list and fulfilment theories) which emphasise more the specific societal benefits of wellbeing. In addition, theories which contain a more hybridised mix of

subjective and objective elements are also reviewed. The latter part of the chapter considers the main curriculum planning and pedagogical practice implication for schools in taking forward contrasting theories of wellbeing.

Policy perspectives on wellbeing

Wellbeing as a distinctive universal feature of education is evident in many national initiatives such as 'Every Child Matters' in England and Wales and the 'Getting It Right for Every Child' programme in Scotland. Therefore, schools are now seen as conduits for addressing a plethora of wider concerns about learners' social, emotional, mental and physical wellbeing, as evidenced, for example, by the Social and Emotional Aspects of Learning programme implemented in just under three-quarters of secondary schools in England by 2010. The two chapters considering policy perspectives review wellbeing developments from both a broader societal context and through a detailed national evaluation of the Scottish specific circumstance.

- Chapter 3 by *Malcolm Thorburn* considers 'The societal prominence of wellbeing and its implications for education policy and practice'. In so doing the chapter compares and contrasts recent policy developments in England, Australia and New Zealand in terms of policy direction and the ways in which curriculum arrangements have engaged with various contested points of concern. These include educational-worthiness claims and the merits or otherwise of a skills-based process-led approach for achieving a range of affirmative educational outcomes.
- Chapter 4 by *Malcolm Thorburn* and *Donna Dey* evaluate policy 'efforts to enhance health and wellbeing' in the Scottish context specifically, as in Scotland health and wellbeing is a key responsibility of all teachers. The chapter reviews support for these policy aspirations along with a critique of practice developments. Evidence to date suggests that the strengths of outlining a learner-centred curriculum model have yet to be fully reflected in health and wellbeing becoming a more central feature of learners' learning and an everyday component of teachers' professional lives.

Professional perspectives on wellbeing

On the basis that teaching is a complex and demanding professional occupation, the policy intention of making wellbeing a more prominent feature of education raises a number of professional issues. These are analysed in the professional perspectives section of the book from the perspective of the: school leader, class teacher, teachers-in-training and those teachers who have an enhanced pastoral remit.

- Chapter 5 by *Christine Forde* on 'The school leader perspective: Integrating schools with the communities they serve' reviews the multiple tasks schools face in creating a shared school vision and establishing values within the culture and ethos of school communities in order to enhance wellbeing, engagement and quality of learning. The chapter examines the work of school leaders in building a shared vision and set of values that support a culture of wellbeing from three perspectives: the task of community building; the emotional labour of leadership; and establishing and sustaining the school culture.

- Chapter 6 by *James MacAllister* considers 'The teacher perspective' in teaching wellbeing and the importance of creating capabilities in schools. The chapter is influenced by the work of Martha Nussbaum who, while not opposed to wellbeing measurement, believes that the focus should be placed on creating wellbeing capabilities. In advancing this critique, *real* wellbeing where learners consider what it might mean to live well and be encouraged to think about and shape the future direction of their lives is contrasted with *pseudo* wellbeing where a narrower perspective of wellbeing is adopted as learners are less encouraged to make sense of wellbeing on their own terms.

- Chapter 7 by *Monica Porciani* reviews the 'The teacher-in-training perspective' and in so doing, considers the types of professional and pedagogical support student teachers require during their undergraduate and postgraduate teacher education programmes. This is an important area to focus on as there is often a gap in schools at present between teachers who are seeking greater pedagogical guidance and national curriculum arrangements which expect teachers to use their decision-making responsibilities to take on greater responsibility for their teaching practices.

- Chapter 8 by *Monica Porciani* considers 'The pastoral perspective: Handling sensitive issues' and reviews some of the main issues associated with wellbeing from the perspective of teachers who have an enhanced remit for pastoral issues and for handling sensitive issues in schools. The chapter reviews asset-based approaches to health creation, where building resilience and working collaboratively with other agencies can provide support for learners and encourage teachers to make more effective use of peer education, social-norms education and interdisciplinary learning.

Practical perspectives on wellbeing

As it is anticipated that promoting the wellbeing of young people will improve educational outcomes, it makes sense for schools to take forward a whole school approach to wellbeing, where the culture, ethos and school environment support learners in realising their full potential. In essence, a virtuous circle exists: the better schools promote wellbeing the greater learners' attainment and achievements are likely to be; accomplishments which will in turn foster enhanced wellbeing. As such, constructive relationships between learners and teachers and among learners can increase sense of belonging and feelings of being safe and valued within the wider school community. Sadly, of course, the opposite it true: learners who lack confidence, self-esteem, organisational and problem-solving skills are more likely to have difficulty with academic engagement, achieve poorer outcomes and experience educational disadvantage.

- Chapter 9 by *Vivienne Smith* and *Sue Ellis* considers 'Wellbeing and educational disadvantage' and highlights how different aspects of language, literacy and literature contribute to wellbeing, and the capacity teachers' pedagogical practices have to enhance the social, emotional and intellectual wellbeing of learners. The chapter explores the importance of rich language experiences and interaction in the early years and how good language and communication promotes attachment and understanding of the wider world. The chapter also explores the ability to imagine new experiences and understand old ones coupled with the advantages for all readers of reading, stories and literature for their social and emotional wellbeing. Finally, the chapter considers the pedagogical challenges of designing literacy instruction and of framing learning activities that are fundamentally empowering.
- Chapter 10 by *Maeve O'Brien* considers 'Wellbeing/welfare, schooling and social justice: Caring relationships with students, parents and community' and argues that the professional responsibility of teachers and schools for supporting learners' wellbeing necessitates an ecological and relational approach that takes seriously the life worlds of the young people in their care. Drawing on interdisciplinary perspectives on equality and schooling, and on her own experiences of working in areas of high social disadvantage, the author outlines some of the current challenges and opportunities that present themselves to schools and teachers in providing an educational environment that meaningfully includes parents and community. Current research with final year student teachers in Ireland informs of the real concerns that 'becoming teachers' have regarding relationships with communities and parents. The chapter also discusses concern for teachers' own wellbeing around the limit of their wellbeing work within educational systems that are reformative and performative. The chapter concludes with a call for more inclusive and relational approaches to wellbeing in schools and for the development of a more just society.

Prospects for further enhancing wellbeing

One challenge in reviewing how learners can flourish in schools is that procedural matters associated with policy and practice implementation can come to dominate time and thinking. This is relative to exploring more widely and creatively the possibilities which exist for enhancing wellbeing. The two chapters in this section aim to rise to this challenge through considering extended ways in which wellbeing can flourish in schools.

- Chapter 11 by *Ina Stan* considers 'Wellbeing, outdoor learning and sustainable living' and how experiential and holistic learning approaches could be a viable way to cultivate wellbeing and raise awareness of environmental sensitivities.

The chapter explores a range of theoretical and practical concerns about how precisely increased opportunities to learn outdoors can help young people to reflect on their experiences and make sound decisions, and particularly focuses on the role of the teacher/facilitator during learners' outdoor-learning experiences. The chapter highlights that it should not be assumed that simply engaging children in the outdoors will benefit wellbeing and reviews the need for teachers to be aware of how their approaches and interactions can impact on children's outdoor learning and wellbeing.

- Chapter 12 by *Christine Doddington* on 'Wellbeing and aesthetic imagination' explores the relationships between wellbeing, aesthetic and imaginative experiences and activity. The chapter draws upon the philosophical work of John Dewey and later interpretations of his ideas on somaesthetics and democratic flourishing.

A personal perspective on wellbeing

The book concludes with a personal review on wellbeing in Scottish schools. This approach is based on utilising a longitudinal perspective where wide-ranging contemplations on professional experience are used as the basis for reflection and review.

- Chapter 13 by *George MacBride* on 'Lessons learned or insufficiently grasped?' considers whether schools provide a caring environment characterised by relationships of mutual respect. The author critically reviews ways in which curriculum, school culture and organisation have developed to promote the growth of the attributes and capabilities which are necessary if learners are to respect themselves and others, be confident and at ease with themselves and play active roles in our society. The chapter is informed by the author's experience as a practitioner (a secondary pupil support teacher in Glasgow), as a contributor to national educational policy formation (particularly in curriculum and assessment) and as a contributor to, and user of, educational research.

How the book is organised

The authors have set about analysing developments in wellbeing in their effort to produce interesting chapters that are highly valuable for a professional readership; framed as they often are by reviews of the links between academic analysis and progress in school-based practices. We occasionally use Scotland as an exemplar context in order to help develop a depth of focus, as in Scotland, policy is explicit in detailing how every teacher has a responsibility for health and wellbeing. We balance this with a width perspective which draws on national curriculum developments in England, Australia and New Zealand in order to support our interest in the range of challenges teachers face in incorporating wellbeing into their learning and teaching and in supporting learner wellbeing more widely. We note, in doing so, key differences in the wellbeing-related terminology used in policies and also issues surrounding the measuring of wellbeing. Our general focus in *Wellbeing, Education and Contemporary Schooling* will be in recognising the need to balance definitions of wellbeing which focus most on skills and capacities e.g. managing our emotions, showing resilience and perseverance (see, for example, Weare, 2004) with contrasting views of wellbeing which value more reflective abilities such as self-awareness and perspective (Tiberius, 2008).

The six-fold focus (*i.e. philosophical, policy, professional, practical, prospective and personal*) enables a comprehensive review of *Wellbeing, Education and Contemporary Schooling* to be undertaken in ways which help readers to engage with the text in various ways; for example through proceeding in a linear way from a general *philosophical* perspective to a review of future wellbeing possibilities *(prospect-based)* via a *policy* review of wellbeing possibilities and through reviewing associated *professional* and *practice* implications. Alternately the layout of the perspectives enables a more selective engagement with chapters that reflect readers' particular areas of professional interest.

Wellbeing, Education and Contemporary Schooling aims to complement other Routledge titles in the broad area of education and professional learning, as it invites readers to broaden their own practice through analysis, reflection and discussions within their professional communities. In providing a conduit between theory and practice, *Wellbeing, Education and Contemporary Schooling* is not a toolkit book which advises teachers on what to teach and how to incorporate wellbeing into their learning and teaching, nor does it provide exhaustive details on underpinning theories of learning and pedagogy. However, by merging ideas from theory and practice, the book engages with current debates on the various viable ways in which wellbeing can become a greater and more central part of contemporary schooling with all the benefits this might yield in terms of supporting compassionate education and developing for the future confident, self-assured and active citizens.

References

All Party Parliamentary Group on Wellbeing Economics. (2014). Retrieved from http://parliamentarywellbeinggroup.org.uk/

Coleman, J. (2009). Well-being in Schools: Empirical Measure, or Politician's Dream? *Oxford Review of Education, 35*(3), 281–292.

Dewhirst, S., Pickett, K., Speller, V., Shepherd, J., Byrne, J., Almond, P., Grace, M., Hartwell, D., & Roderick, P. (2014). Are Trainee Teachers Being Adequately Prepared to Promote the Health and Well-Being of School Children? A Survey of Current Practice, *Journal of Public Health, 36*(3), 467–475.

Ecclestone, K. (2012). Emotional Wellbeing in Education Policy and Practice: The Need for Interdisciplinary Perspectives and a Sociological Imagination, *Research Papers in Education, 27*(4), 383–387.

Formby, E., & Wolstenholme, C. (2012). 'If there's going to be a subject that you don't have to do …' Findings from a Mapping Study of PSHE Education in English Secondary Schools, *Pastoral Care in Education, 30*(1), 5–18.

Layard, R., & Dunn, J. (2009). *A Good Childhood: Searching for Values in a Competitive Age.* London: Penguin.

Soutter, A.K., Gilmore, A., & O'Steen, B. (2011). How Do High School Youths' Educational Experiences Relate to Wellbeing? Towards a Trans-Disciplinary Conceptualization, *Journal of Happiness Studies*, *12*(4), 591–631.

Thorburn, M. (2014). Educating for Well-Being in Scotland: Policy and Philosophy; Pitfalls and Possibilities, *Oxford Review of Education*, *40*(2), 206–222.

Tiberius, V. (2008). *The Reflective Life: Living Wisely with Our Limits*. Oxford: Oxford University Press.

Weare, K. (2004). *Developing the Emotionally Literate School*. London: Paul Chapman.

White, J. (2011). *Exploring Wellbeing in Schools*. London: Routledge.

PART I

Philosophical perspectives on wellbeing

1

WELLBEING, BEING WELL OR WELL BECOMING

Who or what is it for and how might we get there?

Claire Cassidy

Introduction

A book called *Wellbeing, Education and Contemporary Schooling* would not have been likely until relatively recently. Indeed, it has only been in the last fifteen to twenty years that the notions of wellbeing and schooling have been in any way aligned. Education *policy makers* around the world seem to have determined that wellbeing should be a central part of learning and life in schools; see, for example, the Scottish, Australian, Canadian, Japanese and Finnish curricula. Traditionally, schools focused on subject knowledge, what children might need to know or be able to do in order to function in the world of work. Take, for example, the teacher Gradgrind from Dickens' *Hard Times*; he wants his pupils to learn facts and only facts, with no allowance for imagination or creativity, and certainly has no great interest in the children's welfare. While this character is somewhat exaggerated, it is based on common features of schooling in the nineteenth, and even into the twentieth, century in Great Britain and beyond. If the likes of imagination, creativity and thinking were not encouraged in the classroom, then there is little to suggest that children's wellbeing would have been of interest. It makes sense to wonder why there has been this shift.

Certainly, the global political context is an important one. In this age of instant access to world news and information, we are able to see and hear about the lives of our fellow humans, we are able to compare and contrast experiences, but this is not perhaps the main reason there has been a shift in thinking about what happens in schools. Biesta (2009) talks about the need to rethink the purpose of schooling. He situates his discussion in the educational context of outcomes and measurement agendas, suggesting that some thought needs to be given to what is valued in education. Note, too, that he is referring to the notion of education as opposed to schooling, with education perhaps being a broader notion than what happens in schools. Biesta cites the likes of the OECD's Programme for International Student

Assessment (PISA), the Trends in International Maths and Science Study (TIMMS) and the Progress in International Reading Literacy Study (PIRLS) as tools that are used to measure elements of children's academic performance that result in the production of league tables where countries can compete against one another. The results of the studies are further dissected in order that individual countries can use these to 'drive up standards'. While Biesta acknowledges that what happens in education should be based on facts, he cautions that we also need to consider what we want from our education systems and asserts that values have a part to play in determining curricula and learning. This leads to questions, therefore, of what education is for.

Given that wellbeing features so strongly in school curricula, especially in the likes of the Scottish *Curriculum for Excellence* where wellbeing is the 'responsibility of all' teachers and, like literacy and numeracy, is a central plank of what is done in schools, it seems that there has been a move in the purpose of schooling. While the language of measurement and outcomes is ever present in educational discourse, this is not restricted to academic subject areas like science, maths and literacy. Indicators of wellbeing have been produced, and measures are in place to gauge children's wellbeing. In Scotland, Scottish Government policy dictates that every child's wellbeing should be considered against them being safe, healthy, achieving, nurtured, active, respected, responsible and included (http://www.gov.scot/Topics/People/Young-People/gettingitright/background/wellbeing). While the need to determine the purpose of education is important, the question of why wellbeing has become more prominent in school curricula remains. It is to this that the remainder of the chapter will turn.

In 1989 the United Nations Convention on the Rights of the Child (UNCRC) was published, and then subsequently ratified by world governments (with the exception to date of the USA). The treaty asserted fifty-four articles designed to protect and advance children's social, political, civil, cultural and economic rights. Taken together, as the Convention states that the rights are not discrete, the wellbeing of children is at the very core. The need for this specific attention to children draws awareness to why there is a contemporary interest in children's wellbeing. Around the time of the UNCRC, a new academic discipline was emerging, that of Childhood Studies. Childhood Studies explores children's lives, but it also raises questions of childhood and what it is to be a child. These are questions that were little discussed before the 1980s, and it is the emergence of notions of child/childhood, it could be argued, that has led to the view that children's wellbeing is important and should be placed within contemporary schooling.

The chapter will consider the concept of child and why it needs to be considered in relation to wellbeing in schools. It will suggest that there is a disconnect between how children are seen in schools, and society more generally, and the notion of wellbeing. The role of the teacher in the promotion of wellbeing will be discussed before turning our attention to an approach, Community of Philosophical Inquiry, which might allow for teachers' and learners' wellbeing that will support them to live well together.

Main findings

Concepts of child

Childhood, as we currently think of it in Western societies, is a relatively new phenomenon (Cunningham, 2006). Children in mediaeval times, suggests Postman (1994), existed in the same social sphere as adults; they had access to the world of work, the world of entertainment, of politics, religion, news and information. The divide between people was determined by class rather than age and it was with the invention of the printing press in the mid-fifteenth century that the difference between children and adults became more pronounced, mainly because people needed to be taught to read and the way in which this could be achieved was to send some individuals – children – to one place to learn, school. To be clear, not all children attended school and children did have their games and interests that were perhaps different to those of adults, but the suggestion is that in advancing the need to read, a distinction was made between two groups in society – children and adults. However, it was some considerable time after the invention of the printing press when the present notion of child and childhood was advanced.

Writing in 1762, Jean-Jacques Rousseau, a Swiss philosopher, published two texts written to complement one another; one was *The Social Contract*, a treatise on the ideal state, and the other, a manifesto for educating children with the ideal state in mind, *Emile*, or *Education*. What is important in *Emile* is that Rousseau sets out five stages through which children progress in their development and within the early phases he advocates that children are breastfed, that their limbs are freed from the swaddling they are wrapped in and that they are encouraged to learn through experience in the natural world, away from corrupting adult society. He proposes that the time of being a child, childhood, is one that should be prolonged, that it is a time of innocence and that it should be protected. This was arguably the first time in Western thinking that childhood was thought of in such terms and, as a consequence, current thought and practice has adopted this perspective. Jenks (1996) would describe this as the Apollonian view of children, that they are born good and that it is society that corrupts them. Cook (2009) suggests that the view of children and childhood illustrated by Jenks' Apollonian child is advanced and perpetuated because adults want to retain and protect their memories of their own childhood, a romanticised notion of happy and carefree times, an image with its roots in Rousseau's *Emile*. Others such as Ryyst (2010, 2015) caution that we should be aware that as adults we view children/childhood through adult eyes and that we do so with the experiences we have had that children have not. As such, we run the risk of wrongly inferring things from our observations. In her 2010 study, Rysst spoke to ten-year-old girls about why they wanted to buy the kinds of clothes that older sisters or pop stars wore as these could be seen as sexy. However, the children roundly refuted this accusation, saying that they simply wanted to look like the people they admired and those people were grown-up.

Stables (2008) offers us three more ways of thinking about child/childhood that are important to the present chapter. The first way to think about children, he says, is to accept that we are all children because we all have parents. The second is determined by one's age, for example, under Article 1 of the UNCRC a child is an individual under eighteen years of age, unless in their country they have attained the age of majority earlier, and this is usually determined by law. The third model is perhaps the most interesting and is linked to the Aristotelian notion of potential; the child is viewed in terms of its becoming. This notion is one that suggests childhood is a time when children are not yet ready to participate fully in the social world, that they have not learned what they need to learn and that their childhood is a time of preparation. It is what Kohan (2011, p. 342) refers to as 'a revolutionary space of transformation'.

Child as becoming

Children are often not seen as complete beings, they are considered to be in a process of transition and they lack certain – necessary – qualities or attributes that adults possess (Kennedy, 2006; Cassidy, 2007, 2012). Adults, it seems, will rescue children from their childhood by preparing them well, by giving them the tools they will need in their future lives, by telling them what and how to think and behave. This deficit view of children is important in thinking about education broadly, and schooling more specifically. It situates children in positions where they have limited voice, power and influence and this is significant when speaking about children's wellbeing.

The language of becoming is evident in much of the theory and practice around education. Curricula are written with a view to giving children the knowledge and skills they will need in the future, mainly in the world of work. Very little, it appears is done in schools that is not about training children for their roles in society when they have full access to it: their moral behaviour is regulated; they are taught how the world works through the likes of education for citizenship for when they will be able to make decisions; and their academic work is assessed, examined and measured in ways that determine their future paths. Take, for example, the *Curriculum for Excellence* in Scotland which states that the aim is for children to become successful learners, confident individuals, effective contributors and responsible citizens (Scottish Executive, 2004). There is some rhetoric around preparing children for now and in their future lives, but the thrust of the documentation is forward-looking. There is, however, an interesting disconnect between the notion of becoming, as evidenced by school systems, structures and practices, and that is in the area of wellbeing.

Wellbeing and becoming

There is much recent literature related to the notion of children's wellbeing, and what it all has in common is that the authors all agree that there is no consensus in offering a definition of wellbeing (see, for example: Amerijckx and Humblet, 2014; Mashford-Scott, Church and Taylor, 2012; Camfield, Streuli and Woodhead,

2009; Bourke and Geldins, 2007). In fact, what several authors have done is note that defining the concept is a difficult one, so they have asked children about their understanding of wellbeing. While there is not, and perhaps cannot be one fixed definition, there is some commonality. There is agreement that wellbeing relates to one's social, emotional, intellectual, mental and physical wellness, linking wellbeing to health. Features that emerge as important in considering one's social, emotional, intellectual, mental and physical wellness are grounded in the likes of relationships, community, respect, agency, autonomy, happiness, satisfaction and being valued.

Thorburn in Chapter 2 articulates different ways in which wellbeing might be considered. Drawing on Mill's notion of maximising happiness is an attractive one when speaking about wellbeing, particularly when suggesting that one does this by advancing one's own pleasure. Children are often accused of pursuing what may be called a hedonistic approach to wellbeing, but this is to omit an element of pleasure for Mill that is important. Certainly Mill promotes the idea of pleasure, but he speaks of higher and lower pleasures, where the higher, more academic pleasures are ones that should be sought in order to be happiest. More base pleasures such as eating chocolate or reading comics will be less likely to induce pleasure – wellbeing – than the more worthy activities advanced through the higher pleasures. Amerijickx and Humblet (2014) criticise such a hedonistic vision, favouring, instead, a more eudaimonic perspective. The eudaimonic life, for Aristotle, relates to ideas of flourishing, where one strives to live the good life, with this life being considered over the entirety of one's life rather than in the moment, as in the hedonistic view. It is no accident that the idea of child as becoming is Aristotelian in nature; the notion of potential for Aristotle was evident and, we may argue, leads one to suggest that wellbeing is something to strive for, that one may eventually attain. This is not helpful. Children exist in the present and, as Kennedy (1992), suggests, the adult is always travelling within the child, they are not two distinct entities. The *being* element of wellbeing is important.

Wellbeing or being well

While wellbeing is somewhat ill-defined, it may be more helpful to think in terms of *being* well, in other words, how one *is* in the world in terms of one's engagement and interaction with it and those who inhabit it. Being well need not refer to one's health, it goes beyond this to consider the individual as part of a larger whole. This is not to suggest that individuals are not important, but humans do not exist in isolation. Taking a broader view of ourselves in the social context allows us to consider why we are interested in children's wellbeing. It may be argued that much of what is done in schools when seeing the child as becoming or potential, is about socialisation, indoctrination or preparation, depending on one's philosophy of education. Ironically, though, under this view children are treated in an atomistic way; the idea that they are connected to others is limited to ensuring that the end product is as required or desired by adults and each child is monitored, assessed, in isolation.

Children's physical fitness and mental health is explored on an individual level, their welfare is considered aside from the welfare of others, children are expected to reflect and evaluate as single entities who have learned how they are to be in society. Of course it is crucial that individual children's welfare is ensured, and there is no suggestion here that this should not be the case. However, the holistic view of the child only seems to pay attention to *the* child rather than the wider whole as humans situated amongst others.

This leads us to return to the question of who or what education or schooling is for. The view promoted by children being treated as becomings would suggest that education and schooling are not for those being educated or schooled, that the goal is to serve the structures already in place, where adults retain power and children aspire to attain that power. Amerijckx and Humblet (2014) suggest that a binary language is used when discussing children's wellbeing; they illustrate it through examples: positive versus negative wellbeing; objective versus subjective; end state versus process; material versus spiritual; individual versus community, but they do not recognise the more invidious binary of adult versus child. It is in the realm of adult that power resides. Adults measure children's successes, be that in their performance in mathematics or their wellbeing. Despite children being able to articulate, even from a very young age, how well they feel, Mashford-Scott *et al.* (2012, p. 238) are correct to highlight that there is a 'belief that reports of subjective wellbeing are less credible or valid than objective measurements of wellbeing or observable behaviours [which] may contribute to a reluctance to seek children's perspectives on their wellbeing'. The emphasis on measuring children's wellbeing is skewed. The purpose of education and schooling, rather than situating wellbeing alongside health or as a discrete area within the curriculum, should be to support children to *be* well, to live the 'good life'.

The good life

The good life does not mean to lead a morally good life, though that may be part of it. Rather, it means to live *well*; this pertains to one's quality of life. There are elements in children's lives that are beyond their control, but the good life need not mean material wealth or possessions. No, let the material lives of children be the work of the state with overall responsibility for ensuring children's welfare. It is no accident that welfare would link to wellbeing, though it is perhaps a better construct in thinking about the elements that are often measured, such as how children are respected or cared for. The notion of the good life, or living/*being* well, affords children autonomy and power in their lives. The good life allows us to see ourselves as part of a larger picture. Bourke and Geldins (2007) suggest that it is problematic to separate the mental from the physical and social. This exposes one of the problems with wellbeing curricula in schools; discrete lessons or interventions to address specific issues or topics are introduced. In the same way that the individual does not exist outwith society, so too, the social cannot be separated from the mental; for example, in exploring with children the topic of feelings and emotions, it cannot make sense not to situate this conversation in the wider picture of how we engage with others and how they might engage with us.

Conrad, Cassidy and Mathis (2015), in discussing the notion of the good life, identify that there are at least two ways to think of the good life. The first is a subjective notion where one determines what is good, pleasurable or enjoyable for oneself. This relates to one's personal preferences and interests. The second and more objective perspective is one that encourages individuals to strive for what will be as good a life as possible for all. The two are not mutually exclusive because the ideas of fairness or equality emerge quickly in any discussion considering the two perspectives. Conrad *et al.* (2015) point to Krebs (1998) who suggests that the two coincide when we emphasise autonomy. The subjective view of the good life allows one some autonomy of realising a life that one considers good. The second perspective of autonomy is such that it guarantees everyone the opportunity to have the autonomous subjective good life they would choose. Nussbaum (2011) talks of capabilities, meaning what each individual is able to be and to do. Important to Nussbaum's notion of the good life is that one is able to conceive of the good and that one is also able to reflect critically in order to participate in the political world, the world of living with others. For Nussbaum, what is important in society, and those providing the structures for that society, is that support is provided to individuals in order that they might pursue and engage in an autonomous, good life. This is not a view reserved for adults, but is a goal for all, regardless of age.

In striving for the good life, in learning to *be* well, the notion of child as becoming is lost. *Being* is in the present, and being *well* is the good life, the good life is for all and is not something one has to wait for until one reaches adulthood. It would be foolish to suggest that children are able to control all aspects of their lives, but the question of how they think about how to live their lives offers them some autonomy which will, in turn, facilitate their engagement in decision-making about their welfare, general wellbeing and health. In supporting children to *be* well, children will be better able to access their rights, particularly in relation to being able to express their views in matters concerning them, as set out under Article 12 of the UNCRC. Ultimately this will impact on every aspect of their lives while allowing that they need not be in a period of preparation; in *being* well, children exist in the now.

Ryan (2012) suggests that living well is aligned to applying one's knowledge, that one uses this 'wisdom' to engage with ethical and practical challenges and decisions about how one should live one's life. She proposes that living well is necessary in order to be wise. School certainly offers children opportunities to gather information, but to be wise one must be able to apply that information, or knowledge. Aristotle talks of *phronesis*, or practical wisdom that 'implies a broad evaluative ability. It tells us what and what not to do' (Juuso, 1999, p. 21). For Juuso (1999), if we are to be wise and life a good life, critical discussion and judgement are vital. Cassidy (2012) asserts that the idea of practical wisdom requires action if it is to have any impact on how one lives the good life. She situates the place for learning how to engage in critical discussion in schools. This is simply a practical measure since the majority of children attend school, making this learning easier. The learning can then be taken beyond the confines of the school and into wider society, since *being* well, the good life, is not reserved for educational institutions. The manner in which such critical discussion might be practised might be through an approach such as Philosophy with Children.

Philosophy with Children

Given that 'It is the task of philosophy to understand the general nature of human beings and society' (Jusso, 1999, p. 13), a philosophical approach to discussion would seem appropriate. There are many approaches to Philosophy with Children (PwC), but they all have their roots in Lipman's Philosophy for Children (P4C) programme (Lipman, 2003; Pardales and Girod, 2006; McCall, 2009; Vansieleghem and Kennedy, 2011). Unlike academic philosophy that is studied in universities or for exams in secondary schools, PwC is practical philosophy. During PwC sessions children engage in dialogue using a structure that encourages them to make connections between others' contributions by agreeing and disagreeing and offering reasons for those agreements and disagreements. The dialogue is philosophical in nature with children discussing issues related to the likes of justice, fairness, art, the environment, time, language or even what makes a good life (see Conrad *et al.*, 2015). The dialogue is facilitated, usually by an adult with some training in PwC and in academic philosophy.

Gregory (2008, p. 7) notes what children will gain from participating in PwC; they will, he says:

> become aware of the aesthetic or the ethical in their own experience, to share their puzzlement and excitement, to inquire into the problematic and to learn how to make their own sense of it all – to formulate their own judgements about what is what and how things relate, and how their corner of the world could be more just, more beautiful, more meaningful.

In effect, what Gregory has shown us is what it means to live or *be* well. What Gregory is proposing is more than the information or knowledge that is gleaned through attending school, he offers a suggestion of what could be achieved if children are given the tools to think for themselves. Such an approach will support children to engage with the world in a way that will work for its benefit.

Living well demands that one lives well with others. Earlier in the chapter there was the suggestion that wellbeing related to ideas of community, relationships, respect, agency, autonomy, happiness, satisfaction and being valued. Practising PwC addresses each of these elements. The notion of community is essential in PwC; grounded in Dewey's philosophy, the idea of shared meaning making is central. Working collaboratively, though not necessarily in agreement, the participants work to come to some shared understanding of the topic under examination. This does not mean that the participants reach a consensus, since philosophical dialogue would cease were everyone to agree. This is also important; in practising

PwC, children come to learn that people need not agree, that they can live well together while disagreeing and that they are furnished with resilience in accepting that others may disagree with them. Indeed, they will accept that disagreement can be important in exploring what it means to live well, particularly in advancing the good life for themselves and others. This resonates with the need for respect if one's wellbeing is considered to be good. In PwC every participant has an equal voice. In addition, the space to speak – or not – is afforded to everyone and when they speak they will be listened to and their contribution will be taken seriously. While not every contribution will be followed-up by other participants, the contribution is valued because it has come as a consequence of building upon the previous contributions. This sense of having something listened to and that it contributes to a wider purpose, the shared purpose of the community of philosophical inquiry, allows participants to feel valued.

The sense of being valued is important for all, but even more especially perhaps, for those who are more likely to be marginalised. One approach to PwC, Community of Philosophical Inquiry (CoPI) (Cassidy, 2007; McCall, 2009), has been shown to be particularly inclusive for children who are marginalised because of their particular emotional and behavioural needs, including children with autism (Cassidy, Christie, Marwick, Deeney, McLean and Rogers, 2017). The children are able to participate in ways that are different to their usual patterns in class and they have transferred some of the skills acquired during CoPI to other group-work activity. Similarly, Cassidy *et al.* (2015) have been conducting CoPI sessions in secure residential accommodation for children aged between fourteen and seventeen. The participants have reported that they feel listened to, respected and part of a club, or community, when participating in the sessions. They reported that the interest shown in what they had to say, which resulted in a volunteer from outside of the institution coming to work with them and introduce them to practical philosophy, made them feel valued.

This sense of having someone listen to them is suggestive that children generally do not consider themselves to be listened to. This is borne out in the perpetuation of the notion of child as becoming, where they are not yet considered able to participate fully in the society in which they live. Children's sense of agency is promoted when they realise that they are being listened to and that what they say has a bearing on decisions made for and about them. If children's views are taken seriously and action results as a consequence, this can only be an empowering experience that will lead to agency, engagement and an autonomous outlook. Of course children must depend on adults for the provision of certain aspects of their wellbeing such as shelter, food, health, clothing and some areas of their education, but more autonomous children can assert what they consider their needs to be and be more able to assess whether those needs have been met. Acknowledging that one has more autonomy means that one is empowered and, it might be suggested, more satisfied or happy as a consequence.

Like other areas of wellbeing, happiness is not something that is easily measured or quantified, though one ought to be able to say if one is happy or not. Mashford-Scott *et al.* (2012, p. 237) are correct to assert that there ought to be a focus on children's 'own sense of wellbeing [rather than] the demonstrations of particular behaviours'. It may be that participating in philosophical dialogue makes people happy, there are many that attest that it does, but the place of PwC in relation to one's satisfaction or happiness is that one is able to interrogate what it means to be happy or satisfied and gauge to what extent one considers oneself to be so. Further, in engaging in such dialogue, participants are able to explore just what it means to live well or have the good life.

Conrad *et al.* (2015) did just that, holding CoPI sessions with over 130 children between the ages of three and eighteen in Scotland and Switzerland to reach some sense of what the children thought the good life was. Across the age groups and between the two countries there were elements in common: family, friends, fun, equality, fairness, justice and kindness. What emerged in the dialogues, though, was that children saw themselves as distinct from the rest of society and that they did not consider themselves to have influence or autonomy. In other words, the children had already been pulled into accepting the suggestion that children are 'other' to adults and that they are in a period of preparation, of becoming. The strong sense that the good life demanded that people are treated fairly and equitably is important since this illustrates that the children do not see individuals in isolation but that their sense of the good life is one that turns on relationships with and to others. Given that relationships are seen to be important to children's wellbeing, this is significant. The children recognise the need for positive relationships with others if one is to have a good life. In addition, through participating in PwC, children learn how to engage with others and build relationships. This is closely linked to the idea of community. Community of Philosophical Inquiry demands that participants work together, though they may disagree or even dislike one another. The dynamics and relationships created in the likes of CoPI are important, where children learn that they are important members of the community, that they have relationships with the other participants and that the whole is often greater than the parts.

It is in engaging in philosophical dialogue that children 'move beyond the instrumental nature of using philosophy in the classroom to enhance academic performance and allow that it becomes an enriching part of one's life' (Cassidy, 2012, p. 261). A rich life must be one in which one is living, *being* well. It is perhaps through philosophical dialogue, through PwC, where children come together to explore ideas, to examine life and all that it holds, where children engage in what Gregory (2011, p. 212) calls a 'method of wisdom training' that children may come to see what a good life is and what it means to live *well*. It is from here, it is hoped, that children move from thought to action if they are to have a good life, if they are to *be* well.

And what about the teachers?

In an age of measurement and accountability it is not only the children's wellbeing or good life that is called into question. At a time when teachers are under increasing pressure to perform better, meaning to ensure better grades and outcomes from the children with whom they are working, the lives of teachers cannot be dissociated from their work. Acton and Glasgow (2015, p. 110) are clear that there are great 'difficulties in maintaining [teachers'] wellbeing in political times that foreground performativity and competition'. They conclude that it is important to avoid simply 'managing stress, burnout or resilience' (p. 111), that what is required is a positive working environment where happiness is promoted. Teachers, though they need to collaborate, do not always find themselves in a collegiate atmosphere where they are valued and where happiness is a priority. In such an atmosphere, relationships with colleagues and children may not be as rich as they might otherwise be were there to be a focus on *being* well.

Van Petegem *et al.* (2005) note that teachers have often over-estimated the positive relationships they have with the children with whom they work. They emphasise that in order for teachers and children to feel good, a positive classroom environment is needed that situates positive relationships at the centre. Engagement with children that positions them as autonomous and empowered within the classroom, where they are seen as *beings* rather than as becomings might serve to support a positive classroom environment. In addition, in situating the promotion of the good life or being *well* at the centre for all in the classroom, healthy relationships may be engendered. Indeed, this should not be limited to the classroom, but should be practised across the school context. To include the suggestion that practical philosophy is introduced to classrooms would also support the notion of a respectful, happy space that fosters a sense of community where all work to a shared goal of promoting the good life of themselves and others. Indeed, it would be no bad thing to promote practical philosophy with and for teachers and other members of the school community.

So, who or what is it for? And how might we get there?

At the outset of the chapter there was some discussion about the nature of wellbeing and who this was for. While wellbeing may be difficult to define, there is some consensus around elements that constitute wellbeing. Instead, though, what might be more helpful is to reflect on how children are perceived. In empowering children that they may be more engaged with the world it is important to see them as beings rather than as becomings. In considering their wellbeing, it is more helpful, perhaps, to think about *being* or living well and that this resides in the notion of the good life. So, who is the good life for? The good life is for everyone. One cannot *be* well or be *well*, live well or have a good life in isolation. One way we might promote critical discussion that leads to thoughtful action and the good life that treats children as beings and ensures valued and valuable relationships in our schools might be through an approach such as Community of Philosophical Inquiry. In promoting the good life we support children – and their teachers – to recognise they are part of a wider whole and that, as Nussbaum (2011) suggests, one element of the good life is that we would wish to promote conditions that allow for others also to have a good life, to have well *being*.

Future directions

The chapter highlighted that children are often considered as in a state of becoming rather than as beings in and of themselves. It went on to suggest that in order to consider children's *being* well or living *well* was a helpful way of considering the notion of wellbeing. The notion of the good life was seen to be the purpose of *being* well or living *well* and that this was not an individual endeavour. The chapter concluded by proposing that in order to effect a good life, one must be able to engage critically with the world and others and that this may be achieved in part through PwC. In moving research forward, there are at least two areas worthy of further exploration. The first would be to explore the ways in which a programme of PwC might support more positive teacher–children relationships and other features of what are understood as contributing to wellbeing. The second area would be to explore the extent to which engaging in philosophical dialogue impacts on teachers' and children's actions.

Summary of key findings

- Children are usually treated as being in a state of becoming where childhood is a preparation for adult life and full membership of society.
- Notions of *being* well or living *well* may be helpful in trying to understand wellbeing.
- Critical discussion and reflection help towards the good life.
- One does not lead the good life in isolation.
- Philosophy with Children may be one way to promote the good life.

Reflective tasks

- To what extent is it problematic to think of children as becomings?
- What might the differences be between welfare, wellbeing and *being* well?
- What features might a classroom that embraces a philosophical outlook have?
- How might one know if one has a good life?

Further reading

Kennedy, D. (2006). *The Well of Being. Childhood, Subjectivity, and Education.* Albany: SUNY Press.

References

Acton, R., & Glasgow, P. (2015). Teacher Wellbeing in Neoliberal Contexts: A Review of the Literature, *Australian Journal of Teacher Education, 40*(8), 99–114.

Amerijckx, G., & Humblet, P.C. (2014). Child Well-being: What Does it Mean? *Children and Society*, *28*(5), 404–415.

Biesta, G. (2009). Good Education in an Age of Measurement: On the Need to Reconnect to the Question of Purpose in Education, *Educational Assessment, Evaluation and Accountability*, *21*(1), 33–46.

Bourke, L., & Geldens, P. (2007). What Does Wellbeing Mean? Perspectives of Wellbeing Among Young People and Youth Workers in Rural Victoria, *Youth Studies Australia*, *26*(1), 41–49.

Camfield, L., Streuli, N., & Woodhead, M. (2009). What's the Use of 'Well-Being' in Contexts of Child Poverty? Approaches to Research, Monitoring and Children's Participation, *International Journal of Children's Rights*, *17*(1), 65–109.

Cassidy, C. (2007). *Thinking Children*. London: Continuum.

Cassidy, C. (2012). Philosophy with Children: Learning to Live Well, *Childhood and Philosophy*, *8*(16), 243–264.

Cassidy, C., Christie, D., Marwick, H., Deeney, L., McLean, G., & Rogers, K. (2017). Fostering Citizenship in Marginalised Children Through Participation in Community of Philosophical Inquiry.

Cassidy, C., Heron, G., & Christie, D. (2015). Breaking into Secure: Using Philosophy with Children with Vulnerable Young People. *International Council for Philosophical Inquiry with Children Conference, Vancouver, Canada, June 2015*, retrieved from http://icpic2015-educ.sites.olt.ubc.ca/files/2015/06/Abstract-June-16-small.pdf

Conrad, S.-J., Cassidy, C., & Mathis, C. (2015). 'Encouraging and supporting children's voices.' In: J. Tremmel, A. Mason, I. Dimitrijoski & P. Godli (Eds.), *Youth Quotas and Other Efficient Forms of Youth Participation in Ageing Democracies* (pp. 109–124). Cham: Springer.

Cook, D.T. (2009). Editorial: When a Child is Not a Child, and Other Conceptual Hazards of Childhood Studies, *Childhood*, *16*(1), 5–10.

Cunningham, H. (2006). *The Invention of Childhood*. London: BBC Books.

Gregory, M. (2008). Philosophy in Schools: Ideals, Challenges and Opportunities, *Critical and Creative Thinking*, *16*(1), 5–22.

Gregory, M. (2011). Philosophy for Children and its Critics: A Mendham Dialogue, *Journal of Philosophy of Education*, *45*(2), 199–219.

Jenks, C. (1996). *Childhood*. London: Routledge.

Juuso, H. (1999). Ancient Paideia and Philosophy for Children, *Thinking: The Journal of Philosophy for Children*, *14*(4), 9–20.

Kennedy, D. (1992). The Hermeneutics of Childhood, *Philosophy Today*, 44–58.

Kennedy, D. (2006). *The Well of Being. Childhood, Subjectivity, and Education*. Albany: SUNY Press.

Kohan, W.O. (2011). Childhood, Education and Philosophy: Notes on Deterritorialisation, *Journal of Philosophy of Education*, *45*(2), 339–357.

Krebs, A. (1998). Werden Menschen schwanger? Das 'gute menschliche Leben' und die Geschlechterdifferent. In: Holger Steinfath (Ed.): *Was Ist ein Gutes Leben?* Frankfurt: Suhrkamp, 235–247.

Lipman, M. (2003). *Thinking in Education (2nd ed.)*. Cambridge: Cambridge University Press.

McCall, C. (2009). *Transforming Thinking. Philosophical Inquiry in the Primary and Secondary Classroom*. London: Routledge.

Mashford-Scott, A., Church, A. & Taylor, C. (2012) Seeking Children's Perspectives on their Wellbeing in Early Childhood Settings, *International Journal of Early Childhood*, *44*(3), 231–247.

Nussbaum, M.C. (2011). *Creating Capabilities*. Cambridge: The Belknap Press.

Pardales, M.J., & Girod, M. (2006). Community of Inquiry: Its Past and Present Future, *Educational Philosophy and Theory, 38*(3), 229–309.

van Petegem, K., Creemers, B.P.M., Rossel, Y., & Aelterman, A. (2005). Relationships Between Teacher Characteristics, Interpersonal Teacher Behaviour and Teacher Wellbeing, *Journal of Classroom Interaction, 40*(2), 34–43.

Postman, N. (1994). *The Disappearance of Childhood*. New York: Vintage Books.

Ryan, S. (2012). Wisdom, knowledge and rationality, *Acta Analytica, 27*(2) 99–112.

Rysst, M. (2010). 'I Am Only Ten Years Old': Femininities, Clothing-Fashion Codes and the Intergenerational Gap of Interpretation of Young Girls' Clothes, *Childhood, 17*(1), 76–93.

Rysst, M. (2015). Friendship and Gender Identity Among Girls in a Multicultural Setting in Oslo, *Childhood, 22*(4), 490–505.

Scottish Executive. (2004). *Curriculum for Excellence*. Edinburgh: Scottish Executive.

Stables, A. (2008). *Childhood and the Philosophy of Education. An Anti-Aristotelian Perspective*. London: Continuum.

United Nations. (1989). *United Nations Convention on the Rights of the Child*. Geneva: United Nations.

Vansieleghem, N., & Kennedy, D. (2011). What is Philosophy *for* Children, What is Philosophy *with* Children – After Matthew Lipman? *Journal of Philosophy of Education, 45*(2), 171–182.

2

CONTRASTING CONCEPTIONS OF WELLBEING AND THEIR IMPLICATIONS FOR EDUCATIONAL PLANNING AND PRACTICE

Malcolm Thorburn

Introduction

For those involved in education in its widest sense, we naturally wish learners to be happy and *well*. The happier learners are the more likely they are to make good decisions about their wellbeing, their education and their future lives. Thinking along these lines, it could be argued, just makes common sense. However, the term wellbeing is a relatively new one in comparison with a plethora of historically related terms such as welfare, utility and happiness, and is new as well in relation to broader educational considerations such as civic values and cultivating virtues (Thorburn, 2015). This is further evident from a comprehensive literature review on wellbeing and schooling noting that approaches to understanding wellbeing 'have developed in accordance with historical, cultural and philosophical positions, relative to disciplinary traditions and their dominance in research and the academy' (O'Brien, 2008, p. 56). The newness of wellbeing coupled with varied approaches taken towards understanding wellbeing can lead to wellbeing meaning different things to different people. Therefore, as Tiberius and Plakias (2010, p. 402) note, it makes 'a big difference what conception of wellbeing one adopts'. The diverse nature and range of current wellbeing theories is captured by Tiberius (2013a) who highlights five main wellbeing theories. On this basis wellbeing could either be considered as a subjective theory (i.e. based on things which are *intrinsically* good for us) such as *hedonism* (Bradley, 2015), *desire fulfillment* (Griffin, 1986) or *life-satisfaction* (Sumner, 1996) or, as an objective theory (i.e. based on things which are *instrumentally* good for us) such as *human nature fulfillment theory* (Nussbaum, 2000) or *individually driven nature fulfillment theory* (Haybron, 2008). The chapter begins by examining these five theories of personal wellbeing and analyses their relative educational significance in a context where wellbeing is considered as part of everyday learning and teaching; i.e. one where wellbeing is included in holistic learning environments (rather than as a component of a separate subject e.g. Personal and Social Education). Thus, the task being taken forward is to better understand some of the main influences on theories of wellbeing and their implications for educational planning and practice.

In taking this remit forward, the chapter strives to play a part in developing readers' professional curiosity in an area of education which is increasingly central to the realisation of whole school aims, and which (as noted in Chapter 3) is becoming ever more prominent in public policy discussions. On this basis, it makes sense in the busy world of education to free up time as best possible to review the concept of wellbeing, and to understand and clarify what wellbeing is being taken to mean. This is in preference to accelerating past such matters to consider implementation concerns associated with policy, professionalism and practice. This latter point is an important one as by no means does everyone in education consider that wellbeing should feature as prominently as a component of education as it does at present. Ecclestone and Hayes (2009), for example, are highly critical of the supposition that focusing on the emotional wellbeing of learners will lead to more successful educational practices and a broader array of positive affective outcomes for learners. Thus, they remain dismayed by the wide-ranging, therapeutic-type interventions taking place in schools and argue that learners may become *more* not *less* dependent upon educators for their wellbeing under such circumstances. Furthermore, Ecclestone and Hayes (2009) have concerns about levels of engagement with subject knowledge and the claimed crisis in current curriculum theory, where a loss of focus on subject teaching coincides with a downgrading in teachers' instrumental function i.e. that parents 'send their children to school expecting them to acquire the specialist knowledge that they would not have access to at home' (Young, 2014, p. 107). Paterson (2014) has similar concerns and is perplexed by the lack of disciplinary subject-based specialism in Scottish education at present. This is relative to the prominence afforded to learners' motivation (and even more problematically learners' enjoyment). That said, it is noteworthy that in Scotland and many other countries discussed in this book, the motivation of learners, what interests and engages them and their wellbeing more generally is now considered a *responsibility of all* teachers (see Chapter 1).

Main findings

As noted above, exploring wellbeing requires some kind of awareness about what the constituents of wellbeing are. With this in mind, five main theories of personal wellbeing are described and analysed.

Subjective theories of wellbeing

Hedonism

Hedonism theories place a premium on pleasure and with fostering a sense of being pleased with the positive decisions made following experiences. Such thinking has a utilitarian lineage dating back many years to philosophers such as Bentham and Mill who outlined in their various ways that pleasure is the only thing which is intrinsically good for us. Bradley (2015) considers that hedonism has many advantages as a wellbeing theory, as it more than other theories appreciates how well someone's life is going at any particular moment or time (rather than over a whole life). However, hedonism is also a weak theory; as if we ever desire anything other than pleasure then hedonism must be false. For example, throughout life there are many duties we may feel obligated to carry out even though they do not necessarily bring us immediate pleasure. Thus, as Kraut (2007, p. 127) highlights, reasoning that if someone enjoys swimming then 'swimming is the cause and object of his pleasure' is unsatisfactory as there may also be *instrumental* benefits associated with swimming e.g. at the very least, increased personal safety when in water. What is needed therefore is a way of recognising that the goods of wellbeing consist of *flourishing* more than just happiness and pleasure (Kristjansson, 2016). Therefore, as well as feeling satisfied and happy, wellbeing means developing as a person, being fulfilled and making a contribution to the community (Shah and Marks, 2004). John Dewey, who distinguished the simpler states of enjoyment and desire, with reflections which can generate stable, caring and evaluative judgements, was one of the foremost learner-centered educators to review such matters. Dewey's pragmatic emphasis was on merging scientific method, human practices and evolutionary biology in order to better understand human activity in terms of habits, impulses and intelligence, and also in terms of how deep satisfaction could be gained through effort (Thorburn and MacAllister, 2013). Dewey's (1913; 1916) thinking remains important to many educators, as his writings on interest and democracy recognise and prioritise learners' engagement and the need for teachers to reflect this in their planning, practice and evaluations of learning and teaching. However, more generally as most educational contexts nowadays require engagement with specific subject-based objectives, hedonism theorising is best considered as an important contributor to curriculum aims rather than as the overarching rationale for the curriculum.

Desire fulfillment

Desire fulfillment theory is based on the fundamental view that what makes life go well is getting what you want and what makes life go less well is not getting what you want (Bradley, 2015). Desire theory moves beyond hedonism's focus on feelings and pleasure to identify objects (targets) as desires. As such, desire theory is a counterpoint to the reasoning and passion-based philosophies of Plato and Hume; for as Griffin (1996, p. 32) argues, 'reason and desire are not independent enough for one to be the master and the other slave'. The challenge for desire fulfillment theories is to indicate how desires can provide an account of values and worthwhileness which moves beyond merely satisfying individual needs and preferences and which recognises that desires differ in terms of their strength and intensity. Some desires might also be relatively fleeting while others might be more persistent and life changing. Therefore, the capacity of desire fulfillment theories to enable individual variability at the same time as fitting within an overarching unified theory is considered a strength, e.g. some learners might have only a passing interest in playing a musical instrument or taking part in a drama production while others may find participation in these activities to have a much more lasting influence. These effects introduce into desire fulfillment theory the notion of *effort* and *achievement*, and for the *prospect* of achieving desires to motivate and engage learners (Bradley, 2015). So conceived, practical reasoning is not inert but rather something which should be considered as part of our motivation and our desires. In this way, the old interpretation of there being one overarching substantive value should be replaced by a finer-grained teasing-out of what is prudentially valuable for persons (Griffin, 1996).

The main downside of desire fulfillment theories is that people often make irrational or ill-advised judgements. The remedy for this difficulty is to make theorising idealised by outlining how it is only certain informed desires which contribute to personal wellbeing (Griffin, 1986). Thus, a mix of subjective and objective elements can inform judgements and aid coherence provided the advantages of privileging certain desires is not overly constrained by the narrowness of what counts as an informed value. Framed this way, it is possible to see connections with hedonism theorising; as both theories would in an educational context see the merits of a personalised and voluntary engagement with many areas of the curriculum e.g. art, music, literature, languages and science. Furthermore, these opportunities for involvement should be available as an ongoing part of learners' wider education (and not just as part of formal syllabus requirements). As well as this idealised view of desire fulfillment there is also a hybrid view which recognises that certain things are objectively worthy of desire as they are good for us to do. Committing to persevere with certain subjects at school might fit this theory. For example, playing a full and active part in some subjects might not match your idea of what makes life go well for you. However, it might connect with your view on getting to where you want your life to get to (Bradley, 2015).

Life satisfaction

The challenge for life-satisfaction theories is similar to that of desire fulfilment theories i.e. to indicate how self-beliefs can move beyond satisfying individual needs and preferences. The main advocate of life-satisfaction theory, Sumner (1996), considers that authentic happiness provides the endorsement necessary for connecting life satisfaction with welfare values. Authenticity is achieved when a person's own values are central to their evaluation of wellbeing. This occurs through merging an experiential feelings-based review of being fulfilled along with a cognitive review of how well life is going according to your standards. In this way, Sumner (1996) argues that informed life-satisfaction thinking overtakes the main limitation of Griffin's (1986) theorising i.e. that the desires one might have are not necessarily coherent with what is best for one's own personal flourishing. The main problem with life satisfaction theories is that people might be constrained by lack of information or degrees of oppression. As such, the prospects for this theory are dependent on the degree of objective information people have when they make decisions. For example, learners might be moderately engaged in activities which they value to an extent. However, without autonomy (and the chance and opportunity to make full and informed choices) it could be that learners are unlikely to be *wholeheartedly* engaged in activities; and it is wholehearted engagement which leads to flourishing. Knowing in an open and accessible way what might constitute living well has opened up recent strands of theorising which have distinguished values from desires (Raibley, 2010), and which accentuate the need for values to be stable over time and realistic if they are to form the basis of our choices and reviews of how well our lives are faring. However, these benefits can only occur if the information reviewed is important to your wellbeing. Haybron (2008) considers that the possibility exists that the potentially wide-ranging influences on our lives can make our self-analysis misleading. As such, our views on life satisfaction could differ from our wellbeing values. Haybron (2008) cites, for example, how the onset of serious illness would change perceptions of life satisfaction even though our wellbeing values might remain more constant.

Objective theories of wellbeing

A distinguishing feature of desire fulfillment and life-satisfaction theories is that they tend to require idealising (objective) constraints, so that the more unreliable aspects of subjectivism are of limited influence. This is a tricky matter however, as in philosophical rather than psychological contexts values are normative and value-laden. Therefore, the challenge is in ensuring that there is coherence between personal values and those which people aspire towards or which are set for them as targets. To some extent this involves trying to square an impossible circle; for if values require a human evaluation component in order to be explained then our evaluations cannot be considered as objective. Angner (2011) argues that making plausible subjective–objective connections is likely to benefit from identifying adequacy criteria, as these can help provide the required reliability and validity. This line of thinking recognises the historic origins of wellbeing, for as Tiberius (2013a, p. 27) notes, no 'one in the Ancient world thought that what things are good for you would be determined by your own subjective attitudes'. It also recognises that in contemporary times, wellbeing is considered as a dynamic and multi-dimensional construct (Dodge, Daly, Huyton and Sanders, 2012). And (as noted in Chapter 3), those interested in the connections between economics, poverty and wellbeing engage with objective indicators of welfare as well as subjective measures of wellbeing.

Human nature fulfillment theory

The simplest type of objective theory is a list theory against which measurements of wellbeing can be made. The problem with a list is that the criteria specified on the list might not be important to people. To overcome this limitation, two more specific forms of objectively influenced theories have been developed. The first of these – the human nature fulfillment theory – is based on the concept of function; and developments such as Nussbaum's (2011) capabilities approach are an attempt to describe necessary functional (outcome-based) attributes. The ten central capabilities are: *life* (having a normal length of life); *bodily health* (including nourishment and shelter); *bodily integrity* (freedom from violence); *senses, imagination and thought* (including pleasures); *emotions* (attachments and loving relationships); *practical reason* (reflecting on one's life plan); *affiliation* (forming groups, not being discriminated against); *other species* (relationships to nonhumans) and *play and control* over one's political and material environment (Nussbaum, 2011). Comparing progress with these capabilities should make it possible to measure how well a person's life is faring, and of how well a person's life is faring relative to others. Robeyns (2005) notes that the defining characteristics of the capability approach are its broad interdisciplinary focus on wellbeing and the capacity the approach has to highlight the differences there are between the subjective and the objective i.e. between substantive freedoms (capabilities) and outcomes (achieved functionings). Capability approach studies are widely used in analysing many areas of welfare economics and social policy and in an educational context could be used to draw attention to structural (functioning-type) issues such as the influences schools can have on the development of young people's capabilities. Nussbaum (2011, p. 156) further advises that as far as young people's education is concerned that 'governments will be well advised to require functioning of children, not simply capability … (and that consequently) … we should tolerate less deference to individual – or parental – choice'. While some may concur with such reasoning e.g. in areas such as achieving functional levels of literacy and numeracy, it may be less true with regard to personal wellbeing, as not everyone is seeking or desiring the same normative ends.

Individually driven nature fulfillment theory

Individually driven nature fulfillment theories are constructed with a view to determining the extent to which values match peoples' emotional needs and contribute to their happiness (Haybron, 2008). This theory has similarities with life-satisfaction theory (Sumner, 1996), in that happiness must be autonomous in nature and not unduly constrained by lack of information. However, Haybron (2008) argues that authenticity (a key feature of life-satisfaction theory) needs to include *richness*; where richness is taken to mean fully engaging with the complexities of life with all that this entails for defining your nature and individuality within the everyday business of life. This type of theorising might be considered as a form of *pluralism*, whereby objective-type list debates merge with reviewing the various subjective influences which motivate and sustain learners' interest. For example, recent, positive psychology-informed models have measured positive emotions, relationships and accomplishments as part of wellbeing (Seligman, 2011). In an educational sense, measurement might involve reviewing the extent to which learners' nature and individualism are apparent in the way they are engaging with knowledge, cultivating virtues and promoting friendships; three capacities it would be reasonable to argue are useful for developing individually and for functioning in society more generally. One factor with pluralism is that lists are never complete or fixed. They are fluid and can be added to or adapted over time. This leads to problems with *unification* and with attempts to reach a unifying view of the capacities it would be good for learners to develop e.g. Nussbaum's (2011) capabilities approach. Therefore, the current Scottish curriculum, based as it is on developing four generic learning capacities; namely, for young people to become 'successful learners', 'confident individuals', 'effective contributors' and 'responsible citizens', could be read in different ways e.g. either as a help in that its openness, flexibility and lack of definition and explanation encourage inspirational teaching and a degree of personalisation and choice in learning. On the other hand it could be read as rather unhelpful due to its vagueness and lack of satisfactory supporting explanation and justification.

Wellbeing theories and educational planning

Which way forward?

The mix of influences on schooling, not least the requirement in most instances to provide evidence of how learning articulates with assessment arrangements, suggests that a wholly subjective wellbeing theory would be insufficient. Moreover, an objective requirement, especially one which was not overly idealised, could provide the definition required in clarifying the nature of the wellbeing values informing educational planning. Arguably, a hybridised mix of subjective and objective elements, as evident in desire-fulfillment theories (Griffin, 1986) or a values-informed version of life-satisfaction theory (Raibley, 2010), could, if linked to objective criteria which are partly referenced by learners own emotional needs, represent the most productive prospect for education-related theorising. Moving forward on this basis would help learners appreciate that wellbeing is more than happiness and something which connects with flourishing as a person *and* with making a positive contribution to the community and wider society (Shah and Marks, 2004). Progress in this way might overtake many of the limitations highlighted by Ecclestone and Hayes (2009) about learners becoming dependent on support as a result of emotional wellbeing programmes in schools. Instead, learners could become empowered, resilient and responsible as a result of engaging with experiences, where personal experiences merge with wellbeing values and a liberal-based and partially subject-defined education.

The benefits of reflective wisdom

The work of Tiberius (2008) is useful to consider in this respect as it outlines a reflective wisdom framework for reviewing how to make good choices in order to live well and wisely. Even though Tiberius's theorising is not written with education contexts specifically in mind, her thinking provides a helpful account of the virtues of reflectiveness, perspective and self-knowledge. Tiberius's (2008) four chosen values (attention flexibility, perspective, self-awareness and realistic optimism) aim to balance achievable standards in normative areas such as personal growth and relationships with others while also recognising the subjective importance of being absorbed in experiences which fully engage with our interests, skills and capacities. This mix appreciates the virtues people continue to endorse as being personally fulfilling, as well as recognising the changing influences on society e.g. the need for people to take on a more constructive attitude towards managing their overall health. This line of theorising suggests that through better-quality reflection people can make stable values connections, and as cognition and emotion develop together, people can progressively endorse and justify the decisions they make. Tiberius (2008) considers that her reflective wisdom framework avoids the significance problems attached to hedonist accounts of wellbeing and also the problems of being too closely aligned with objectivist-informed normative measures that make too many presumptions about the worthlessness of subjective experiences. Moreover, as the wellbeing values identified by Tiberius (2008) are relatively conservative in nature, based as they are on a cognitive-inclined and reflective perspective on wellbeing, it could be argued that this aids rather than detracts from their connection to the subject-based schooling arrangements which exist in most countries. In a Scottish context, Thorburn (2014) and Thorburn and Horrell (2014) provide two extended model-based examples of how Tiberius's (2008) chosen values could support a holistic context for learning which connects learning tasks with whole-school curriculum planning and evaluation arrangements.

Challenges to reflection

However, there are concerns that Tiberius's commitment towards using 'our experience as the only source of answers to our normative questions' (Tiberius, 2008, p. 6) is problematic in a number of respects. The first relates to the difficulty there might be in using self-beliefs as the normative device for providing an account of wellbeing values, as a subjective-informed account may prove shallow and insufficiently action guiding. Angner (2011) argues, for example, that subjectively experienced mental states are indirect and imperfect measures of wellbeing. The contribution of Annas (2011) might allay these types of concerns as she considers that practising practical skills can become the situated context for developing expertise, and as practical expertise improves, so does practical reasoning. Thus, following Griffin (1996), if we are sufficiently motivated by improvement we should be able to use our improved abilities to reflect and to become more expert at reviewing the reasons underpinning the decisions we make. In this respect, the coupling Annas (2011) makes between expertise in practical skills and expertise in practical reasoning supports Tiberius's (2008) thinking; as evident by the endorsement Annas (2011) provides for arguing that improved practical reasoning is helpful in explaining the reasons we choose to justify the decisions we make about how we wish to live our lives.

A second related challenge to Tiberius' (2008) account of wellbeing is that the premium afforded to rational reflection might not be merited, as reflection can be prone to bias, inaccuracy, confusion and distortion. Kornblith (2012) does not believe that reflection has special powers and instead considers that reflection suffers from problems of infinite regress. Thus, if we have problems in our lives, secondary reflection will not rectify these primary problems. If it does, then there is a problem with the accuracy of our secondary reflections. The upshot of this line of thinking is that reflective scrutiny is not required in order to make personal beliefs more reliable. Instead, Kornblith (2012) considers that what matters is whether beliefs are reason-responsive, rather than whether they are accompanied by reflection. Keller (2011) has similar concerns, noting that living a life which you value on reflection may be different to a life based on your initial values, and to what made these comparable or distinctive relative to other people in the first place. For this reason, Keller (2011, p. 789) doubts that our personal values can play a foundational role in moving from 'reflective endorsement to the values of self-direction and life-satisfaction, and then to the life of reflective wisdom'. Moreover, from a moral psychology perspective, studies have also shown that people often rely on their gut instinct and even on reaffirming convictions which are shown to be inaccurate. This scattered approach to values decision-making owes little to reflection and also highlights how there is often a conflict between unreflective and reflective responses (Doris, 2009). In light of this criticism, Tiberius (2013b, p. 224) has launched 'a defense of reflection against what seems like an increasingly hostile environment for reflection and reasoning'. Tiberius (2013b, p. 230) responds by noting that we cannot separate reflection and values and consequently we cannot resolve 'a conflict one way rather than another without reflections on what's appropriate given certain norms and standards'. As such, it is not possible to make a normative assessment of whether we are making the right type of values decisions without recourse to subjective-based practical reasoning on why our decisions are appropriate. Therefore, those who are less practised in reflection are more likely to make shallow or normatively imprecise values justifications.

Educating for wellbeing: Improving curriculum gains and pedagogical practices

Ideas for integrating wellbeing into everyday learning and teaching and whole school planning

O'Brien (2008, p. 179) considers that fostering wellbeing in schools necessitates a 'holistic approach to the development of students' competencies and to their learning'. This chapter, despite the multiple challenges involved, concurs, as making progress on this basis should ensure that teachers are more likely to focus on making sound and plausible connections between learners' previous learning experiences, their wellbeing values and subject knowledge imperatives. However, as noted, one of the problems surrounding wellbeing theorising is recognising that people often make poor choices. Thus, in educational (as in other) contexts, progress in unlikely to be linear and uncomplicated. This can create uncertainty for teachers; for in certain situations teachers need to recognise learners' values at the same time as acknowledging the norms and expectations of their professional role. These difficulties are evident in multiple everyday teaching situations, where teachers find themselves both encouraging learners to cultivate their reflective abilities (relevance and context) and then engaging with them on the appropriateness (validity) of the choices they make. Such instances can arise in situations where learners are making decisions which trigger some degree of personal/professional dubiety/unease with teachers. This could happen, for example, in outdoor learning contexts where learners were considered to be displaying undue ecological sensitivity towards their local habitat and/ or intolerance of other learners' values on such matters. The sense of being in a pedagogical quandary can also exist as a form of institutional paternalism as well; for example, in situations where teachers are expected to endorse wider school values on matters such as school uniform arrangements, even though their own value preferences may be relatively *laissez-faire* or more stringent relative to school expectations. Davies (2013, p. 475) has elaborated on these dilemmas by teasing out teachers' institutional and educative roles and by characterising school teaching as being not just a complex activity 'but a complex set of different activities co-located in one place and engaged in by the same agents'. This line of thinking highlights the importance of teachers being able to blend two contrasting professional perspectives; the need for individual accountability with a commitment to a shared collaborative concept of whole school professionalism. Furthermore, it is important that teachers are patient and confident in their teaching; in short, to reflect Higgins' (2011) belief that the multiple challenges teachers face should not become so onerous or constraining that their own self-cultivation is impaired.

Ideas for improving pedagogical practices

Given the above complexities, the intention is to say something more on some of the most pressing pedagogical issues teachers might face in helping learners to see the importance of wellbeing as part of their education. The position taken here largely follows MacIntyre's (2007) Aristotelian-informed view that it is from inside practices that learners and teachers can encounter 'distinctive notions about what it is worthwhile to participate in, excellent to achieve and admirable to become' (Higgins, 2011, p. 50). The term 'communities of practice' does not feature in MacIntyre's (2007) work as it does in Wenger's (1998) account of this area, however as McLaughlin (2003, p. 341) notes 'the general implications of the notion are inherent in MacIntyre's concept of a practice'. In practice settings, learners should aim to become increasingly adept at cultivating the right types of stable value judgements; in short, of displaying practical wisdom as evident through their focus on achieving excellences of character. Similarly, teachers need to move beyond being effective and efficient in a technical sense and become concerned as well with the moral dimensions of education and with learners flourishing (Carr, 2006). Viewed this way the goods internal to practice have transferable gains, as engaging in practice can increase the ways in which learners make expert-informed value judgements. For example, with regard to understanding accurately the science informing ecological debates on local inhabits, a mix of subjective relevance and objective accuracy gains can help learners to make sensitised and principled personal decisions, which not only outline their own views but which also recognise and appreciate the contested and different beliefs others may have on these types of matter. If formal high-stakes assessment is required, Thorburn (2008) found that a blended assessment approach consisting of a first-person informed account of the activity (subjective) which merges with the reporting of factual (objective) knowledge is a viable and authentic method to adopt.

MacIntyre's views on practice have enjoyed something of a pre-eminence among philosophers of education based on the identification of the key features of practice and their 'invitation to a certain kind of self-involving and self-transformative co-operative engagement … (combined with) … deep-seated intuitions about the nature and value of teaching, properly conceived, particularly in opposition to technicist and instrumentalist conceptions of the activity' (McLaughlin, 2003, p. 347).

Pivotal to a MacIntyrian concept of practice is achieving a shared and coherent sense of excellence which emphasises to learners the need to use time constructively. Thus, following MacIntyre's (2007) view of practice, learners need to extend their human powers as well as recognise the authority of the standards which govern practice arrangements. To help learners do so requires teachers to facilitate discussion and help learners to critically engage with their experiences, recognise available choices and discern viable ways forward. In brief, to follow standard Aristotelian-informed plans for teaching where there is a threefold emphasis on the requirement for practice, the need for teachers to exemplify the virtues and to present extended opportunities for learners to exercise reflection and deliberation (Arthur and Carr, 2013). Progress in this way enables learners to make greater sense of their world, with their uncertainties and hunches informing the establishment of more rounded conceptual understandings which are both accurate (objective) plus relevant to their lives (i.e. having a subjective/intrinsic value). Furthermore, over time and via ongoing interactive questions and discussion, learners could be encouraged to critically engage with their emotional needs in learning environments where their experiences enrich their overall perspective of how their lives are faring. Teachers, with practice, would become increasingly expert at judging the size and scope of learning tasks and better able to think through when to intervene and ask questions, and when to wait longer for answers to emerge. Progress on these lines could match Tiberius' (2013b, p. 234) intention that cultivating reflection has sufficient flexibility to be 'a rough recipe, a loose grouping of ends or values arranged in a network or web, or a set of very general principles that require great sensitivity to context for their application'.

A further word on John Dewey

The final part of the chapter considers how the contribution of philosopher of education, John Dewey, might help in connecting the learning process with the realisation of set learning outcomes *and* with enhancing learners' wellbeing. Dewey was frustrated by entrenched traditional and progressive movements in education in the first third of the twentieth century and attempted to navigate a *via media* between them. The traditionalists, Dewey felt, attended more to subject matter than learners' own experiences and by contrast, progressives sought learning environments where learners overly drove experiences and process. Thus, while Dewey applauded progressive interest in child development and self-realisation, he criticised the way these approaches undervalued the role of the educator and the curriculum and argued that a link needed to be found that balanced curriculum goals with the lives and experiences of learners. Dewey employed two interrelated principles to navigate a middle way: continuity and interaction. The principle of continuity argues that learning is a fluid process, for Dewey (1938) observed that outside of formal education learners naturally integrate past and present experiences. A learners' understanding of the world is therefore constantly developing and adjusting. Thus, Dewey recognised the need to connect curriculum to learning which is already underway. Dewey's second principle, interaction, points to the interplay between what Dewey (1938) called the objective and internal conditions of experience (Table 2.1). For Dewey, objective conditions make up the aims and content of the experience. In addition to these objective gains, Dewey was concerned with the learners' internal conditions, or unique mental map of the world. Consequently, Dewey aimed to engage learners in educational experiences (objective conditions) beginning from their foundation of past experiences and perceptions (internal conditions). By deploying the principles of continuity and interaction, Dewey was able to preserve learning as a process while still aiming at achieving predetermined outcomes. Awareness of these mutually dependent principles – continuity and interaction – challenges the educator to both 'survey the capacities and needs of the particular set of individuals' and simultaneously 'arrange the conditions which provide the subject matter or content for experiences that satisfy these needs and develop these capacities' (Dewey, 1938, pp. 18 and 24).

Two brief examples of holistic learning environments where there are connections between wellbeing values, subject knowledge and learners' previous experiences

Following Thorburn and Marshall (2011) two outdoor learning-based interdisciplinary examples: one relating to a walk for primary age learners (5–11 years) and the second a half-day river kayak journey for secondary age learners (12–18 years) are described. Briefly, the forest walk involves learners visiting a forest within walking distance of the school. Once there they have opportunities to make decisions about route planning with a partner and in groups, develop their communication skills and a sense of independence through packing their own resources and carrying a small rucksack. These experiences are designed to engage learners holistically as they connect with cognitive, psychomotor, emotional and social domains of learning. This approach recognises that learning is a complex process which is framed by learners' previous related learning experiences, preferred modes of learning, the context for learning and the nature of the tasks involved. For the kayak journey, completing a local river descent involves practising basic kayaking skills and discussing habitats and conservation issues with further connections drawn with other school experiences. The excursion represents a chance for 'real' practice on a moving river and the opportunity to work together and develop camaraderie with others. The journey involves learners responding appropriately to the demands of the task in conjunction with their prior kayaking experiences, emotional disposition and social engagement.

Future directions

The chapter has argued that wellbeing learning and teaching in schools would benefit from a clearer engagement with recent theorising on wellbeing values. Contrasting theoretical influences on wellbeing were reviewed (hedonism, desire fulfillment, life satisfaction, human nature fulfillment theory and individually driven nature fulfillment theory) with arguments developed on how a mixed approach which blended subjective and objective influences might best suit school-based developments. This is provided the wellbeing values chosen articulate clearly with related educational aims and with how learning and teaching are intended to take place. On this basis, the chapter has advanced a series of ideas and suggestions on how curriculum planning and pedagogical progress could be achieved in holistic learning environments, where wellbeing values are integrated with subject-knowledge imperatives and learners' prior learning experiences. This, it was argued, was a realistic ambition for schools to try and achieve as wellbeing in this light would be pivotal in supporting learners' wider achievements and contribution to formal records of educational attainment. As Chapter 3 highlights, making progress on these matters could help overtake some of the policy problems there are at present, where a lack of elaboration on the planning and practice issues associated with wellbeing is impacting on the quality of learners' learning experiences (Formby and Wolstenholme, 2012; Thorburn, 2016).

Summary of key findings

- Wellbeing can be difficult to define. So be curious and review critically definitions of personal wellbeing used in education.
- Subjective theories of wellbeing focus on things which are *intrinsically* good for us.

TABLE 2.1 Dewey's objective and internal conditions exemplified alongside wellbeing values through a forest walk and kayak journey exemplar

	Dewey's principles	Wellbeing-related values	Forest walk	Kayak journey
Objective conditions	Development of related skills	Practical reasoning; clear decision-making; on-task	Making individual and shared decisions about route planning	Paddling techniques; reading river flow
	Application of knowledge	Practical wisdom; objective accuracy	Assessing terrains for safe travel; group safety issues in forest	Safety considerations; reviews of river-based habitat and conservation issues
	Personal and social development	Personal growth; relationships with others; stable values	Being responsible; working as part of a team on group tasks; improving independence on personal tasks	Confidence and self-reliance; cooperative spirit among learners; teacher–learner relational depth
Internal conditions	Past experiences, perceptions, and understanding of the world	Relevant; worthwhile; motivated; interested; strong feelings; rich experience	Excited about being in forest; concerns about darkness in forest; inter-class tensions; out-of-school issues	Lack of confidence in water; interpersonal issues with some learners; dealing with issues at home
	Expectations of new experiences	Achievement; prospect; realistic expectation	Strong feeling for local travel; link to class work	Interdisciplinary learning connections; social excursion

- Objective theories of wellbeing focus on things which are *instrumentally* good for us.
- A hybridised mix of subjective and objective elements, could if linked to objective criteria which are partly referenced by learners own subjective needs, represent the most productive prospect for education-related theorising.
- Learners who are practiced in reflection are more likely to make normatively precise justifications for their values.
- Incorporating wellbeing into everyday learning and teaching is a complex task requiring planning and practice.
- Wellbeing-related learning and teaching requires teachers to review their educative role alongside their institutional role.
- Teachers need to look after their own wellbeing as well as the wellbeing of learners.

Reflective tasks

- To what extent is it a good educational idea to incorporate wellbeing into everyday learning and teaching?
- Could you incorporate a focus on wellbeing into learning and teaching without comprising levels of formal attainment?
- Do some of the theories of wellbeing described have more to recommend themselves than others?
- To what extent should teachers exemplify the wellbeing values they are trying to help learners cultivate?
- Should extended opportunities be provided for learners to exercise reflection and deliberation as part of their education?

Further readings

Seligman, M. (2011). *Flourish – A New Understanding of Happiness and Well-Being – and How to Achieve Them*. London: Nicholas Brealey Publishing.
White, J. (2011). *Exploring Wellbeing in Schools*. London: Routledge.

References

Angner, E. (2011). Are Subjective Measures of Wellbeing 'Direct'?, *Australasian Journal of Philosophy*, *89*(1), 115–130.
Annas, J. 2011. *Intelligent Virtue*. Oxford: Oxford University Press
Arthur, J. and Carr, D. (2013). Character in learning for life: a virtue-ethical rationale for recent research on moral and values education, *Journal of Beliefs and Values*, 34(1), 26–35.
Bradley, B. (2015). *Well-Being*. Cambridge: Polity Press.
Carr, D. (2006). Professional and Personal Values and Virtues in Education and Teaching, *Oxford Review of Education*, *32*(3), 171–183.
Davies, R. (2013). After Higgins and Dunne: Imagining School Teaching as a Multi-Practice Activity, *Journal of Philosophy of Education*, 47(3), 475–490.

Dewey, J. (1913/1969). *Interest and Effort in Education*. Bath: Cedric Chivers.

Dewey, J. (1916/1980). 'Democracy in education.' In: J. A. Boydston (Ed.), *John Dewey: The Middle Works (1899–1924) Volume 9*. Carbondale: Southern Illinois Press.

Dewey, J. (1938). *Experience and Education*. New York: Macmillan.

Dodge, R., Daly, A., Huyton, J., & Sanders, L. (2012). The Challenge of Defining Wellbeing, *International Journal of Wellbeing*, *2*(3), 222–235.

Doris, J. (2009). Skepticism about Persons, *Philosophical Issues*, *19*(1), 57–91.

Ecclestone, K., & Hayes, D. (2009). *The Dangerous Rise of Therapeutic Education*. London: Routledge.

Formby, E., & Wolstenholme, C. (2012). 'If There's Going to be a Subject That You Don't Have to Do …' Findings from a Mapping Study of PSHE Education in English Secondary Schools, *Pastoral Care in Education*, *30*(1), 5–18.

Griffin, J. (1986). *Wellbeing: Its Meaning, Measurement and Moral Importance*. Oxford: Clarendon Press.

Griffin, J. (1996). *Value Judgement: Improving our Ethical Beliefs*. Oxford: Clarendon Press.

Haybron, D. (2008). *The Pursuit of Unhappiness*. Oxford: Oxford University Press.

Higgins, C. (2011). *The Good Life of Teaching: An Ethics of Professional Practice*. Chichester: Wiley-Blackwell.

Keller, S. (2011). Social Psychology and Philosophy: Problems in Translation. Critical Study of Valerie Tiberius, the Reflective Life: Living Wisely With our Limits, *Nous*, *45*(4), 776–791.

Kornblith, H. (2012). *On Reflection*. Oxford: Oxford University Press.

Kraut, R. (2007). *What is Good and Why: The Ethics of Well-Being*. London: Harvard University Press.

Kristjánsson, K. (2016). Recent Work on Flourishing as the Aim of Education: A Critical Review, *British Journal of Educational Studies*. Retrieved from http://dx.doi.org/10.1080/00071005.2016.1182115

MacIntyre, A. (2007). *After Virtue: A Study in Moral Theory*. London: Duckworth.

McLaughlin, T.H. (2003). Teaching as a Practice and a Community of Practice: The Limits of Commonality and the Demands of Diversity, *Journal of Philosophy of Education*, *37*(2), 339–352.

Nussbaum, M. (2000). *Women and Human Development: The Capabilities Approach*. Cambridge: Cambridge University Press.

O'Brien, M. (2008). *Well-Being and Post-Primary Schooling*. Dublin: National Council for Curriculum and Assessment.

Paterson, L. (2014). Competitive Opportunity and Liberal Culture: The Significance of Scottish Education in the Twentieth Century, *British Educational Research Journal*, *40*(2), 397–416.

Raibley, J. (2010). Wellbeing and the Priority of Values, *Social Theory and Practice*, *36*(4), 593–620.

Robeyns, I. (2005). The Capability Approach: A Theoretical Survey, *Journal of Human Development*, *6*(1), 93–114.

Seligman, M. (2011). *Flourish – a New Understanding of Happiness and Well-Being – and How to Achieve Them*. London: Nicholas Brealey Publishing.

Shah, H., & Marks, N. (2004). *A Well-Being Manifesto for a Flourishing Society*. London: The New Economics Foundation.

Sumner, L.W. (1996). *Welfare, Happiness and Ethics*. Oxford: Clarendon Press.

Thorburn, M. (2008). Articulating a Merleau-Pontian Phenomenology of Physical Education: The Quest for Active Student Engagement and Authentic Assessment in High-Stakes Examination Awards, *European Physical Education Review*, *14*(2), 263–280.

Thorburn, M. (2014). Educating for Wellbeing in Scotland: Policy and Philosophy; Pitfalls and Possibilities, *Oxford Review of Education*, *40*(2), 206–222.

Thorburn, M. (2015). Theoretical Constructs of Well-Being and Their Implications for Education, *British Educational Research Journal*, *41*(4), 650–665.

Thorburn, M. (2016). Evaluating Efforts to Enhance Health and Wellbeing in Scottish Secondary Schools, *Journal of Curriculum Studies*. Retrieved from http://dx.doi.org/10.1080/00220272.2016.1167246.

Thorburn, M., & Horrell, A. (2014). Grand Designs! Analysing the Conceptual Tensions Associated with New Physical Education and Health and Wellbeing Curriculum, *Sport, Education and Society*, *19*(5), 621–636.

Thorburn, M., & MacAllister, J. (2013). Dewey, Interest and Well-Being: Prospects for Improving the Educational Value of Physical Education, *Quest*, *65*(4), 458–468.

Thorburn, M., & Marshall, A. (2011). 'Evaluating adventure education experiences: The outside view.' In: M. Berry & C. Hodgson (Eds.), *Adventure Education: An Introduction* (pp. 105–125). London: Routledge.

Tiberius, V. (2008). *The Reflective Life: Living Wisely with Our Limits*. Oxford: Oxford University Press.

Tiberius, V. (2013a). 'Recipes for a good life: Eudaimonism and the contribution of philosophy.' In: A. Waterman (Ed.), *The Best within Us: Positive Psychology Perspectives on Eudaimonic Functioning* (pp. 19–38). Washington, D.C.: American Psychological Association.

Tiberius, V. (2013b). In Defense of Reflection, *Philosophical Issues*, *23*(1), 223–243.

Tiberius, V., & Plakias, A. (2010). 'Wellbeing.' In J. Doris (Ed.), *The Moral Psychology Handbook* (pp. 402–432). New York: Oxford University Press.

Wenger, E. (1998). *Communities of Practice: Learning, Meaning and Identity*. Cambridge: Cambridge University Press.

Young, M. (2014). Overcoming the Crisis in Curriculum Theory: A Knowledge-Based Approach, *Journal of Curriculum Studies*, *45*(2), 101–118.

PART II
Policy perspectives on wellbeing

3

THE POLICY PROMINENCE OF WELLBEING AND THE IMPLICATIONS FOR EDUCATION

Malcolm Thorburn

Introduction

In earlier chapters (Chapters 1 and 2) we have highlighted how a greater conceptual awareness of wellbeing may help educators ensure that young people's lives are more fulfilling and meaningful. The task now is to consider how wellbeing plans are being taken forward in public policy and the extent to which these policies are clear, satisfactory and adequate, as in recent years there has been an increased expectation that schools can be a pivotal force for good in helping young people's lives to become more satisfying and noteworthy (White, 2011). These intentions reflect the heightened global interest there is in wellbeing and the aspirations there are in educational policies to try and constructively connect wellbeing with whole school curriculum planning and pedagogical advice. Within the general discussion of the aims and purposes of wellbeing policy, a review of whether wellbeing could (and should) be measured and the extent to which this might benefit learners' progress is also considered. In addition, the chapter contrasts developments across the Anglophone world (predominantly in England, Australia and New Zealand) in order to better understand policy direction and planning arrangements over recent years. For as Sinnema (2016, p. 966) notes, the policy focus in England and Australia is much more based on a 'tightening of national control, prescription and regulation over curriculum, with expanding curriculum content and a more explicit emphasis on core knowledge', whereas in New Zealand the focus is more on teachers using their professional autonomy to make decisions about curriculum content and implementation.

The two chapters in this section of the book therefore review the broad societal prominence of wellbeing and their implications for educational policy making and practice (Chapter 3) prior to focusing on a detailed evaluation of policy efforts to enhance health and wellbeing in Scottish secondary schools (Chapter 4). This width and depth focus is designed to add to the current evidence base on wellbeing as part of education policy and to identify some of the problematic issues which remain outstanding if wellbeing is to contribute to a range of positive outcomes for young people. As highlighted in the opening two chapters, defining wellbeing is problematic, so the intention is not to reengage with these concerns and arguments but rather to note that from a policy perspective it matters what definition and view of wellbeing policy makers are taking forward. For as Coleman (2009) attests, how wellbeing is defined influences how wellbeing is audited as part of school inspection regimes and how wellbeing progress is reviewed relative to similar curriculum initiatives e.g. programmes relating to social and emotional learning, character education and citizenship.

Focusing on some of the theories and issues informing policy can aid understanding of public policy. Making progress on this basis requires reviewing the most fundamental matters e.g. what policy measures exist for wellbeing, what types of theoretical thinking informed their development and what might this mean for teachers' future professional roles. A further issue is the role of the policy community in driving policy direction, and of how precisely wellbeing policies are framed with regard to educational agendas and with regard to the social and political views of different supra-national bodies and third-sector groups (i.e. national organisations comprising non-governmental and non-profit-making associations, including charities, social enterprises, voluntary and community groups and cooperatives) who view education systems as a way of improving world circumstances. Therefore, while Cairney (2012) notes that the policy process is invariably complex, messy and unpredictable, he also recognises that issues of policy governance are likely to impact on the relationships between *policy conditions* (e.g. the specific wellbeing challenges policy makers face), *structural considerations* (e.g. schooling arrangements such as the school day/week/year) and *agency considerations* (e.g. the capacity of teachers to bring about the types of improvements to wellbeing which are intended).

Why is wellbeing part of public policy?

The prominence of measuring policy in areas such as health, economics and employment has broadened out in recent years to include wellbeing as a more subjective feature of public policy. For example, Layard, Clark, Cornaglia, Powdthavee and Vernoit (2013) conceive that a happy and successful adult life is likely to be founded upon a number of interconnected issues including: family background (e.g. economic, psycho-social factors); adult outcomes (e.g. income, educational level, employment, physical and emotional health) and childhood influence (e.g. intellectual development, school life and wellbeing). In this context, schools are considered as pivotal in relating education to learners' social, emotional, mental and physical wellbeing and to broader childhood influences 'as education is seen as a key factor in developing capacities not only for work and civic engagement, but also for experiencing a flourishing life' (Soutter, O'Steen and Gilmore, 2012, p. 112). Coleman (2009) notes there are many influences at work here including the general emotional literacy of learners (Chapter 9), improving social justice and reducing inequalities (Chapter 10) and a broader focus on health promotion in schools (Chapter 4). This breadth of perspective highlights the multi-various influences there are on achieving a happy and successful life. However, it also needs to be noted that there are those with an interest in political liberalism who argue that 'liberal societies should not base policy on comprehensive religious, moral or philosophical doctrines that many reasonable citizens may not accept' as this may advantage some citizens at the expense of others (Wren-Lewis, 2013, p. 2). Nevertheless, even authors such as Wren-Lewis (2013) recognise that there are good grounds for wellbeing policies promoting the public good and this is very likely to include areas such as education and health policy.

Main findings

A feature of analysing wellbeing policy is trying to understand the thinking which informs policy. Often, thinking can remain rather unacknowledged in policy with statements asserted rather than explained and justified. Dolan, Layard and Metcalfe (2011) advise that for an account of wellbeing to be useful in policy it needs to satisfy three general conditions, namely that it is: *theoretically rigourous, policy relevant and empirically robust*. By theoretically rigourous, Dolan *et al.* (2011) mean that the account of wellbeing provided is underpinned by sound philosophical theory. By policy relevant the authors mean that accounts provided for wellbeing are politically and socially acceptable as well as straightforward to understand. By empirically robust, the authors consider that the account of wellbeing policy chosen can be measured in quantitative ways that are reliable and valid. Three areas of thinking which may have the potential to inform policy are discussed relative to the three criteria for effective wellbeing policy set out by Dolan *et al.* (2011). Thereafter, a review of wellbeing policy-related developments underway in England, Australia and New Zealand are discussed with a particular focus on policy relevance and coherence.

The task therefore for readers during the main part of the chapter is to review:

- the extent to which the three theorising influences on wellbeing discussed are *theoretically rigorous* and underpinned by sound philosophical theory;
- whether wellbeing policy-related developments underway in England, Australia and New Zealand are *policy relevant* in terms of being politically and socially acceptable; and
- whether the review of theorising influences and policy developments in England, Australia and New Zealand provide the basis for collecting *empirically robust* findings which can be measured in quantitative ways that are reliable and valid.

Wellbeing theorising influences – objective and/or subjective measurements of wellbeing

Wellbeing as part of interconnected public policy contains *objective* influences (e.g. peoples, income levels, quality of housing, health and transport) and more *subjective* influences (e.g. level of happiness and other psychological indicators). Haybron and Tiberius (2015) consider that one farsighted example of *objective* and *subjective* influences working together is in Bhutan (a small landlocked country in the Eastern Himalayas in Central Asia with a population of less than one million people) where they reference wellbeing as part of their gross national happiness (GNH) index. The index is comprised of responses to questions in nine areas: psychological wellbeing, population health, education, living standards, good governance, community vitality, time use, ecological resilience and diversity, and cultural resilience and diversity (Centre for Bhutan Studies, 2015). Findings showed that less than one in ten citizens (8.8%) were unhappy, with the remaining citizens being to various degrees happy. Within this broad finding it was noted more specifically that men were happier than women, people living in urban areas were happier than rural residents, educated people were happier and farmers were less happy than other occupational groups (Centre for Bhutan Studies, 2015). By contrast, the more typical measure used in the Anglophone world is to quantitatively (objectively) measure countries' economic activity (i.e. the monetary value of all goods and services produced within a nation's geographic borders over a specified period of time) as a way of defining a country's gross domestic product (GDP). At face value, we might consider that the GNH index is a more sensitised and enlightened measurement i.e. based on the type of wellbeing-related values chosen and the idea of public-goods policy highlighted by Wren-Lewis (2013). However, within complex Western countries with large populations others might consider there is a need to more obviously measure *economic* (e.g. level of economic activity, income levels, transport infrastructure) and *public* (e.g. wellbeing in education) policy goals, as economic arguments play a considerable part in deciding whether people can satisfy their preferences and achieve their life goals. Therefore, for those in the Anglophone world, analysing wellbeing policy often involves considering economic *and* public influences on policy. For example, the Legatum Institute (2014), an independent non-partisan public policy organisation whose research advances ideas and policies in support of free and prosperous societies around the world, argue for a *prosperity* index based on measuring wealth and wellbeing as it recognises 'that the era of GDP being the unique measure is now over' (Legatum Institute, 2014, p. 16).

One of the main policy devices used for collecting economic and public policy information is to collect large sets of *(objective)* data e.g. through large surveys. Potentially this allows general findings to emerge which can then be scrutinised in more specific ways in order to identity and profile a broad range of *(subjective)* influences on wellbeing. The main challenge with such approaches at the level of wellbeing policy is that while people may have similar objective profiles e.g. similar levels of income and health, they could have very different levels of subjective wellbeing based on their relative levels of confidence, happiness and self-esteem (McLellan and Stewart, 2015). Thus, there is a need for a degree of caution if predominantly using objective measurements of wellbeing as the main basis for policy planning – relative to using a mixed methods approach (quantitative and qualitative) where objective and subjective information is collected e.g. through collecting a broad range of data via survey-type set questionnaire responses and merging this with open-ended questions and/or interview findings with a smaller sample of people. Such an approach is likely to yield more insightful findings provided acknowledgement is taken of the research context e.g. through considering the interrelationship between policy conditions and structure and agency considerations (Cairney, 2012). This would be evident, for example, when collecting data which acknowledged the importance of school catchment area, legal status, curriculum specialism, learner selection criteria, type of academy as well as other factors such as gender and age and stage of learners (McLellan and Stewart, 2015).

Among the largest ongoing collection of data on children's wellbeing is the series of *Good Childhood* reports collated by The Children's Society in collaboration with the University of York. Findings for the reports were achieved using a mixed method research approach through merging children's responses to set survey questions while also allowing space for children to include their answers to more open-ended questions. Furthermore, the survey has evolved over the last decade in response to topics and themes which have emerged from earlier findings. This approach enables progress and trends in children's wellbeing in England and findings in England relative to evidence from children in 14 other countries worldwide to inform the research design (The Children's Society, 2015). This research approach enables policy stakeholders to *diagnostically* review research findings in order to inform future policy. If effective, the policy process can *proactively* highlight how aspiration and arguments for change are drawing upon research concerns identified. In relation to the international comparison data collected from a representative sample of children aged 8/9 years, 10/11 years and 12/13 years, evidence from The Children's Society (2015) highlights that children in England had relatively low levels of subjective wellbeing compared with young people in the majority of other countries. For example, in 24 of the 30 aspects of life questions asked about children in England responses were in the lower half of countries sampled. Responses were of particular educational concern with regard to: life satisfaction (14th out of 15 countries), self-confidence (15th out of 15 countries), relationships with teachers (14th out of 15 countries), school experience (12th out of 15 countries), health (13th out of 15 countries), relationships with other children in the class (14th out of 15 countries) feeling positive about the future (11th out of 15 countries), and happiness in the last two weeks (11th out of 15 countries). In fact, it was mostly in areas which are indirect to schools e.g. friends (6th out of 15 countries), freedom (8th out of 15 countries) and amount of opportunities (8th out of 15 countries) where more average comparisons were evident. It is not the purpose of this chapter to discuss the detail of these findings at length, beyond registering the importance of policy communities (however established and influenced) avoiding complacency when presented with this type of evidence. It is also worth noting that the validity and reliability of these findings is enhanced by the ongoing *monitoring* and *benchmarking* of children's subjective wellbeing, as this approach enables young people's wellbeing to be tracked over time and strategies designed to enhance wellbeing. Studies such as The Children's Society series of reports also highlight the benefits of further research e.g. in areas such as the extent to which learners feel connected with school, learners' relationships with teachers and the extent to which schools are an enabling institution which is a closely integrated part of the learning community (Gray *et al.*, 2011; Noble and McGrath, 2015).

Wellbeing theorising influences: pragmatic subjectivism

In order to know more about the multiple factors which might influence wellbeing, Haybron and Tiberius (2015) consider that *pragmatic subjectivism* offers constructive possibilities for informing wellbeing policy. This is on the basis that public decision-making procedures for wellbeing should, where possible, be subjective in practice, as this 'represents a workable approach given the diversity of values in modern democratic societies' (Haybron and Tiberius, 2015, p. 714). Thus, while the authors recognise that there are other approaches to wellbeing such as capabilities approaches (Nussbaum, 2011) they argue that promoting wellbeing should be among the approaches policy makers consider adopting. This is based on a definition of wellbeing which recognises that bettering people's lives should take place according to people's own standards. Therefore, pragmatic subjectivism encourages policy makers to use the best available research and information of what people value and to consider this closely in the framing of policy objectives. Such an approach effectively rules out the use of comprehensive (objective-type) metrics of wellbeing. Instead, what are required are more partial measures which cover important aspects of wellbeing. In spirit, pragmatic subjectivism (based as it is on treating people's values with respect) is a lot closer to the GNH (Bhutan) approach used to measure personal welfare values than the GDP statistics which more often inform economic approaches to policy. However, the difficulty of pragmatic subjectivism is that it can be problematic for policy makers to simply help 'themselves to a highly tendentious and sharply contested theoretical position in a field where they have no significant competence' (Haybron and Tiberius, 2015, p. 718), especially when diverse theories of wellbeing exist (see Chapter 2). Therefore, reflecting Wren-Lewis (2013), Haybron and Tiberius (2015) take the view that governments should not endorse any particular conception of wellbeing and should instead advise that person-respecting welfarism (pragmatic subjectivism) should defer to individuals' own conceptions of wellbeing in promoting their interests. This position raises issues about how subjective wellbeing data can be collected and measured. In this respect, the OECD (2013) in considering that subjective wellbeing is an important component of a better life (along with various objective wellbeing influences) have produced extended advice on how methodologically survey-based data on subjective wellbeing can be collected, measured and analysed.

Wellbeing theorising influences: strengths-based approaches

Recently, there has been a move across a range of public services to utilise *strengths- (or asset-) based approaches* as a more effective way of helping people identify the factors which enhance their lives (Matthews, Kilgour, Christian, Mori and Hill, 2015).

Strengths in this respect are considered as part of something which is connected with salutogenic health theory (Antonovsky, 1996) where health and wellbeing influences are multi-dimensional and holistic in nature i.e. encompassing social, psychological, spiritual and physical dimensions. As such, the foundations of salutogenic approaches are as much a theory of human beings as a theory of health, especially if health messages are presented as a set of fixed (and often unachievable) pathogenic end-goals to aspire towards. For as McCuaig, Quennerstedt and Macdonald (2013) note, under salutogenic thinking achieving your goals does not involve reaching a definite end point; rather it is part of something which is much more dynamic: a lifelong learning process or journey. On this basis, strengths-based thinking offers possibilities for connecting education with associated wellbeing concerns, as reflected in educational practices which, in part, emphasise learners' self-confidence, self-awareness and empathy for others. A similar approach is utilised in the aforementioned Children's Society reporting where one the three research questions informing the research is 'to consider positive aspects of children's lives rather than just negative behaviours' (The Children's Society, 2015, p. 12). Arguably, as well, following a strengths-based approach to wellbeing might help placate the concerns of Ecclestone and Hayes (2009), who, as noted in Chapter 2, are dismayed by the therapeutic-type interventions taking place in schools and the tendency for learners to become dependent upon educators for their wellbeing under such circumstances. In this context, a strengths-based approach to wellbeing might be considered more constructive as it would focus on the health and wellbeing advantages you have rather than over dwelling on the health and wellbeing concerns you have. Strengths- (or asset-) based approaches contrast with deficit-based models of health improvement where public and professional services are designed to support individual and community needs. Friedli (2013) is critical of asset-based public health policies as the advantages they might create for particular individuals and social groups are overtaken by the *structural* issues which exist in societies and which create material inequalities e.g. poor housing. These inequalities contribute to profound disadvantages in communities and to people having a lack of *control* over how to positively influence their lives. These problems are compounded by neo-liberal welfare economics which 'sound the drum beat for the retreat of statutory, state provision of both public services and public health' (Friedli, 2013, p. 140).

These concerns notwithstanding, Matthews *et al.* (2015) used strengths- (or asset-) based thinking to inform their mixed method research design, through using the Personal Wellbeing Index – School Children, designed by Cummins and Lau (2005) alongside focus group interviews with learners aged between 11–16 years in one comprehensive school in South Wales. Findings were consistent in many instances with The Children's Society (2015) report e.g. learners valued their independence, their friends and their material freedom. However, school transition stages (i.e. moving to secondary schools, impending exams and reviewing plans for after compulsory education) were linked to a lowering of subjective wellbeing. Findings from reports such as The Children's Society (2015) and Matthews *et al.* (2015) invite review over whether wellbeing is having a positive influence over young people's lives within existing curriculum planning and pedagogical approaches in schools.

Wellbeing policy and practice: The context in England

In England, personal, social, health and economic (PSHE) education is a non-statutory subject where it is considered unnecessary to provide standardised frameworks or programmes of study, as teachers are best placed to understand the needs of learners. Within these flexible curriculum arrangements, where wellbeing is part of PSHE, the expectation is that where appropriate teachers will make links with statutory curriculum requirements e.g. in areas such as the importance of physical activity and diet for a healthy lifestyle. Citizenship education is by contrast a compulsory part of the curriculum at Key Stages 3 and 4 and focuses on improving understanding of democracy and justice, rights and responsibilities and identities and diversity. This is noted as a further area where wellbeing might make constructive curriculum connections (Department for Education, 2013). Under current plans, funding has been provided to the PSHE association (as the lead national body) to work with schools to advise them on how best to design their curriculum arrangements and improve the quality of learning and teaching. In their online FAQ section on curriculum guidance, in answer to the question 'How do I fit PSHE education into the curriculum?' the response is 'We recommend that PSHE education should be taught in discrete lessons, supported by other learning opportunities across the curriculum, including the use of enhancement days where possible. This is the position taken by Ofsted' (PSHE, 2016).

Formby and Wolstenholme (2012) found that secondary schools frequently used discrete lessons and enhancement-type days as teaching approaches rather than integrating wellbeing with subject knowledge and learners' prior learning experiences. Formby and Wolstenholme (2012) also found that teachers often viewed wellbeing-related teaching as more of an obstruction than a benefit to the academic life of the school and therefore of little, if any help, in raising learners' attainment. Thus, in only a few schools did the authors find evidence of learners' subjective perspective on their needs being seen as a constructive contributor to their educational achievement. Furthermore, Formby and Wolstenholme (2012) identified that teachers often felt uncomfortable and lacking in confidence when engaging learners in discussions about their personal values and decision-making. Similarly, Byrne et al. (2016) found that with regard to teaching particular health issues that proportionately fewer preservice, newly qualified and early career teachers considered themselves knowledgeable, skilled and confident when covering sensitive topics such as sex and relationship education relative to other topics such as healthy eating. Therefore, while the PSHE association do move on to mention the possibilities for integrated learning approaches as a supplement to discrete lessons, it may be that without more formal curriculum advice (and arguably statutory curriculum status) that wellbeing-related outcomes become one among many of the priorities schools face. This raises the possibility of variability in how schools take wellbeing agendas forward and also the possibility of quality assurance metrics, such as those set out in Ofsted (2015) school inspections guidelines defining how schools measure their progress. This is potentially problematic, as it could be argued that under the grade descriptors for personal development, behaviour and welfare (see criteria high-lighted below), there are relatively few distinguishing differences between schools classified as 'outstanding' and 'good'.

Outstanding (Ofsted, 2015)	Good (Ofsted, 2015)
Pupils can explain accurately and confidently how to keep themselves healthy. They make informed choices about healthy eating, fitness and their emotional and mental well-being. They have an age-appropriate understanding of healthy relationships and are confident in staying safe from abuse and exploitation.	The school's open culture promotes all aspects of pupils' welfare. Pupils are safe and feel safe. They have opportunities to learn how to keep themselves safe. They enjoy learning about how to stay healthy and about emotional and mental health, safe and positive relationships and how to prevent misuse of technology.
Pupils' spiritual, moral, social and cultural development equips them to be thoughtful, caring and active citizens in school and in wider society.	Pupils' spiritual, moral, social and cultural development ensures that they are prepared to be reflective about and responsible for their actions as good citizens.

Ofsted (2015, pp. 52–53).

School-based reviews against the expectations of Ofsted (2015) might make it difficult for teachers to know what areas of wellbeing are reasonable to address and measure at certain ages and stages of learning, and how such developments can be evaluated. It might also run the risk that the focus becomes one of achieving objective measurement metrics rather than dwelling on the subjective experiences of each particular child (Watson, Emery and Bayliss, 2012).

By contrast, it could be argued that the flexibility available within wellbeing (as part of the broader area of PSHE) is quite an enlightened approach to take as within the messy complexity of schools 'one-size-fits-all policies (can) run aground when hitting the rocks of real life' (Ball, MacGuire and Braun, 2012, p. 149). Therefore, schools might consider building on the broad advice provided by Weare (2015) who outlined in generic terms the types of planning and practice ideas schools should consider taking forward when promoting wellbeing. Central to advice is adopting a whole school approach which emphasises strengths and capacities and which is sustained by supportive classroom climates and ethos. Adopting this longer-term approach is considered preferable to shorter-term interventions such as the enhancement-type thematic days PSHE (2016) recommends but which Formby and Wolstenholme (2012) found to be ineffective. Consistent with this approach is ensuring that teachers are *well* and have access to professional learning support (Bryne *et al.*, 2016) and, in addition, that learners and parents/carers are involved in sharing their wellbeing aspirations. Weare (2015, p. 5) recognises however that within 'the complex world of the secondary school, whole school approaches need to be developed incrementally, with the total commitment of the senior leadership team, starting small with realistic expectations and proceeding strategically'. This brief review of wellbeing as part of PSHE in England has shown that there is only a partial tightening of national control and regulation at this time (Sinnema, 2016) with the challenge being for schools to maximise the curriculum flexibility presently available at the same time as ensuring national quality assurance standards are met.

Wellbeing policy and practice: The context in Australia

In Australia, preparations for the first national curriculum adopt a seven-fold generic-capabilities approach as a device for enhancing cross-curriculum learning and teaching (Australian Curriculum Assessment and Reporting Authority [ACARA], 2015). The closest of the seven capabilities to wellbeing – personal and social capability – is underpinned by self and social references in ways similar to Nussbaum's (2011) capabilities approach, where there is an attempt to merge central capabilities with necessary functional (outcome-based) attributes. Comparing progress across capabilities should make it possible to measure how well a person's life is faring, and of how well a person's life is faring relative to others (see Chapter 2). The key ideas for personal and social capability are organised into four interrelated elements: self-awareness, self-management, social awareness and social management (ACARA, 2015). Under self-awareness learners are encouraged to develop a well-grounded awareness of their own emotional states, needs and perspectives, and as part of self-management, learners are supported in their attempts to develop metacognitive skills strategies to manage themselves in a range of situations in order to achieve their goals. As part of social awareness, learners are encouraged to recognise others' feelings and to know how and when to assist others within a rights-respecting culture, and under social management learners are supported in their attempts to work effectively with others and to resolve conflict with positive outcomes. The self- and social-awareness and management focus is redolent of Nussbaum's (2011) notion of the good (capable) life being one where young people can reflect critically in order to participate in the political world and the world of living with others (functionings).

The policy intention is that personal and social capability skills are addressed across all learning areas and at every stage of learners' schooling (ACARA, 2015). That said, health and physical education is specifically highlighted as the learning area with the highest proportion of content linked to personal and social capability. Within health and physical education policy the advice is that adopting a strengths-based approach (one of five propositions that shape the entire health and physical education curriculum) is a helpful way for learners to develop a range of interpersonal skills such as communication, negotiation, teamwork and leadership, and an appreciation of diverse perspectives (ACARA, 2015). As the introduction of the first national curriculum in Australia is still ongoing it will be a little while before evidence gathered from practice filters back and informs the extent to which policy plans are being coherently implemented. For the present, it is worth noting that in wellbeing specifically, a psychologically-informed focus on capabilities e.g. personal attributes such as resilience, courage and determination and social dimensions such as group learning is very different from the cognitive perspective on wellbeing which emphasises more the importance of reflecting critically on happiness and personal decision-making (see Chapter 2). Furthermore, there may be concerns about how developmental accounts such as a capabilities/functionings approach (with a focus on social awareness and social management) can articulate with a focus on personal value judgements (with a focus on self-awareness and self-management). This is especially so when national arrangements need to coherently link with state- and territory-based responsibilities for curriculum implementation.

Wellbeing policy and practice: The context in New Zealand

In New Zealand, from the early 1990s onwards there have been various revisions to their outcomes-focused national curriculum arrangements. These revisions have enabled academic and policy evaluations to comment on progress and consider their implications for education and schooling. Soutter *et al.* (2012) in exploring the language used in the New Zealand curriculum, consider that there is now a clear alignment between New Zealand curriculum arrangements and contemporary wellbeing scholarship, as evident through policy advice emphasising the importance of coherence and of making natural and feasible (rather than forced) integrated curriculum connections across learning areas. However, in similar ways to Formby and Wolstenholme (2012), Soutter *et al.* (2012) also found that as learners progressed through secondary schooling there was increasing evidence of learning experiences being dominated by assessment-related subject tasks. Therefore, quite how a heightened emphasis on testing and evaluation can merge with wellbeing curriculum intentions (and their supporting theory and policy advice) is likely to be an important matter in the future, as currently wellbeing related areas are insufficiently evident in learners' qualifications records (see Chapter 4). Thus, Soutter *et al.* (2012, p. 135) consider there is a need to 'provide a feasible and flexible structure for holistic assessment of student achievement, resulting in a multi-faceted view of academic success that encompasses wellbeing'.

Fuelled by an interest in improving outcomes for young people aged 12 to 19 years with, or at risk of developing, mild to moderate mental health issues (estimated to be around one-fifth of young people during their adolescent years), the New Zealand Government (2015) completed a wellbeing review of progress in 68 secondary schools. The review found that support for wellbeing varied across schools, with 11 of the 68 schools (16.2%) sampled being well-placed to promote and respond to learners' wellbeing while 39 schools (57.3%) had elements of good practice that could be built on. The remaining 18 schools (26.5%) faced more major challenges with some schools being overwhelmed by various issues and unable to adequately promote learners' wellbeing. Therefore, while there was evidence of rights–respecting relationships and connecting care information with academic guidance when identifying and responding to wellbeing issues, learners would benefit from more teachers asking them about their experiences and involving them in decisions about the quality of their school life as 'student voice' varied from school to school. Learners would also benefit from schools being more deliberate in promoting wellbeing in the curriculum. To improve matters it is considered that the Ministry of Education should provide examples of possible approaches to learners' wellbeing which are strongly aligned to the health and physical education learning area and which support the development of the key competencies. Additionally, promoting meaningful and innovative assessment practice should help deliver more manageable assessment arrangements (New Zealand Government, 2015).

Even though it is possible that emphasising the particular contribution of health and physical education for improving learners' wellbeing could run counter to a more obvious school approach (see Chapter 6), it is worth reviewing some of the interrelated policy-planning-pedagogy issues associated with wellbeing *through* health and physical education, as this is also the approach being taken in Australia. Sinkinson and Burrows (2011) consider that, as areas such as mental health cover sensitive concerns like diversity, discrimination, body shape and relationships, it clearly matters how learning and teaching takes place. In this respect, Sinkinson and Burrows (2011, p. 58) bemoan the twinning of health and physical education, as it leaves the teaching of health education prone 'to the mercy of physical education teachers' whims'. While no empirical data is produced to support this assertion, it does raise the question of the contrast there might be between a teacher as subject-knowledge expert and teacher as health professional when it comes to engaging with sensitive issues (see Chapter 8) and when it comes to wellbeing being seen as a whole-school responsibility for all teachers (see Chapter 4). Sinkinson and Burrows (2011) – as with Formby and Wolstenholme (2012) – are concerned that in this context, teachers might play it safe and stay within their comfort zones, with as a consequence learning becoming increasingly shallow and dull. If this happens, it would 'in the face of inequalities in youth health and wellbeing … (become) … a highly political statement about priorities, privileges and disadvantages' (Sinkinson and Burrows, 2011, p. 61). In terms of how health education might be redefined to provide greater recognition of societal and global wellbeing ambitions, Sinkinson and Burrows (2011) recommend a more learner responsive approach, where teachers are committed to diversity, school improvement and teacher effectiveness; a series of ambitions which are broadly similar to those outlined by Weare (2015).

Future directions

Surrounding this chapter are arguments about the extent to which wellbeing policies make a public good difference. Inevitably, this is a complex area to consider as without clear criteria and goals it is often difficult to define wellbeing (*in theoretically rigourous ways*), elaborate on its connections with education and society (*policy relevance*) and to measure progress (*empirically robust findings*). These various challenges are likely to impact on policy implementation, and it is not surprising that what emerges from a review of developments in England, Australia and New

Zealand are variable degrees of policy coherence and clarity. More positively however, it could be argued that within our ever more complex, dynamic and interconnected lives it is good that public policies are trying to engage with a broader and more nuanced conception of wellbeing within a policy context which recognises the limitations of relying more narrowly on certain fixed measurements of health and economic satisfaction. In this light, it is also helpful that education is a key component of wellbeing policies. Furthermore, findings such as those from The Children's Society (2015) provide a useful benchmark reference for tracking future progress, and for identifying emerging wellbeing-related priorities requiring policy attention. Following this line of progress, the potential exists for the aspirations of policy stakeholders to more closely connect with the structural arrangements operating in schools and with teachers' professional role, and most crucially, with the vital matter of what young people think about their wellbeing.

Summary of key findings

- Wellbeing is increasingly prominent in public policy – albeit in different guises and driven by different objective and subjective influences.
- The public policy process is frequently complex and subject to multi-various influences e.g. policy conditions, structural considerations and agency considerations.
- Wellbeing is of interest to a range of government departments as well as policy stakeholders in different supra-national bodies and third-sector groups.
- Three areas of theoretical thinking (objective and/or subjective measurements of wellbeing, pragmatic subjectivism and strengths-based approaches) which have the potential to inform policy were reviewed.
- Wellbeing policy and practice developments in England, Australia and New Zealand reveal contrasting theoretical influences, planning intentions, strategies for pedagogical engagement and approaches for measuring wellbeing.
- Reviewing whether good policies are theoretically rigourous, relevant and empirically robust is an effective way of analysing policy coherence.

Reflective tasks

- Do you consider that wellbeing should become an increasingly prominent part of educators' professional responsibility?
- Are you surprised by the findings of The Children's Society (2015) report?
- Is it possible (and wise) to let learners decide on what is important for their own wellbeing (pragmatic subjectivism)?
- Do you think learners' wellbeing should be measured in schools?
- Is it possible for teachers to be a subject knowledge experts as well as health and wellbeing professionals?

Further readings

Gray, J., Galton, M., McLaughlin, C., Clark, B., & Symonds, J. (2011). *The Supportive School: Wellbeing and the Young Adolescent*. Cambridge: Cambridge Scholars.
Nussbaum, M.C. (2011). *Creating Capabilities*. Cambridge: The Belknap Press.
White, J. (2011). *Exploring Wellbeing in Schools*. London: Routledge.

References

Antonovsky, A. (1996). The Salutogenic Model as a Theory of Health Promotion, *Health Promotion International, 32*(1), 11–18.
Australian Curriculum, Assessment and Reporting Authority. (2015). *Australian Curriculum*. Retrieved from http://www.australiancurriculum.edu.au/
Bryne, J., Pickett, K., Rietdijk, W., Shephard, J., Grace, M., & Roderick, P. (2016). A Longitudinal Study to Explore the Impact of Preservice Teacher Health Training on Early Career Teachers' Roles as Health Promoters, *Pedagogy in Health Promotion*. Retrieved from http://php.sagepub.com.ezproxy.is.ed.ac.uk/content/early/2016/05/19/2373379916644449.full.pdf+html
Cairney, P. (2012). *Understanding Public Policy: Theories and Issues*. London: Palgrave Macmillan.
Centre for Bhutan Studies. (2015). Bhutan's 2015 Gross National Happiness Index. Retrieved from http://www.bhutanstudies.org.bt/publicationFiles/2015GNH/Summary of 2015 GNH Index.pdf
Coleman, J. (2009). Well-being in Schools: Empirical Measure, or Politician's Dream?, *Oxford Review of Education, 35*(3), 281–292.
Cummins, R. A., & Lau, A.D.L. (2005). *Personal Wellbeing Index: School Children (PWI-SC)* (3rd ed). Melbourne: Deakin University.
Department for Education. (2013). National Curriculum in England: Framework for Key Stages 1 to 4. Retrieved from https://www.gov.uk/government/publications/national-curriculum-in- england-framework-for-key-stages-1-to-4
Dolan, P., Layard, R., & Metcalfe, R. (2011). *Measuring Subjective Wellbeing for Public Policy*. London: Centre of Economic Performance, London School of Economics and Political Science.
Formby, E., & Wolstenholme, C. (2012). 'If there's going to be a subject that you don't have to do ...' Findings from a Mapping Study of PSHE Education in English Secondary Schools, *Pastoral Care in Education, 30*(1), 5–18.
Friedli, L. (2013). 'What we've tried, hasn't worked': The Politics of Assets Based Public Health, *Critical Public Health, 23*(2), 131–145.
Gray, J., Galton, M., McLaughlin, C., Clark, B., & Symonds, J. (2011). *The Supportive School: Wellbeing and the Young Adolescent*. Cambridge: Cambridge Scholars.
Haybron, D., & Tiberius, V. (2015). Well-being Policy: What Standard of Well-being? *Journal of the American Philosophical Association, 1*(4), 712–733.
Kosutic, I., & McDowell, T. (2008). Diversity and social justice in family therapy literature: A decade review. *Journal of Feminist Family Therapy*, 20(2), 142–165.
Layard, R., Clark, A.E., Cornaglia, F., Powdthavee, N., & Vernoit, J. (2013). *What Predicts a Successful Life? A Life-Course Model of Well-being*. London: Centre of Economic Performance, London School of Economics and Political Science.
Legatum Institute. (2014). *Wellbeing and Policy*. London: Legatum Institute.
McCuaig, L., Quennerstedt, M., & Macdonald, D. (2013). A Salutogenic, Strengths-based Approach as a Theory to Guide HPE Curriculum Change, *Asia-Pacific Journal of Health, Sport and Physical Education, 4*(2), 109–125.

McLellan, R., & Stewart, S. (2015). Measuring Children and Young People's Wellbeing in the School Context, *Cambridge Journal of Education, 45*(3), 307–322.

Matthews, N., Kilgour, L., Christian, P., Mori, K., & Hill, D.M. (2015). Understanding, Evidencing, and Promoting Adolescent Well-being: An Emerging Agenda for Schools, *Youth and Society, 47*(5), 659–683.

New Zealand Government. (2015). *Wellbeing for Young People's Success at Secondary School.* Retrieved from http://www.ero.govt.nz/assets/Uploads/ERO-Wellbeing-SecondSchools-web.pdf

New Zealand Ministry of Education. (2016). *The New Zealand Curriculum online.* Retrieved from http://nzcurriculum.tki.org.nz/

Noble, T., & McGrath, H. (2015). *The PROSPER School Pathways for Student Wellbeing: Policy and Practices.* New York: Springer.

Nussbaum, M.C. (2011). *Creating Capabilities.* Cambridge: The Belknap Press.

Organisation for Economic Co-operation and Development. (2013). *OECD Guidelines on Measuring Subjective Well-being.* Retrieved from http://dx.doi.org/10.1787/9789264191655-en

Ofsted. (2015). *School Inspection Handbook.* Retrieved from https://www.gov.uk/government/publications/school-inspection-handbook-from-september-2015

PSHE Association. (2016). *Curriculum Guidance.* Retrieved from https://www.pshe-association.org.uk/curriculum-and-resources/curriculum

Sinkinson, M., & Burrows, L. (2011). Reframing Health Education in New Zealand/Aotearoa Schools, *Asia-Pacific Journal of Health, Sport and Physical Education, 2*(3–4), 53–69.

Sinnema, C. (2016). 'The Ebb and Flow of Curricular Autonomy: Balance between Local Freedom and National Prescription in Curricula'. In: Wyse, D., Hayward, L., & Pandya, J. (Eds.) *The Sage Handbook of Curriculum, Pedagogy and Assessment* (pp. 965–983). London: Sage.

Soutter, A.K., O'Steen, B., & Gilmore, A. (2012). Wellbeing in the New Zealand Curriculum, *Journal of Curriculum Studies, 44*(1), 111–142.

The Children's Society. (2015). *The Good Childhood Report.* London: The Children's Society.

Watson, D., Emery, C., & Bayliss, P. (2012). *Children's Social and Emotional Wellbeing in Schools: A Critical Perspective.* London: Policy Press.

Weare, K. (2015). *What Works in Promoting Social and Emotional Well-being and Responding to Mental Health Problems in Schools?* London: National Children's Bureau.

White, J. (2011). *Exploring Wellbeing in Schools.* London: Routledge.

Wren-Lewis, S. (2013). Well-being as a Primary Good: Towards Legitimate Well-being Policy, *Philosophy and Public Policy Quarterly, 31*(2), 2–9.

4

EVALUATING EFFORTS TO ENHANCE HEALTH AND WELLBEING

A review of policy aspirations and practice developments in Scottish secondary schools

Malcolm Thorburn and Donna Dey

Introduction

Chapter 3 highlighted the increased policy expectation there often is nowadays for schools to be a pivotal force for good in helping young people to live more stable and rewarding lives. However, as Chapter 3 also outlined, these aspirations have been supported by variable degrees of policy coherence and clarity. Accordingly, the focus in this chapter is to analyse health and wellbeing (HWB) developments in Scotland, in order to understand better in the context of one country the policy formation process, learning and teaching in HWB, the contribution of HWB towards learners' wider achievement as well as a broader evaluation of HWB as part of Curriculum for Excellence (CFE). This review aims to provide insights into the multiple challenges which exist in and between policy guidelines and policy enactment in schools. Approaching the chapter in this way enables consideration to be taken of the 'overall texture and rhythms of teachers' work – the different times of year in schools and the deadening tiredness with which teachers often grapple' (Ball *et al.*, 2012, p. 5). The review is also timely, as since 2004, CFE – in essence, a progressive set of all-encompassing national curriculum guidelines and arrangements covering learners between 3 and 18 years – has moved from being a broad set of policy aspirations to full implementation in 2010–2011. As such, there should be in place by now a heightened emphasis on active learner engagement alongside an encouragement for teachers to make greater use of their professional autonomy and curriculum decision-making responsibility (Scottish Government, 2008). Sinnema (2016, p. 966) considers that Scotland (like New Zealand but unlike England and Australia), is one of the leading examples of where schools 'are asked to address the challenges inherent in designing and implementing a local curriculum in a manner that also ensures they give effect to a national curriculum'. Moreover, the current period has been identified as a 'watershed moment' for CFE, as the first five-year cycle of programme implementation is nearing completion (OECD, 2015, p. 100).

Thus, there is a major opportunity to evaluate whether a greater policy engagement with dynamic learning and teaching in HWB is being taken forward or not.

In brief, Scotland has made use of its post-1999 devolved-governmental powers to update curriculum aims and address health inequalities. As Allan (2003) notes, the policy-making culture became one where conservatism and caution were replaced by innovation and forward thinking. Cairney (2009) found, when researching the health-related area of tobacco control, that internal politics became bound-in with forward thinking, as politicians were keen to trump each other in order to highlight how devolution was making a constructive difference in Scotland. This situation is in marked difference to previous times when educational policy thinking was more centralised and controlled (Bryce and Humes, 2008). Within this dynamic policy context, HWB came to occupy a prominent curriculum role, as along with literacy and numeracy, it is one of three cross-curriculum responsibilities of *all* teachers due to its capacity to promote 'confidence, independent thinking and positive attitudes and dispositions' (Scottish Executive, 2006a, p. 10). Furthermore, it is a new disciplinary area alongside the more familiar subject areas of language, mathematics, science, expressive arts, social studies, technologies and religious and moral education (Scottish Executive, 2006a). As such, HWB has a dual curriculum role in that it is both a general responsibility for all teachers and a subject-based responsibility of some teachers – typically Guidance, Home Economics and Physical Education teachers) who have an enhanced subject remit for HWB.

CFE is considered one of the most ambitious programmes of educational change ever undertaken in Scotland (Scottish Government, 2008) and is based on developing four generic learning capacities; namely, for young people to become 'successful learners', 'confident individuals', 'effective contributors' and 'responsible citizens'. The current design arrangements reflect a partial engagement with the type of therapeutic culture ambitions which are a particular concern of governments and supra-national bodies with an interest in equity, social justice and the emotional wellbeing of young people (Thorburn, 2016). This is evident through the merging of a traditional subject-based curriculum with four newly framed generic contexts for learning (i.e. the ethos and life of the school as a community, curriculum areas and subjects, interdisciplinary learning and opportunities for personal achievement) which are collectively designed to help learners identify and take on more responsibility for their progress (Scottish Government, 2008). Within the HWB context specifically what is evident (relative to the theorising influences for wellbeing outlined in Chapter 2) is that Scotland mostly perceives HWB as part of a wider asset-based approach to learning. Therefore, the endorsement for HWB reflects an interest in the development of the whole child and of Scottish aspirations to replicate a Scandinavian-type model of public policy, where there is an ongoing commitment to comprehensive schooling and to all learners (Lingard, 2008). Needless to say, enacting these intentions is not without its considerable challenges, with McLaren (2013, p. 431) noting, for example, that the responsibility of all teachers for HWB commitment 'is over-simplistic and, unless there is some further consideration of roles and remits, it will become the responsibility of no-one'.

Given the HWB as part of CFE context outlined, the chapter focuses on five key aspects of policy and practice. These are a:

- descriptive account of policy formation;
- critical review of the policy-making process;
- critical review of HWB pedagogy and practices;
- critical review of the connections between HWB and wider achievement;
- wider evaluation of HWB, CFE and young peoples' lives.

As secondary schooling is the stage of schooling which has tended to have the most difficulty in introducing many CFE imperatives (Humes, 2013), our focus is mostly in this area. For international readers predominantly, Scotland occupies the northern third (approximately) of the United Kingdom (UK) mainland and has a population of 5.35 million – 8% of the UK population, most of whom live in the urbanised centre of Scotland. Scotland currently has 361 secondary schools for learners of 11–18 years with school education being compulsory until 16 years with over three-quarters of learners continuing their school education until 18 years (Scottish Government, 2015a). Local (unitary) authorities (councils) retain an operational responsibility role for managing most schools as market models of education 'run against the grain ... (as) ... democratic values, comprehensive schools, equality of access and positive discrimination have long been distinguishing hallmarks of national and local authority policies' (MacBeath, 2013, p. 1014). As such, there is little school diversification in Scotland e.g. according to legal status, curriculum focus or pupil selection, and the independent (private school) sector is also small (i.e. less than 5% of pupils).

Main findings

Educating for health and wellbeing in Scotland

A descriptive account of policy formation

As noted earlier, health improvement quickly became a key policy area in twenty-first-century Scotland with the Scottish Health Promoting Schools Unit already involved in the process of embedding HWB into schools, through the launch of the policy 'Being Well, Doing Well' (Learning and Teaching Scotland [LTS], 2004). This health promoting framework consisted of a variety of aspirational statements to support all schools becoming health-promoting schools by 2007. A related report on helping children to be safe and achieve their potential (Scottish Executive, 2005) contained the first mention of the eight SHANARRI indicators (safe, healthy, achieving, nurtured, active, respected, responsible and included), the broad equivalent of the 'Every Child Matters' programme in England and Wales. Consequently, HWB became identified as one of the main measures by which CFE would be better able to meet the educational outcomes of all young people (Scottish Government, 2008), as policy ambitions recognised that curriculum aims can best be achieved if children are healthy, emotionally secure and psychologically at ease with themselves. During the policy formation process, policy attention focused on articulating how the four CFE capacities could be developed. A series of *Building the Curriculum* publications between 2006 and 2011 contained an emphasis on curriculum areas (Scottish Executive, 2006a), learning and teaching (Scottish Government, 2008) and a framework for assessment (Scottish Government, 2011a).

Furthermore, LTS (a public body organisation responsible for the development and support of the Scottish curriculum prior to its merger with Her Majesty's Inspectorate for Education to form 'Education Scotland' in 2011), issued principles and practice advice on HWB for all teachers to consider as part of their remit (LTS, 2009a). The brief support notes (four pages) offered a blend of aspirational and entitlement statements coupled with an outline of the general expectations of teachers e.g. teachers are advised that their responsibilities include 'establishing open, positive, supportive relationships across the school community, where children and young people will feel that they are listened to, and where they feel secure in their ability to discuss sensitive aspects of their lives' (LTS, 2009a, p. 2). In the same year, six areas of HWB covering 51 experiences and outcomes statements on: mental, emotional, social and physical wellbeing; planning for choices and changes; physical education, physical activity and sport; food and health; substance misuse and relationships, sexual health and parenthood were identified (LTS 2009b). The links to subject areas are most immediately identifiable in the last four of the six areas. These first two areas are more generic in nature and represent the newest of the challenges for all teachers in terms of supporting their school environment, promoting positive behaviour and encouraging learners to make informed choices about their HWB. However, unlike the vast majority of other curriculum areas, many of the HWB experience and outcome statements were not progressive, but repeated verbatim across successive stages of development. The continuing emphasis on HWB is evident in the Scottish Government's (2015b) draft National Improvement Framework for Scottish Education and later (following consultation) in the full framework (Scottish Government, 2016b). The Scottish Government (2015b, p. 8) report advises that 'improvement in children and young people's health and wellbeing' is one of four national priorities. In addition, it is stated that during 2016 the Scottish Government will consult with a wide range of stakeholders 'as part of the development of the new children and young people's health and wellbeing survey on what constitutes the most appropriate measures of health and wellbeing for children and young people at different ages and stages' (Scottish Government, 2015b, p. 13).

A critical review of the policy-making process

Echoing earlier theoretical concerns (see Chapters 1 and 2) a feature of initial CFE documentation was the general lack of definition of what precisely was meant by HWB (Thorburn, 2014; 2015). Arguably, the lack of curriculum precision and definition is evident in the retention of repetitious experience and outcome statements, even though Education Scotland (2014a, p. 10), when highlighting emerging issues for teachers to review when making curriculum links to HWB, claim that 'it would seem counterproductive to designate a particular level for a learner's achievement in health and wellbeing, where the learner's development and progress is dependent on a variety of factors and life circumstances which can change quickly'. Nevertheless, Reform Scotland (2013), a Scottish-based public policy institute, were sufficiently concerned on this point to argue that it was unfortunate that the outcomes 'relating to the responsibilities of all teachers for HWB almost entirely lack progression of any kind ... (before noting that) ... there is no reason why the weaker examples cannot be replaced or improved' (p. 15). The concern over definition and outcomes is part of a larger debate over whether the generic and streamlined form of policy elaboration CFE has adopted has been effective or not. In this respect, it is noteworthy that in 2013 two Education Scotland reports analysed the relative benefits and limitations of current HWB practice (Education Scotland, 2013a) and associated key strengths and aspects for development (Education Scotland, 2013b). The shorter impact report (Education Scotland, 2013b) summarised 17 key strengths and 18 aspects for development under the headings of culture (supportive ethos and high quality relationships), systems (shared focus, improving outcomes) and practice (sense of teamwork and productive environments). This more extended approach towards policy guidance contrasts with the earlier streamlined approach e.g. LTS (2009a). Part of this disconnection could be due to the general vagueness about what precisely the intentions of CFE are with regard to learners' wellbeing. The OECD (2015, p. 11) addresses these types of concerns and advises that CFE would benefit from focusing on 'curriculum and related assessment and pedagogy' rather than being viewed as part of a wider-ranging set of societal reforms. This getting closer to learning, teaching and assessment-type definition supports notions of teacher autonomy and extended professional license to be creative in their teaching relative to being more passive and reactive in responding to professional advice on how to engage with wider societal HWB-related concerns.

That said it would appear helpful nevertheless if the HWB experiences and outcomes more clearly articulated with the wider societal ambitions emphasised through the 'Getting it Right for Every Child' (GIRFEC) programme (Scottish Executive, 2006b) and the SHANARRI indicators which are outlined as being the responsibility of all teachers as part of their HWB remit (LTS, 2009a). For example, it was not until Education Scotland's (2014a) report that the connections between GIRFEC, SHANNARI and HWB were exemplified in an integrated way. Teasing out these connections makes it easier for schools to evaluate their progress, especially as Education Scotland's self-evaluation toolkit 'How Good Is Our School' now contains wellbeing as an aspect of self-evaluation (Education Scotland, 2014b). More recently, the National Improvement Framework for Scottish Education (Scottish Government, 2016b, p. 3) connected its dual emphasis on excellence through raising attainment and achieving equity via an updated GIRFEC wheel in order to highlight how 'every young person has the right to expect appropriate support from adults to allow them to grow and develop and reach their full potential'.

Thus, it is only relatively recently that school-based HWB programmes have more fully articulated with asset-based approaches to learning which encourage learners to take on greater responsibility for their learning and wider achievement. This is an important matter, for as Porciani (2013) notes, research has consistently advocated taking more account of the complex and varied circumstances of the communities in which young people live.

In this respect the extensive mentioning there is in recent policy reporting (Scottish Government, 2016b) for literacy and numeracy relative to HWB might cause unease. For example, plans from 2017 onwards are for national and local authority level data to be collected on literacy and numeracy achievement at four age stages across primary and secondary schooling with teachers having new nationally standardised assessment materials to help inform their judgements. These plans appear more advanced than HWB plans to 'monitor health behaviours and wellbeing between different groups of children and take action to improve equity' (Scottish Government, 2016b, p. 17). The detail of plans for collecting survey-based monitoring information remains slightly underwritten at present even though 'improvement in children and young people's health and wellbeing' remains one of four key priorities identified (Scottish Government, 2016b, p. 7).

A further outstanding issue is the extent to which the focus on personal wellbeing is the right one relative to the focus on citizenship education (see Chapter 3). Ecclestone (2013) considers that the general privileging of personal wellbeing dispositions in Scotland undermines the importance of subject knowledge and alters the ways in which teachers interpret curriculum reforms and relate to learners. Biesta (2013) is also concerned that the personal focus on wellbeing makes it more difficult for learners to focus on the underpinnings of democratic citizenship. This is despite the comprehensive schooling ideal remaining dominant in Scotland, even though the version of wellbeing being advanced is, as noted, more focused on personal wellbeing than collective moral goodness (Biesta, 2013). Furthermore, in pledging to improve HWB learning experiences for all learners there is a supposition that teachers have the capacity to enhance learners' HWB, either through their teaching or as part of their wider whole school input. However, as Bok (2010) highlights, teachers are not generally well-positioned to provide experiences that help learners lead more satisfying lives, as most secondary school teachers are not sufficiently expert in psychology to evaluate learners' wellbeing. In addition, Bok (2010) considers that encouraging learners to emphasise the positive in life can lead to unwarranted optimism in ways which limit genuine engagement with suitably serious issues.

A critical review of health and wellbeing in practice

As mentioned earlier, CFE guidance predominantly focuses on how broad declarations of ambition can be realised within a tightly defined experience- and outcomes-based curriculum framework. Drawing upon Kelly's (1999) theorising on the need to acknowledge the planning considerations which underpin curriculum ideologies, Priestley and Humes (2010) conclude that CFE is not the process-based curriculum it purports to be, but rather a mastery curriculum where the retention of curriculum areas supports the status quo in schools. In this guise, CFE is representative of a style of policy making where neo-liberalist interests (with an emphasis on retaining subject-based learning) continue to be pursued under a new progressive education pretext (Priestley, 2011). The retention of subjects and concerns for knowledge-informed teaching can lead to teachers having difficulty in engaging in a thorough review of learner-centered practice ideas. Porciani (2013), for example, considers in a HWB context that teachers are seeking pedagogical guidance on matters such as active learner engagement at the same time as national organisations expect teachers to take on greater responsibility for their teaching practices. Education Scotland (2013a, p. 10) agrees, noting that many teachers 'are not yet clear about their role in delivering the aspects of health and wellbeing'. An open question therefore is the extent to which the merging of national priorities for promoting health and reducing health inequalities for young people have benefited through their association with HWB in schools. Is it the case that the fusion of health and education thinking has become rather diluted and unclear as a result of policy priorities merging?

In the meantime schools are trying to take forward HWB learning and teaching during a period when there are relatively few curriculum and pedagogical directives and an emphasis instead on guidelines. Secondary schools are therefore experimenting with a range of arrangements for organising the broad area of HWB, especially with regard to how it articulates with Personal and Social Education (PSE) as part of HWB. Some schools are opting for 'vertical' systems, where learners in the same house across S1–S6 (11–18 years) meet together, while other schools are enlarging more familiar 'horizontal' (same age/year) meeting arrangements. These new arrangements tend to result in a greater proportion of teachers taking on a more active HWB-related role with longer meetings with the same group of learners happening each week (McLaren, 2013). These meetings, known by a host of names, are typically a method of helping learners review a broad range of whole-school, cross-curriculum and subject issues as well as their wider achievements more generally. One challenge is in ensuring that these various approaches avoid HWB being effectively seen as PSE and not as a larger and more integrated and coherent part of learners' overall curriculum. A further concern for learning and teaching in HWB is the possibility of implementation regression due to assessment pressures in the senior school (age 15–18 years) having a backwash effect on the development and progress of HWB across the earlier school years (Thorburn, 2016). As Bloomer (2014, p. 21) notes, by 'opting for examination reform, government ensured that attention would be almost wholly diverted from the lower secondary where the need for change was greater and more urgent'. A supplementary concern is whether formally assessing HWB is beneficial for learners and can be easily managed by teachers. Issues exist, for example, about whether teachers are suitably expert to make judgements e.g. in areas such as learners' mental, social and emotional wellbeing (Bok, 2010), and of whether assessment is worthwhile for learners and avoids learners 'parroting phrases provided for them … (with notions of learner-centredness being effectively) … hollowed out by the removal of the child's agency' (Reeves, 2013, p. 69).

As far as integrating learning, teaching and assessment is concerned, Thorburn (2016) found when discussing efforts to enhance HWB with a range of key policy stakeholders (comprising head teachers, teacher education academics and staff with national and local authority quality improvement remits) that there was evidence of variability. School progress was often characterised by schools who were early adopters of change and other schools who were more prepared to delay implementation until more certainty was available. The latter approach often proved difficult in supporting teachers to take on a more rounded view of HWB due to competing subject demands and teachers perceived lack of expertise and confidence in knowing how to make connections across learning e.g. in terms of increasing learners' self-esteem, social interaction and engagement in learning conversations. This often led to schools continuing with 'health weeks' where suspended timetable arrangements applied and where the focus was predominantly on increasing health-related activities. These annual interventions were criticised by Education Scotland (2013b, p. 2) as they leave 'insufficient opportunities for follow up' on cultivating the more integrated learning, teaching and assessment connections intended. Associated with this variable approach to implementation was evidence that most schools were not formally assessing HWB. Some schools were assessing the more objective outcomes in Physical Education and Home Economics while other areas e.g. mental, emotional, social and physical wellbeing were occasionally mentioned in school reports but not graded. These findings support the view that 'greater clarity is needed about how success and progress in health and wellbeing is evaluated, recorded and communicated' (Education Scotland 2013b, p. 2).

There was nevertheless evidence of innovation in line with the many of the broader aspirations of CFE. In one school, Thorburn (2016) found that HWB was helping learners to develop leadership across the school through a peer tutoring system whereby younger learners (S2–S3, 13–15 years) visited associated primary schools and helped support lessons on drugs and alcohol awareness as well as sex education and further aspects of personal and social education. In the upper school (S5–S6, 16–18 years) some learners had a HWB-related school prefect remit involving leading assemblies and chairing focus group meetings; initiatives which were designed to enhance links with community partners and support school-based weekly health fairs. The same school invited S1–S3 pupils (12–15 years) to complete a Pupil Attitude to Self and School psychometric (*objective*) questionnaire with questions based on feelings about school, perceived learning capability, self-regard, preparedness for learning, attitudes to teachers, general work ethic, confidence in learning, attitude to attendance and response to curriculum demands. Results indicated, through a green, amber and red colour scheme, areas of relative concern. The results provided objective-type HWB evidence which could be used for reporting to parents/carers and sharing with partners such as Pupil Support Officers and Educational Psychologists.

An additional issue to consider is whether developments in HWB are as far advanced in practice as they are for literacy and numeracy. For as the OECD (2015, p. 22) note, 'the ultimate location of quality and change – which all other reforms are seeking to influence – is teaching and learning, in classrooms and out-of-school settings'. A recent comparison of teacher education courses highlights that only half (50%) of student teachers considered their courses to be very useful or useful for HWB relative to nearly three-fifths of student teachers considering literacy (56%) and numeracy (56%) to be very useful or useful (Scottish Government, 2016a). This raises questions about how teachers and student teachers can be better supported in terms of conceptions of HWB (Chapters 1 and 2) and also in terms of their teacher education and career-long professional learning (Chapter 7).

This review of HWB developments in practice broadly reflects the all-too-familiar situation with policy enactment, where there is a mix of 'policy ad-hockery, borrowing, building, re-ordering, displacing, constructing and re-constructing, and patterns of compliance and standardisation … (combined with) … a process of complex iterations between policies and across policy ensembles that generate forms of institutional transformation and regeneration' (Ball, 2015, p. 309). Within the Scottish context specifically, Priestley and Minty (2013) have noted a concern that teachers' high level of first-order engagement for CFE contrasts with their later second-order level of engagement once it becomes apparent the scale of the professional and pedagogical changes required. The emergence of an implementation gap, familiar to many studies of policy and practice, does highlight with regard to HWB the continuing need to indicate to teachers the positive differences they can make with regard to learners' HWB.

A review of the connections between health and wellbeing and wider achievement

As mentioned earlier, 'opportunities for personal achievement' is one of the four CFE-identified contexts of learning (Scottish Government, 2008). This is consistent with CFE intentions to establish broader policy connections with wider achievement where 'every child and young person in Scotland should be clear on how well they are progressing and what support is in place to help them succeed, and that support should be carefully planned to meet their needs' (Scottish Government, 2015b, p. 2). However, relatively little is known on the detail of the interrelationship between HWB and wider achievement, and this makes it difficult to draw clear conclusions about causality and how these goals can be effectively integrated within educational frameworks (Public Health England, 2014; McLellan and Steward, 2015). For example, Soutter, O'Steen and Gilmore (2012, p. 135) argue, in the broadly similar New Zealand policy context, that there is a need to 'provide a feasible and flexible structure for holistic assessment of student achievement, resulting in a multi-faceted view of academic success that encompasses wellbeing'. Therefore, what appears to be needed in Scotland at present is research studies which investigate both the *subjective* experiences of learners' confidence and the quality of their relationships with teachers and sense of belonging in schools as well as *objective* studies which manage to measure the aforementioned types of issues with a larger research sample which is selected according to age, gender, academic ability and other key learner characteristics. Research on this basis would enable learners' experiences to be understood in greater detail, and when allied with a larger data set containing details of teachers' values and practices, would enable more insightful in-school evaluations of practice to take place, see for example, Thorburn and Dey (2016). This, in turn, could contribute to wider scale evaluations of policy enactment and reviews of school effectiveness. Such research studies appear necessary given that the OECD (2015, p. 10) is concerned that liking school drops sharply among secondary students and reported belonging in school among Scottish teenagers has dropped since 2003 … (and that) … national surveys show a higher incidence of low achievement against expected level among secondary pupils than previously.

Wider evaluations of health and wellbeing, Curriculum for Excellence and young peoples' lives

In 2013, the Cabinet Secretary for Education commissioned the OECD to evaluate the introduction of CFE. Their report *Improving Schools in Scotland: An OECD perspective* (OECD, 2015) bisected the draft national framework for education (Scottish Government, 2015b) and the publication of the full framework (Scottish Government, 2016b). The latter report welcomed the OECD recognition that CFE 'is an ambitious and far-sighted reform which has put Scotland in a strong position to compete with the best education systems in the world if we realise its potential and address some key issues' (Scottish Government, 2016b, p. 4). Taking the OECD (2015) report as the main stimulus for a wider review of HWB, CFE and young peoples' lives, the following evaluation focuses on the international and national evidence drawn upon to inform the OECD (2015) review and on the key issues which emerge from their findings. The predominant section of the OECD (2015) report where HWB is elaborated on in relatively specific ways is 'Quality and Equity in Scottish Schools' (pp. 49–90).

The *international* evidence draws frequently on a longitudinal Health Behaviour in School-Aged Children (HBSC) quantitative study which collects field data from many European and North American countries every four years at three age stages: Primary 7 (11–12 years) and at the second and fourth years of secondary schooling, 13–14 years and 15–16 years (Currie, *et al.*, 2015). In broad terms the HBSC data complements the experience and outcome areas defined for HWB, enabling viable comparisons to be made between the two. Findings showed that over four-fifths

(87%) of young people are highly satisfied with their life (90% of boys, 84% of girls) however there is a decrease in life satisfaction among girls (from 92% at 11 years old to 84% at 13 years old to 76% at 15 years old). These figures are consistent over time (i.e. between 2002 and 2014) and indicate little change in in life satisfaction for either boys or girls. Similarly, when it comes to feeling confident more boys 'always' feel confident (21%) than girls (11%) with these gender differences being particularly apparent between the ages of 13 and 15. However, unlike for 'life satisfaction' the proportion of boys and girls reporting that they always 'feel confident' has been in decline over the last decade. In terms of the school environment more specifically, relative to most OECD countries the evidence in Scotland is of positive attitudes towards schools and high classmate support (62% of young people), even though this latter figure has been in gradual decline since 2002. Furthermore, while nearly a third of learners (30%) report high teacher support, perceived teacher support was considered as being substantially lower in secondary schools relative to primary schools (Currie *et al.*, 2015).

The *national* evidence the OECD (2015) report drew upon was predominantly from two studies: the Scottish Schools Adolescent Lifestyle and Substance Use Survey (which broadly complements the HBSC study and provides quantitative data on smoking, alcohol and substance misuse), and the qualitative Behaviour in Scottish Schools study. However, these studies, relative to the experiences and outcomes described for HWB, provide modest evaluation evidence. Therefore, in order to support learners' experiences in school in more all-encompassing ways there is a need for research interventions which help schools to evaluate, for example, school relationships, rights-respecting pro-social behaviour and a range of factors influencing learners' confidence and sense of belonging in schools in much more clearly defined and precise ways.

Future directions

The OECD (2015) report comes at a pivotal time. It endorses a learner-centered view of education during a period of sustained economic austerity and has resisted the temptation to argue for the lessening of broad general educational ambitions in favour of the narrower pursuit of high-stakes examination success. As the report states

> A major challenge is how to stay bold and to build on what has already been accomplished in a way that is as persuasive to the public as it is to the profession, and that can achieve greater equity for all pupils sooner than later.
>
> *(OECD, 2015, p. 16)*

This chapter considers a similar boldness is required if HWB is to become a clearer responsibility of all teachers and more central to curriculum planning and learners' wider achievement (Thorburn, 2014). If successful, it would help reduce the overly diverse ways in which schools currently engage with HWB (Thorburn, 2016). We consider that these are not unrealistic aspirations for HWB, as in most respects it is consistent with the OECD (2015, p. 11) intention that CFE can be 'managed from the centre and become more a dynamic, highly equitable curriculum ... built constantly in schools, networks and communities with a strengthened middle in a vision of collective responsibility and multi-layer governance'. Key to achieving this aspiration will be how well professional learning can support practice and collaborative working at a time when a considerable number of challenging 'culture', 'systems' and 'practice' aspects of HWB development need to show greater evidence of impact (Education Scotland, 2013b). The Scottish Government (2016a) five-years-on evaluation of the impact of the implementation of Teaching Scotland's Future (The Donaldson Report) (Scottish Government, 2011b) highlights a number of positive professional developments, including: teachers being more engaged with professional learning; a greater focus on the impact of professional learning on learners; a consensus that teachers are engaging in professional dialogue more often and that there has been an increase in sharing experiences and a willingness to talk more openly about pedagogy and practice. These encouraging signs of progress potentially equip schools with the capacity to review how well they are articulating with initiatives covering such issues as how schools can promote HWB and lessen inequalities e.g. through considering reports such as Better Relationships, Better Learning, Better Behaviour (Scottish Government, 2013) and Better Eating, Better Learning (Scottish Government, 2014), and with new ideas in education such as restorative approaches to promoting harmonious relationships (McCluskey *et al.*, 2008). Making progress on this basis could help achieve something more coherent than a scattergun approach to engaging with policy initiatives. This could prove productive in terms of tackling ongoing HWB concerns e.g. learners' diminishing confidence and sense of belonging and concerns over teachers' quality of support in secondary schools (OECD, 2015) as well as other policy-related matters highlighted in this chapter e.g. the benefits of policies being more theoretically explicit about the influences which have informed their development.

Summary of key findings

- Multiple challenges exist in and between policy implementation planning and policy enactment in schools.
- Making plausible learning connections between GIRFEC, SHANNARI and HWB can be a complex learning task.
- Schools are engaging with various approaches in order to make HWB a more integrated and coherent part of the overall curriculum.
- Integrating formative and summative assessment with learning and teaching as part of enhancing HWB has proved problematic to date.
- Professional learning is key for improved practice and collaborative working in schools.

Reflective tasks

- Is it a good educational idea for *all* teachers to have a responsibility for learners' HWB?
- Is the merging of a traditional subject-based curriculum with newly framed generic contexts for learning an effective curriculum model for HWB? What are the advantages or disadvantages of this intention?
- What forms of professional learning would help improve HWB in schools?
- Has HWB as part of CFE in secondary schools played a constructive part so far in reducing health inequalities? If so, why is this the case? If not, why is this the case?
- Has HWB as part of CFE in secondary schools played a constructive part in promoting wider achievement? If so, why is this the case? If not, why is this the case?

Further readings

Ecclestone, K., & Hayes, D. 2009. *The Dangerous Rise of Therapeutic Education.* London: Routledge.

White, J. (2011). *Exploring Well-being in Schools.* London: Routledge.

References

Allan, J. (2003). Daring to Think Otherwise? Educational Policymaking in the Scottish Parliament, *Journal of Education Policy, 18*(3), 289–301.

Ball, S. (2015). What Is Policy? 21 Years Later: Reflections on the Possibilities of Policy Research, *Discourse: Studies in the Cultural Politics of Education, 36*(3), 306–313.

Ball, S., Maguire, M., & Braun, A. (2012). *How Schools Do Policy: Policy Enactment in Secondary Schools.* London: Routledge.

Biesta, G. (2013). 'Responsible citizens: Citizenship education between social inclusion and democratic politics'. In: M. Priestley & G. Biesta (Eds.) *Reinventing the Curriculum: New Trends in Curriculum Policy and Practice* (pp. 99–115). Bloomsbury: London.

Bloomer, K. (2014). 'Two cheers for Curriculum for Excellence'. In: *First Class: From Nursery to University: Essays on Improving Scottish Education* (pp. 15–25). Scottish Conservative and Unionist Party: Edinburgh.

Bok, D. (2010). *The Politics of Happiness: What Government Can Learn from the New Research on Wellbeing.* Princeton: Princeton University Press.

Bryce, T.G.K., & Humes, W.H. (Eds.) (2008). *Scottish Education.* Edinburgh: University of Edinburgh Press.

Cairney, P. (2009). The Role of Ideas in Policy Transfer: The Case of UK Smoking Bans Since Devolution, *Journal of European Public Policy, 16*(3), 471–488.

Currie, C., Van der Sluijs, W., Whitehead, R., Currie, D., Rhodes, G., Neville, F., & Inchley, J. (2015). HBSC 2014: Survey in Scotland National Report. Child and Adolescent Health Research Unit (CAHRU), University of St Andrews.

Ecclestone, K. (2013). 'Confident individuals: The implications of an 'emotional subject' for curriculum priorities and practices'. In: M. Priestley & G. Biesta (Eds.) *Reinventing the Curriculum: New Trends in Curriculum Policy and Practice* (pp. 75–97). Bloomsbury: London.

Education Scotland. (2013a). Health and wellbeing: The responsibility of all 3–18. Retrieved from http://dera.ioe.ac.uk/18519/7/HealthandWellbeing3to18_tcm4-814360_Redacted.pdf

Education Scotland. (2013b). Health and wellbeing: The responsibility of all 3–18. Curriculum impact report summary of key strengths and aspects of development. Retrieved from https://education.gov.scot/improvement/Documents/hwb14-summary-impact-report.pdf

Education Scotland. (2014a). Health and wellbeing: The responsibility of all. Making the links … making it work. Retrieved from https://education.gov.scot/improvement/hwb30-making-links

Education Scotland. (2014b). How good is our school? Retrieved from https://education.gov.scot/improvement/Pages/frwk2hgios.aspx

Humes, W.H. (2013). 'The origins and development of Curriculum for Excellence: Discourse, politics and control'. In: M. Priestley & G. Biesta (Eds.) *Reinventing the Curriculum: New Trends in Curriculum Policy and Practice* (pp. 13–34). London: Bloomsbury.

Kelly, A.V. (1999). *The Curriculum: Theory and Practice.* London: Sage.

Learning and Teaching Scotland. (2004). *Being well, doing well: A framework for health promoting schools in Scotland.* Retrieved from http://www.educationscotland.gov.uk/Images/Beingwelldoingwell_tcm4-121991.pdf

Learning and Teaching Scotland. (2009a). Health and wellbeing across learning: Principles and practice. Retrieved from https://education.gov.scot/Documents/hwb-across-learning-pp.pdf

Learning and Teaching Scotland. (2009b). Health and wellbeing outcomes. Retrieved from https://www.education.gov.scot/Documents/health-and-wellbeing-eo.pdf

Lingard, B. (2008). 'Scottish education: Reflections from an international perspective'. In: T.G.K. Bryce & W.H. Humes (Eds.), *Scottish Education* (pp. 968–981). Edinburgh: University of Edinburgh Press.

MacBeath, J. (2013). 'Scenarios for the future of schooling and education.' In: T.G.K. Bryce, W.H. Humes, D. Gillies & A. Kennedy (Eds.) *Scottish Education* (pp. 1012–1022). Edinburgh: University of Edinburgh Press.

McCluskey, G., Lloyd, G., Kane, J., Riddell, S., Stead, J., & Weedon, E. (2008). Can Restorative Practices in Schools Make a Difference? *Educational Review, 60(4),* 405–417.

McLaren, D. J. (2013). 'Personal support and PSE in the secondary school'. In: T.G.K. Bryce, W.H. Humes, D. Gillies & A. Kennedy (Eds.) *Scottish Education* (pp. 423–433). Edinburgh: University of Edinburgh Press.

McLellan, R., & Steward, S. (2015). Measuring Children and Young People's Wellbeing in the School Context, *Cambridge Journal of Education, 45(3),* 307–322.

Organisation for Economic Co-operation and Development. (2015). *Improving schools in Scotland: An OECD perspective.* Retrieved from http://www.oecd.org/education/school/Improving-Schools-in-Scotland-An-OECD-Perspective.pdf

Priestley, M. (2011). Whatever Happened to Curriculum Theory? Critical Realism and Curriculum Change, *Pedagogy, Culture and Society, 19(2),* 221–237.

Priestley, M., & Humes, W. H. (2010). The Development of Scotland's Curriculum for Excellence: Amnesia and Déjà Vu, *Oxford Review of Education, 36(3),* 345–361.

Priestley, M., & Minty, S. (2013). Curriculum for Excellence: 'A brilliant idea, but …' *Scottish Educational Review, 45(1),* 39–52.

Porciani, M. (2013). 'Health and wellbeing in secondary education'. In: T.G.K. Bryce, W.H. Humes, D. Gillies & A. Kennedy (Eds.) *Scottish Education* (pp. 567–572). Edinburgh: University of Edinburgh Press.

Public Health England. (2014). *The Link between Pupil Health and Wellbeing and Attainment.* London: Public Health England.

Reeves, J. (2013). 'The successful learner: A progressive or an oppressive'. In: M. Priestley & G. Biesta (Eds.) *Reinventing the Curriculum: New Trends in Curriculum Policy and Practice* (pp. 51–74). London: Bloomsbury.

Reform Scotland and Centre for Scottish Public Policy. (2013). *The Commission on School Reform final report*. Retrieved from http://reformscotland.com/public/publications/bydiversemeans1.pdf

Scottish Executive. (2005). *Happy, Safe and Achieving Their Potential: A Standard of Support for Children and Young People in Scottish Schools. The Report of The National Review of Guidance 2004*. Edinburgh: Scottish Executive.

Scottish Executive. (2006a). *Building the Curriculum 1: The Contribution of Curricular Areas*. Edinburgh: Scottish Executive.

Scottish Executive. (2006b). *Getting it Right for Every Child Implementation Plan*. Edinburgh: Scottish Executive.

Scottish Government. (2008). *Building the Curriculum 3: A Framework for Learning and Teaching*. Edinburgh: Scottish Government.

Scottish Government. (2011a). *Building the Curriculum 5: A Framework for Assessment Reporting*. Edinburgh: Scottish Government.

Scottish Government. (2011b). *Teaching Scotland's Future: Report of a Review of Teacher Education in Scotland*. Edinburgh: Scottish Government.

Scottish Government. (2013). Better relationships, better learning, better behaviour. Edinburgh: Scottish Government. Retrieved from www.gov.scot/Publications/2013/03/7388

Scottish Government. (2014). Better eating, better learning. Edinburgh: Scottish Government. Retrieved from http://www.gov.scot/Resource/0044/00445740.pdf

Scottish Government. (2015a). Summary statistics for schools in Scotland. Retrieved from http://www.gov.scot/Resource/0049/00490590.pdf

Scottish Government. (2015b). *Creating a Smarter Scotland: A Draft National Improvement Framework for Scottish Education*. Edinburgh: Scottish Government.

Scottish Government. (2016a). *Evaluation of the Impact of the Implementation of Teaching Scotland's Future*. Edinburgh: Scottish Government.

Scottish Government. (2016b). *National Improvement Framework for Scottish Education: Achieving Excellence and Equity*. Edinburgh: Scottish Government.

Sinnema, C. (2016). 'The ebb and flow of curricular autonomy: Balance between local freedom and national prescription in curricula'. In: Wyse, D., Hayward, L., & Pandya, J. (Eds.) *The Sage Handbook of Curriculum, Pedagogy and Assessment* (pp. 965–983). London: Sage.

Soutter, A.K., O'Steen, B., & Gilmore, A. (2012). Wellbeing in the New Zealand Curriculum, *Journal of Curriculum Studies*, *44*(1), 111–142.

Thorburn, M. (2014). Educating for Well-being in Scotland: Policy and Philosophy; Pitfalls and Possibilities, *Oxford Review of Education*, *40*(2), 206–222.

Thorburn, M. (2015). Theoretical Constructs of Well-being and Their Implications for Education, *British Educational Research Journal*, *41*(4), 650–665.

Thorburn, M. (2016). Evaluating Efforts to Enhance Health and Wellbeing in Scottish Secondary Schools, *Journal of Curriculum Studies*. Retrieved from http://dx.doi.org/10.1080/00220272.2016.1167246

Thorburn, M., & Dey, D. (2016). Health and Wellbeing and Wider Achievement: An Analysis of Teachers' Practices and Learners' Experiences in Scottish Secondary Schools, *Studies in Educational Evaluation*. Retrieved from http://www.sciencedirect.com/science/article/pii/S0191491X16300906

PART III

Professional perspectives on wellbeing

5

THE SCHOOL LEADER PERSPECTIVE

Integrating schools with the communities they serve

Christine Forde

Introduction

Leadership is a significant focus in educational policy largely because it is perceived as being critical in the enhancement of the culture and ethos of a school and, as a consequence, the wellbeing and learning of pupils. Based on the research literature, Leithwood *et al.* (2008, p. 27) make seven claims about school leadership, the first claim being that 'school leadership is second only to classroom teaching as an influence on pupil learning'. This is not a direct influence on pupil learning but one which is mediated through the organisation and culture of a school and through teacher behaviour and classroom practice. Day *et al.* (2016) propose that a combination of leadership approaches is important in bringing about improvement in pupil learning experiences and outcomes. Thus, 'instructional leadership' is focused more specifically on improving the quality of the learning experiences of pupils while 'transformational leadership' is focused on building engagement across a school community to bring about change – winning of 'hearts and minds'. In the area of wellbeing, school leaders have two broad areas of concern and so exercise both forms of leadership. First, school leaders have to exercise pedagogic leadership through leading and enhancing the curriculum and providing professional learning opportunities for teachers to ensure that the quality of curriculum provision enables pupils to develop their understandings, skills and attitudes in this area. Second, school leaders have to exercise transformational leadership to build and sustain a school community in order that the culture of the school promotes the wellbeing of all.

This chapter considers how school leaders exercise that influence to build a school community that enhances the wellbeing of all its members from three perspectives. The first perspective relates to the role of school leaders in community building. Sergiovanni (1994) highlights the importance of school leaders making connections between the school and the communities it serves. Roland-Martin's (1992) notion of the 'school-home' also underlines the importance of the school building nurturing relationships for a significant proportion of learners in order to create those experiences historically provided in families. Increasingly, schools are the centre of communities especially for disadvantaged communities and communities in crisis, where the school holds possibilities for regeneration. If the learning needs of all learners are to be met it is vital that school leaders engage the staff and pupils in building a nurturing culture and reach out beyond the boundaries of the school to work with parents and carers, other schools, agencies and the wider community.

The second perspective is concerned with the emotional work of school leaders who play a critical role in managing the emotions of others. Schools are social organisations and so at their heart lie relationships: the quality of these relationships determines the quality of the learning experiences of pupils and shapes the motivation and commitment of staff. Crawford (2009) contends that 'leadership cannot operate without emotion' (p. 10) and part of the work of school leaders is to engage in, what Hochschild (2002) has termed, 'emotional labour' to create a culture where all feel engaged.

The third perspective follows on from the idea of emotional labour and considers the building of a school's culture. In a typology of school cultures, Hargreaves (1995) argues that a welfare culture and an academic culture can become polarised, leading to the neglect of either academic achievement or pastoral care. There remains a tension between a focus on academic achievement and what Ecclestone and Hayes (2008) see as the rise of 'therapeutic education'. However, it is important not to see the two aspects of cognitive and affective development as mutually exclusive. The chapter examines ways in which school leaders can purposefully create a school culture that promotes wellbeing and engagement alongside learning and academic achievement.

Main findings

Building community

While it is now common to refer to the 'school community', there remains a lack of clarity about what we mean by this term: is the school community those who come to work and learn, that is, the pupils and staff, or does the school community include other groups, notably parents, professionals such as youth support services and social workers who work with the school to support learners, local authority officers and school governors, all of whom can have a significant influence on the culture of the school? This lack of clarity is part of what school leaders have to grapple with. Increasingly the boundaries of a school are permeable with different groups contributing to the learning of the young people and exercising influence on the purposes and culture of a school. Therefore, while staff and pupils are the core of the school community, part of the task of school leaders is to recognise and value the contribution of different groups.

Determining who is part of the community of the school is one aspect but we need to probe deeper our understanding of the notion of 'community'. Fendler (2006) takes a critical stance in relation to the concept of community, arguing that in the literature this is a broad and sometimes vague idea. There is a tendency for community to be allied with notions of 'commonality' and so in her view, '[t]he problem with community is that its assumptions may serve to exclude others' (p. 304). Fendler identifies three different ideological stances, 'discursive strands' (p. 305) which help us to appreciate both the potential of regarding the school as a community and some of the issues school leaders need to address in order to build community for the wellbeing of all in the school. The first discursive strand relates to community-as-an-alternative to either the large nation state or a market-driven society, the idea of community is about local autonomy which provides mutual support among its members. The idea of self-governance might seem attractive but Fendler sees within this construction a strong impulse to normalisation. In such communities there is a danger that differences are not tolerated and those who are different might be deemed not to belong. Sergiovanni (1994) is similarly critical of a community that may appear to be inclusive but masks a tendency towards 'exclusion, censorship and normalization' (Fendler 2006, p. 309). Therefore, a key task for school leaders in developing wellbeing is to actively work to create and sustain a genuinely inclusive community.

The second discursive strand is that of community-as-solidarity and has its roots in trade unionism with the coming together of individuals to achieve a common cause. Again, community-as-solidarity has potential for the building the school as a community where there is a strong sense of a common purpose. However, there is a tension here between the recognition of difference and the demands of assimilation within a community. For Fendler, schools that are underpinned by a sense of community as solidarity could serve only to reinforce existing inequalities. A key question is how far a particular community enables different individuals and groups to actively shape the purposes of the community within the school (Halsey *et al.*, 1997). To create a context for the promotion of the wellbeing of all, school leaders have to build a common vision where different groups are fully engaged in shaping the community.

The final discursive strand is that of community-as-emotional-bonding, where members of the community feel a particular affinity with one another. Here, Fendler criticises the idea of the affective discourse around community for a number of reasons. First, aligning the idea of community with that of emotional bonding, in her view, reinforces the separation of emotion and reason, setting ideas of care, trust and safety as defining features of 'community' which she argues are culturally bound and happen in specific circumstances but not necessarily in all contexts. Therefore, in the building of trust, care and safety to foster a sense of affinity among members of the school community, school leaders need to also understand and manage conflict and tensions around difference that will arise within a school context. Furthermore, school leaders have to be alert to the dangers of strong emotional bonds which can serve to distance those outside the community. Communities that have strong emotional bonds are often communities that have come together in terms of turmoil and crisis to combat a common enemy. Such an attitude can limit the regard held for others not part of the school community and intensify the sense of exclusion.

From Fendler's critique of the idea of community, there are three significant tensions that school leaders need to grapple with in order to build a school community founded on the promotion of the wellbeing of all. The first issue relates to how far community is seeking to ensure commonality rather than embrace and work with difference. This potentially can have a radical effect on a school community. In a hierarchical organisation, those with less power – pupils, different groups of staff – have less opportunity to contribute. Building participation requires a more open and democratic school. The second issue relates to the participation of minority groups or those such as pupils, who in hierarchical organisations have limited opportunities to contribute. The third issue relates to the attitude towards those not part of the community or who exist on the periphery of the community. Here, school leaders must build a sense of respect and regard for those not within the immediate school community.

Engagement of different groups is central to the promotion of wellbeing. However, genuine engagement can only be fostered if there is the recognition of the importance of the circumstances of each pupil, and so part of the role of school leaders is to appreciate the differences in the young people's experiences, to recognise their needs without being overly judgemental, and to build these understandings across staff groups and indeed across the full school community. Only in this way can a school create what Auerbach (2012a) calls 'authentic partnerships' (p. 5) for wellbeing. Auerbach (2012b) questions the purpose of many existing partnership strategies: if these are largely focused on raising attainment then such strategies can become very instrumental and 'do little to enfranchise marginalized groups and have instead solidified entrenched power' (p. 33). School leaders must remain conscious of wider issues of marginalisation, minority status and poverty and the ways in which such issues impact on wellbeing and achievement. Auerbach (2012b) sees leaders adopting one of four different strategies: leadership can (1) prevent partnerships, (2) adopt a tokenistic approach to partnership, (3) build traditional partnerships where the inequalities of power and autonomy remain and (4) foster authentic relationships. Authentic relationships have to be based on respectful alliances, where all parties are regarded as having a positive contribution to make. These partnerships are about building relationships and sharing power across the partners and are essential to secure the wellbeing of all members of the community.

A key task for school leaders then, is to build a school community that is genuinely inclusive by building family and school partnerships. As part of this, school leaders have to seek to engage particularly those pupils and parents that are hard to reach. Lueder's (2011) description of a family/school partnership aligns with Auerbach's (2012b) authentic partnerships: 'A family/school partnership is a collaborative relationship between family and school designed primarily to produce positive educational and social effects on the child, while being mutually beneficial to all other parties involved' (Lueder 2011, p. 21). Lueder argues that many of the activities schools establish to foster home and school links can become dominated by confident and already advantaged, often middle class, parents who understand the school system. While their contribution is important, Lueder argues that schools need to be concerned for what he calls 'the missing families' (p. 4) and puts forward 'The Self-Renewing Partnership Model' (p. 4) which has two dimensions 'energy-in' activities and 'energy-out' activities. 'Energy-in' strategies are based on activities to build pupil wellbeing through curricular programmes and pastoral activities in the school. The energy-out dimension consists of the use of four intervention strategies which can be utilised in the fostering of wellbeing:

- a connecting strategy used to help reduce the barriers between the school and families;
- a communicating strategy to establish two-way communication flow;
- a coordinating strategy to ensure that school and community resources go to needy families;
- a coaching strategy to enhance the family's ability to play their parent partner role (p. 5).

These strategies are powerful but make significant demands on school leaders and their wider leadership team particularly in relation to their interpersonal abilities and the emotional demands of working closely with families, some of whom may be in severe crisis. This takes us onto the second perspective with regard to school leadership and the fostering of wellbeing, that of emotional leadership.

Emotional dimensions of schools and the role of the school leader

The emotional dimensions of school leadership are a vital component of the promotion of wellbeing of learners as well as staff. The issue of teacher emotional wellbeing has become a policy concern particularly against the backdrop of significant numbers of teachers leaving the profession (Asia Society, 2011). Galton and MacBeath (2008), drawing from their series of UK studies on teacher work and from studies of teacher workload conducted in Canada, Hong Kong, Australia and New Zealand, report that that 'across the globe research indicates that the lives of teachers are more stressful and that there is a growing imbalance between their work and personal lives' (p. 21). From Galton and MacBeath's studies, it is evident that teacher stress is an issue associated with increased accountability and bureaucracy across many educational systems. Increased expectations with regards to pupil attainment side-by-side with the increased diversity of learner needs has led to teachers feeling a loss of autonomy and an intensification of workload. In addition, the teachers reported that demands in two areas had increased significantly: dealing with parents and dealing with issues related to pupil behaviour. Collie *et al.* (2012) in a study of school climate and teacher stress found that teachers' perceptions of pupil motivation and behaviour were critical in the level of stress they reported which in turn impacted on their job satisfaction. Experiences of intensification and loss of autonomy are having an impact not only on the levels of stress and burnout experienced by teachers but their remaining in the teaching profession. Leithwood *et al.* (1999) point to the consequences of staff burnout for both 'the organisation' and the individual: 'teachers who experience burnout are less sympathetic toward students, less committed to and involved in their jobs, have a lower tolerance for classroom disruption, less apt to prepare adequately for class and generally less productive' (p. 85). The challenge facing school leaders is how create a context in which teachers remain engaged and enthusiastic about their role in order to promote the wellbeing and learning of pupils: 'how can leaders work with the emotional experience of their institutions to create them as places where creativity and innovation are welcomed and where there is a passion for the work of educating young people' (James, 2004, pp. 263–264). Thus, part of the role of school leaders is to manage the emotional aspects of organisational life.

Crawford (2009) proposes that 'understanding the emotions of leadership is a key to long-term sustainability and high functioning in headship' (p. 10). Hochschild (2002) indicates that a key dimension of the emotional labour of leadership is to ensure the members of the school community have positive experiences but this can often be at a cost to the school leader. In her in-depth study of the experiences of Canadian school leaders, Beatty (2004, p. 205) noted that:

> In the educational setting, the freedom to communicate openly at work about their own emotions has all but been eliminated replaced by a repertoire of more emotionally managed techniques … this was ultimately accepted by the participants as the way power and control is maintained in leadership.

The participants reported a range of both positive and negative emotions in their role and a significant finding was the degree to which the participants worked to control, almost deny, their emotions and the emotions of others. This was accepted as the way things were despite reporting 'emotional authenticity', that is, recognising and being able to express genuine emotions, was a very positive experience. What comes out strongly from Beatty's study is not only the control of emotions to ensure a detachment and to depersonalise difficult situations but also the need to display only specific emotions such as trust and determination. Hochschild (2002) claims that sustaining such an approach where school leaders express sets of emotions, whether genuine or not, over a longer period can create a lost capacity of school leaders to listen to their own feelings and sometimes even to feel at all.

Two aspects are interlinked: part of the task of school leaders is to be self-aware and understand the role emotions play in their own leadership as well as to look to strategies to underpin their task of emotional labour particularly in their management of staff. One particularly important aspect is an awareness on the part of school leaders of the impact of their behaviours on staff. Evans (1999) argues that a headteacher can either 'fire teachers with enthusiasm for their job and enable them to fulfil their potential' or can make teachers 'dread going to work every Monday morning' (p. 18). Blasé and Blasé's (2002) study of the 'dark side of leadership' looking at teachers' perceptions of mistreatment, illustrates that while abusive behaviours can have devastating consequences for the individual teacher the impact is far wider: 'Over time principals' mistreatment resulted in far reaching, destructive effects on schools, particularly with regard to relationships between and among teachers, their instructional work in classrooms and collective decision making processes' (p. 245). While such cases might be seen as extreme circumstances, it is insufficient for school leaders simply not to engage in abusive behavior. Instead, school leaders, as Beatty (2004) argues, need to ensure support for staff and build their autonomy through 'distributed leadership and collaborative synergy' (p. 203). Part of this will be about the management of emotions but this is not about the suppression of these feelings. Instead, as Crawford argues (2009, p. 24),

> In an emotionally safe school, headteachers need to be able to call upon personal reserves in times of crisis and enable their staff to express their own feelings and emotions in a way that is helpful to them and to the school as a whole.

Goleman (1996) in his work on emotional intelligence identifies a number of elements that link to the role of school leaders in promoting a culture of wellbeing: self-awareness, self-regulation of one's own emotions, strong commitment, empathy and constructive social skills. These elements are important in the way school leaders engage with different members of a school community. However, the idea of emotional intelligence and the particular aspects Goleman proposes have been much debated. Fineman's (2000) criticism is pertinent to this discussion of the role of school leaders in leading their school community to foster the wellbeing of all members. Fineman argues that emotional intelligence promotes a form of managerial behaviour and proposes instead that we need to look at the whole culture of the organisation and the values of its stakeholders. Therefore, while the behaviours of an individual school leader are deeply significant, Fineman argues that the idea of 'connectedness with others' in the organisational setting assumes great importance. Creating an inclusive culture for all members of the school community is a challenging task for school leaders and Hargreaves' (2008) construct of 'emotional geographies' helps us to explore the ways in which some members maybe become more or less distanced from the community.

Hargreaves (2008) also sees emotions embedded in relationships which are relations of power and uses the idea of emotional geographies to explore some of these relations of power. Emotional geographies are the patterns where distance or closeness in relationships in an organisation will shape our emotions and our experiences. Hargreaves identifies five key emotional geographies where school leaders can determine the sense of distance or closeness that individuals and groups feel in relation to the vision and core values of a school community. These emotional geographies can determine the sense of engagement or distance from a vision and values for wellbeing:

- political leadership where different degrees of power are held by different groups and individuals in a school;
- cultural geographies where emotions are culturally inscribed and pupils and parents from different cultures may express emotions differently;
- professional geographies which can act as a barrier to openness and transparency and so distance relationships;
- physical geographies, which are the organisational decisions about timetable, the allocation of teachers and pupils to classrooms, the position and composition of staff rooms, all of which shape the day-today experiences of the school community;
- moral geographies which highlight the importance of the core purposes of the school.

James (2004, p. 265) argues that, in addition to the emotional geographies pointed out by Hargreaves, we need 'to take into account the unconscious'. James's premise is that schools, for a variety of reasons associated with their purpose, are educational institutions where change, risk and relationships are fundamental, and so are places of high levels of anxiety and emotion. In such circumstances we work to protect ourselves, we use 'social defenses' (p. 267) such as 'resistance, repression, regression, covert coalitions, identifications, reaction formation, denial, organizational rituals, splitting and protection' (p. 270). These different forms of emotional geographies can serve to either foster the engagement of different groups and individuals in a school community or distance them from the core purposes of the school. Therefore, school leaders need to create a secure framework within which the work of the school can take place, and so among the strategies James (2004, p. 271) proposes are:

- continual exploration and explanation of what might lying behind the behaviours and responses of different individual and groups;
- modelling;
- learning to identify defensive behaviour;
- talk to people about their experiences not their defences;
- facing up to and resolving conflict;
- checking out that their new feelings are theirs and not introjected of others.

Building feelings of belonging is crucial in the school leader's management of emotion. Crawford (2009, p. 79) argues that:

> every member of a school whether pupil or teacher needs to feel he or she belongs to at least one sentient group or a group of people working together who are able to respond to each other emotionally as well as intellectually.

However, this is not a straightforward process because how individuals and groups experience school life can be very different. As schools become larger and more complex these differences can become significant. Therefore, a critical task for school leaders is to build and sustain a culture in which all members have a sense of belonging. This raises the question of what we mean by culture.

Building a culture of wellbeing

Das (2008, p. 33) proposes that culture can be organised into three different groups of factors we need to consider:

- historical factors such as the history, traditions, beliefs and ceremonies of the school, the latter covering the symbols, rituals, stories and myths that are reiterated within the practices of a school;
- behavioural factors including norms and values, expectations and attitudes, goal and purpose, code of conduct and sense of identity;
- organisational factors comprised of group dynamics, structures that divide work and define relationships and systems of communication.

In essence then, a school culture relates to the values, traditions, social roles and norms and behaviours of members of that specific school community. A school's culture is complex because it 'has very unique and idiosyncratic ways of working' (MacNeill et al. 2009, p. 74) but it can be actively managed through creating a clear sense of purpose and direction. However, as Peterson and Deal (1998, p. 28) note, there are some schools which over time have 'become unproductive and toxic'. These are schools where staff groups 'are extremely fragmented, where the purpose of serving students has been lost to the goal of serving the adults, where negative values and hopelessness reign' (p. 28). However, though we talk of the school culture as if there was only one culture within a school, Day (2016) reminds us that 'how school culture influences the health and well-being of its staff and pupils is mediated through a rich and complex series of social interactions between its component subcultures' (p. 207). Day identifies three broad subcultures: teacher cultures, leadership cultures and pupil cultures. In toxic cultures, pupil wellbeing is often set in opposition to teacher wellbeing. However as Roffey (2012, p. 11) suggests, 'What is in students' best interests is also likely to be in the interests of teacher wellbeing'. Therefore, as Sergiovanni (1994) argues, we need to move beyond seeing a school as simply an organisation and instead propose that there is a need to build purposeful communities which are defined as schools where there are clear bonds among the different members of the community, a shared ideology and unified action to achieve a shared purpose.

Conclusion: Purposes and values

The significance of a shared purpose is illustrated by MacNeill et al. (2009, p. 74):

> When an organisation has a clear understanding of its purpose, why it exists and what it must do and who it should serve the culture will ensure that

things work well. When the complex patterns of beliefs, values, attitudes, expectations, ideas and behaviours in an organization are inappropriate or incongruent the culture will ensure that things work badly.

Part of what school leaders have to grapple with relates to the need to reify the educational dimensions of the vision of the school where the central focus is on the learning of all pupils. However, we need to consider what we mean by 'learning', a much-contested idea. There is considerable discussion about the improvement of student learning outcomes, but what outcomes should we seek to develop? The Organisation for Economic Co-operation (OECD) exerts considerable influence on educational policy in its member states, including the UK, and is driving the idea of a knowledge economy. From this perspective, schools should develop the high cognitive skills, technological and information skills and personal abilities (Asia Society, 2011) to enable young people to enter the workforce of a knowledge-intensive economy. Is learning in a school predominantly about enabling each learner to develop sufficient knowledge, skills and attributes to be able to make an economic contribution to society? This economic driver is a critical aspect of educational policy but is only one dimension of learning. With increased globalisation and migration on an unprecedented scale, there are concerns about social conflict, fragmentation and exclusion. Is learning in a school predominantly about each learner developing the knowledge, understandings, skills and attitudes to contribute constructively to the development of a more cohesive and equal society? The two imperatives of economic development and social cohesion might seem competing purposes in education but they co-exist in educational policy in the UK. A third area is becoming increasingly more significant when we look at policy drivers in education, that of education to build sustainability in the context of climate instability and environmental change (Mansilla and Jackson, 2011). The outcome of these three policy drivers is to produce young people who can exercise 'global competence':

> The growing global interdependence that characterizes our time calls for a generation of individuals who can engage in effective global problem solving and participate simultaneously in local, national, and global civic life. Put simply, preparing our students to participate fully in today's and tomorrow's world demands that we nurture their *global competence*.
> (*Mansilla and Jackson, 2011, p. xiii, italics in the original*)

In the development of global competences a culture of wellbeing in a school will make a considerable contribution. In such ideas about the wider purposes of education a focus on the holistic development of young people including their psychological and physical wellbeing can sit well. However, as 'success' – of a school and of an individual learner – is still related to performance in examination, there is a danger that such imperatives get reduced to attainment of targets set externally to the school and for which schools and school leaders are held to account. Sergiovanni (1994) argues that one of the critical first steps in building a purposeful community is 'to identify and commit to a set of core values' (p. 72). Therefore, part of what school leaders have to grapple with relates to the need to reify the educational dimensions of the vision of the school where the core values of the school focus on these expansive understandings of the learning of all pupils.

Thus, a primary concern of school leaders is to build a school community founded on a core set of values through which wellbeing is nurtured. However, this demands change on the part of all members of the school community. 'Building community in schools is about a shared quest to do things differently to develop new kinds of relationships, to create new ties, to make commitments' (Sergiovanni, 1994, p. 153). In a study of Flemish primary schools exploring capacities of schools to develop and implement policy on wellbeing, Van Gasse *et al.* (2016, p. 353) report that while attributes among the staff team such as 'openness, collaboration, loyalty, involvement and motivation of the team members' are important, teachers reported that it was school cultures that were adaptive and flexible that could better address issues related to pupils' wellbeing. This flexibility and adaptability demands of school leaders and teachers a responsiveness to individual pupils. Roffey (2012), in her exploration of the relationship between pupil and teacher wellbeing, found that how school leaders treated staff then influenced how staff treated each other and in turn how they treated pupils: 'in practice the relational values of respect, acceptance and care had to extend both from and to all staff. Everyone needed to feel positive about being in the school and this was everyone's responsibility' (p. 11).

A central ideal underpinning work on nurturing a culture of wellbeing is that of care. The educational philosopher Nel Noddings (1984) explores the idea of an ethic of care as the foundation of a genuinely inclusive school community. Noddings (1984) argues that the core purpose of education is to produce ethical individuals and the school community is the medium to achieve this. Noddings (2010, p. 267) notes that the notion of community has both positive as well as negative dimensions and argues that 'Students need not only to belong to a community; even more, they need to know what it means and can mean to belong to a community'. Therefore, the community of the school needs to be based on core values around relational ethics, 'an ethic of care' (Noddings 1984). The implications of adopting an ethic of caring for education are profound, helping us to explore the exercise of school leadership with regard to values, ethos and relationships within a school community and practices, the core of which is building relationships. In a caring relationship there are two roles, the carer, that is the 'one caring' and the one who receives the care 'the one cared-for'. While teachers play a key role as the 'one caring', Noddings argues that part of the task of education is to enable pupils not only to receive care but also to be able to enter into caring relationships with peers and ultimately with all other members of the school community where they become the one caring for another. Sergiovanni (1994), drawing from Noddings (1984), argues that caring in a relationship is about:

- receiving the perspective of the other person;
- responding to the awareness that comes from receiving;
- remaining in the caring relationship for a length of time.

Thus to build a culture of wellbeing, a key element of the role of school leaders is to build an inclusive community and this is a community based on an ethic of care and where the core of the educational process is to foster care.

Future directions

In this discussion three aspects of community, emotions and culture have been identified as being critical to the task of school leaders in building a nurturing school where the wellbeing of all is central to the purposes and values of the school. There is a substantial literature on stress and burnout both on the part of teachers and school leaders and increasingly the impact of mental ill-health on the development and learning of young people. While these are major concerns that need to be grappled with, part of the discussion in this chapter has been to suggest a wider understanding of wellbeing. One of the barriers to placing wellbeing at the core of a school community is the result of a historical separation of the curriculum and pastoral support. Wellbeing has to be viewed as the foundation for effective learning in a school. A question to be explored then is what would be the features of a culture of wellbeing in a school? Further, how do school leaders engage with staff to create a culture of wellbeing within each classroom?

One of the keynotes of Auerbach's (2012b) discussion of building partnerships is that of 'authenticity'. A question then to be pursued is how we build authentic partnerships within a school. In this chapter it is argued that the idea of community is very powerful and offers much in viewing the school as an inclusive place, but at the same time there are dangers, particularly exclusion, the pressure towards normalisation and conformity as well as the possibility of creating negative attitudes towards those not part of a school community. Noddings (2010) is alert to some of these tensions and in advocating relational ethics, that is an ethic of caring as the basis for the purpose and values of a school, provides us with the means to address some of these challenges. However, in this Nodding poses a challenge about how we can systematically build the ethic of caring across staff groups and pupils. Again, this raises a number of questions that might be considered: in what ways would expectations on staff change and how might this redefine our understandings of teacher professionalism? Furthermore, how can school leaders enable staff to go about the task of building development opportunities systematically in order that pupils acquire the skills and habits of caring as well as being cared for?

Summary of key findings

- Wellbeing is a key concern for school leaders and has to be an integral part of the role of school leaders in building a culture for learning.
- A critical element of promoting wellbeing is building a sense of belonging among teachers, support staff and pupils.
- Wellbeing can only be promoted through authentic partnerships with parents and the school's community.

- The emotional aspects of school life have to be engaged in constructively in order that school leaders can promote wellbeing across the school community.
- Wellbeing is a critical dimension of the common purpose and shared set of values of a school and is based on an ethic of care.

Reflective tasks

Think about your own school or a school you have recently been involved in.

- How would you define the community of the school? Who are members of this school's community?
- To what degree are the different members engaged in the life of the school?
- Are there significant groups who are on the periphery of the school's life?
- What is the impact of being on the periphery on these groups and on the learning of pupils?
- How might these often hard-to-reach groups be engaged?

Identify two schools you are familiar with and consider the cultures of each.

- In what ways are these cultures similar and in what ways do they contrast?
- Which school promotes better a culture of wellbeing and what do you base this judgement on?

Think about the ethic of care proposed by Noddings.

- What is your response to this concept of 'an ethic of care'?
- What demands would this make on you as a teacher?
- How might you construct learning opportunities through which pupils can develop the skills and habits of care?

Further readings

Briner, R., & Dewberry, C. (2007). *Staff Well-being is Key to School Success*. London: Worklife Support Ltd/Hamilton House. Retrieved from http://www.worklifesupport.com/sites/default/files/uploaded-documents/5902BirkbeckWBPerfSummaryFinal.pdf

Martin, C.R., Fleming, M.P., & Smith, H. (2016). *Mental Health and Well-being in the Learning and Teaching Environment*. Auchtermuchty, Fife, Scotland: Swan and Horn.

The Children's Society. (2016). *The Good Childhood Report 2016*. London: The Children's Society. Retrieved from http://www.childrenssociety.org.uk/sites/default/files/pcr090_mainreport_web.pdf

References

Asia Society. (2011). *Improving Teacher Quality Around the World: The International Summit on the Teaching Profession*. Retrieved from http://asiasociety.org/global-cities-education-network/worlds-education-leaders-support-teachers

Auerbach, S. (2012a). 'Introduction: Why leadership for partnerships?' In S. Auerbach (Ed.), *School Leadership for Authentic Family and Community Partnerships: Research Perspectives for Transforming Practice* (pp. 3–10). New York: Routledge.

Auerbach, S. (2012b). 'Introduction: Why leadership for partnerships?' In S. Auerbach (Ed.), *School Leadership for Authentic Family and Community Partnerships: Research Perspectives for Transforming Practice* (pp. 3–9). New York: Routledge.

Beatty, B.R. (2004). 'Feeling like a leader: The emotions of leadership'. In Tomlinson, H. (Ed.) *Educational Management: Major Themes in Education*, (pp. 179–207). Abingdon: RoutledgeFalmer.

Blasé, J., & Blasé, J. (2002). The Dark Side of Leadership: Teacher Perspectives of Principal Mistreatment, *Educational Administration Quarterly*, *38*(5), 671–727.

Collie, R. J., Shapka, J. D., & Perry, N. E. (2012). School Climate and Social-Emotional Learning: Predicting Teacher Stress, Job Satisfaction, and Teaching Efficacy, *Journal of Educational Psychology*, *104*(4), 1189–1204.

Crawford, M. (2009). *Getting to the Heart of Leadership: Emotion and Educational Leadership*. London: Sage.

Das. S. (2008). 'What is school culture'. In T. Townsend & I. Bogotoch. (Eds.), *The Elusive What and the Problematic How: The Essential Leadership Questions for School Leaders and Educational Researchers* (pp. 33–55). Rotterdam: Sense Publishing.

Day, C., Gu, Q., & Sammons, P. (2016). The Impact of Leadership on Student Outcomes: How Successful School Leaders Use Transformational and Instructional Strategies to Make a Difference, *Educational Administration Quarterly*, *52*(2), 221–258.

Day, S. (2016). 'The impact of institutional culture'. In C.R. Martin, M.P. Fleming, & H. Smith (Eds.), *Mental Health and Well-being in the Learning and Teaching Environment* (pp. 199–210). Auchtermuchty: Swan and Horn.

Ecclestone, K., & Hayes, D. (2008). *The Dangerous Rise of Therapeutic Education*. London: Routledge.

Evans, L. (1999). *Managing to Motivate*. London: Cassell Publishing.

Fendler, L. (2006). Others and the Problem of Community, *Curriculum Enquiry*, *36*(3), 303–326.

Fineman, S. (2000). 'Emotional arenas revisited'. In Fineman, S. (Ed.), *Emotion in Organizations*, (pp. 1–24). London: Sage.

Galton, M., & MacBeath, J. (2008). *Teachers Under Pressure*. London: Sage.

Goleman, D. (1996). *Emotional Intelligence*. London: Bloomsbury.

Halsey, A.H., Lauder, H., Brown, P., & Stuart Wells, A. (1997). *Education: Culture, Economy and Society*. Oxford: Oxford University Press.

Hargreaves, A. (2008). 'The emotional geographies of educational leadership'. In B. Davies & T. Brighouse (Eds.), *Passionate Leadership in Education* (pp. 129–150). London: Sage.

Hargreaves, D.H. (1995). School Culture, School Effectiveness and School Improvement, *School Effectiveness and School Improvement: An International Journal of Research, Policy and Practice*, *6*(1), 23–46.

Hochschild, A.R. (2002). 'Emotional labour'. In S. Jackson & S. Scott (Eds.), *Gender: A Sociological Reader* (pp. 192–195). Abingdon: Psychology Press.

James, C. (2004). 'The work of educational leaders in building culture and passionate schools and colleges'. In H. Tomlinson (Ed.), *Educational Management: Major Themes in Education*, (pp. 263–276). Abingdon: RoutledgeFalmer.

Leithwood, K., Harris, A., & Hopkins, D. (2008). Seven Strong Claims About Successful School Leadership, *School Leadership and Management, 28*(1), 27–42.

Leithwood, K. Jantzi, D., & Steinbach, R. (1999). *Changing Leadership for Changing Times.* Buckingham: Open University Press.

Lueder, D.C. (2011). *Involving Hard-to-Reach Parents: Creating Family/School Partnerships.* Lanham, Maryland: Rowman and Littlefield Education.

MacNeil, A.J., Prater, D.L., & Busch, S. (2009). The Effects of School Culture and Climate on Student Achievement, *International Journal of Leadership in Education, 12*(1), 73–84.

Mansilla, V.B., & Jackson, A. (2011). *Educating for Global Competence: Preparing our Youth to Engage the World.* New York and Washington: Asia Society and Council of Chief State School Officers.

Noddings, N. (1984). *Caring: A Relational Approach to Ethics and Moral Education.* California: University of California Press.

Noddings, N. (2010). *The Maternal Factor: Two Paths to Morality.* California: University of California Press.

Peterson, K.D., & Deal, T.E. (1998). How Leaders Influence the Culture of Schools, *Educational Leadership, 56*(1), 28–31.

Roffey, S. (2012). Pupil Wellbeing – Teacher Wellbeing: Two Sides of the Same Coin?, *Educational and Child Psychology, 29*(4), 1–17.

Roland-Martin, J. (1992). *The School-Home.* Cambridge: Harvard University Press.

Sergiovanni, T. (1994). *Building Community in Schools.* San Francisco: Jossey-Bass.

Van Gasse, R., Vanhoof, J. & Van Petegem, P. (2016). The Impact of School Culture on Schools' Pupil Well-being Policy-Making Capacities, *Educational Studies, 42*(4), 340–356.

6

TEACHING FOR WELLBEING

On the importance of creating capabilities in schools

James MacAllister

Introduction

Schools across the globe have long tried and often succeeded in contributing to the wellbeing of children and young persons who attend them. However, the last ten to fifteen years have seen a heightened policy focus on education for wellbeing in the UK and elsewhere (see Chapter 3). As White notes, 'before the millennium, the term "wellbeing" barely figured in the educational lexicon, a decade later its use is ubiquitous' (White, 2011, p. 12). In this chapter I will consider some of the reasons why this may be so. I will also discuss how teachers in schools might respond to the recent education for wellbeing agenda. I will first consider the role of the Organisation for Economic Cooperation and Development (OECD) in promoting wellbeing measurement in nations and states. I note how the work of Amartya Sen has influenced the OECD's mission to measure wellbeing across the globe. After charting three distinctions Sen makes between agency, being well off and being well, I document the views of Nussbaum, who like Sen, advocates the development of wellbeing capabilities. I observe that the OECD mostly appears interested in *compiling statistics on wellbeing*. This is in contrast to Nussbaum, who is not opposed to wellbeing measurement but nonetheless believes the focus should be placed on *creating wellbeing capabilities for all persons*.

The chapter is thereafter pulled together via a consideration of the role of the teacher in creating wellbeing capabilities in schools. I argue that teachers (and schools) will only be able to help students to 'be well' if both teachers and students are clear about the sort of wellbeing they aspire to achieve. Here, I draw a distinction between schooling for *real* and *pseudo* wellbeing. In the case of real wellbeing, teachers in schools support the creation of diverse wellbeing capabilities in learners. All children and young persons are treated with dignity and encouraged to think about the shape and direction of their own lives with a focus on their long-term wellbeing and that of others. When learner wellbeing is real, it is integral to much, if not all, aspects of school experience. In the case of pseudo wellbeing a more limited perspective of wellbeing is adopted. A narrow focus on exams prevails. Students might be encouraged to reflect upon and gratify their own desires but there is no need for them to show active concern for the wellbeing of others. Three different pedagogies for wellbeing are thereafter delineated and their advantages and disadvantages discussed.

- The *measurement model* where teacher-led instruction in examinable bodies of knowledge and skills is regarded as the best way to promote wellbeing.
- The *subjective model* where the curriculum is built up from the current interests and desires of learners and where a premium is placed upon supporting young persons to learn how to satisfy their own subjective wellbeing preferences.
- The *capabilities model*, where teaching for wellbeing is held to be a matter of ensuring that all learners have opportunities to develop the ten central capabilities.

Following Nussbaum, it is argued that if teachers in schools want to promote genuine wellbeing, a balance of different pedagogies will need to be adopted, where the fostering of wellbeing capabilities in all is nonetheless vital.

The rise of wellbeing as an aim of schooling and the role of the OECD

Wellbeing has a certain intuitive appeal as an educational aim, perhaps especially for those who think education should be about more than the testing of examinable knowledge. Parents and teachers after all usually want the children in their worlds to do well in life (de Ruyter, 2015). However, children and young people ultimately need to realise their own wellbeing – their parents and teachers cannot do this for them (de Ruyter, 2015). What parents and teachers can however try to do is create conditions where children and young people are given the best possible chance of flourishing. But if schools can only indirectly pursue wellbeing for children and young people, why has wellbeing become more of a priority for schools in recent times? In *Exploring Wellbeing in Schools: A Guide to Making Children's Lives More Fulfilling*, John White maintains that three developments have brought renewed focus to the educating for wellbeing agenda in the UK: the *Every Child Matters* (2003) policy, wellbeing becoming a curriculum aim and the appearance of lessons specifically devoted to improving learner wellbeing. The *Every Child Matters* policy initiative placed an imperative upon schools to foster wellbeing in five areas: health, safety, enjoyment and achievement, the ability to make 'positive contributions' and economic wellbeing (White, 2011). Meanwhile, pupil wellbeing has become a prominent curriculum aim in England, Scotland and elsewhere, albeit with different points of emphasis in different places (White, 2011; Thorburn, Chapter 3, this volume). White notes how social welfare concerns, curriculum reforms and the positive psychology of Seligman (promoted by the Wellbeing Institute in Cambridge) have all influenced the emergence of specific lessons in wellbeing. White speculates that the popular work on the 'science' of happiness by the economist Richard Layard may also have helped fuel a shift in societal views about what really makes life worth living – a shift from *economic growth* to *wellbeing*.

White's discussion of the factors that have given rise to wellbeing becoming an educational priority is illuminating but it does not take into account the role played by the OECD. Their role merits consideration however, as the OECD have, since the publication of White's book, become a driving force behind the agenda to foster wellbeing in people, regions and countries rather than mere economic prosperity alone. By their own admission 'the OECD has been heavily engaged in international work to advance the statistical agenda on measuring wellbeing' (OECD, 2015, p. 38). The OECD framework for measuring wellbeing was launched in 2011. They hope that the framework will help in the development of 'better policies for better lives'. The framework is highly ambitious and aims to support the collection of a vast amount of statistical data about wellbeing across the globe. The OECD maintain wellbeing needs to be understood as a multi-dimensional concept. Being well they suggest is more than being economically well off. As such, the OECD has identified 11 key indicators of wellbeing that are grouped into two categories, namely: *material conditions* and *quality of life*. The former category includes income and wealth, jobs and earnings, and housing. The latter includes health status, work–life balance, education and skills, social connections, civic engagement and governance, environmental quality, personal security and subjective wellbeing (OECD, 2015, p. 23). The latest evidence on wellbeing suggests that OECD countries have diverse wellbeing strengths and weaknesses.

Predictably however, there are discernible wellbeing inequalities between countries and between populations in different regions of the same country (OECD, 2015). Here, populations ranked in the top third in terms of gross domestic product per capita (GDP) generally score higher in the overall wellbeing indicators than those ranked lower in terms of GDP. However, even countries that score highly on GDP can have weaknesses in terms of job security, air quality, housing affordability and work-life balance (OECD, 2015). Significantly there are large inequalities in child-wellbeing that are likely to persist into adulthood (OECD, 2015). Children from better off families have better health, are less likely to be bullied at school and form better relationships with parents and peers (OECD, 2015). As Cassidy points out in Chapter 1 systems are now in place to measure the wellbeing of children and not just their performance in exams. The OECD's wellbeing agenda opens up some vital educational questions though. Should schools promote pupil wellbeing as a central aim? If so how might they? If they can how would anyone, including the OECD, really know if they had succeeded in improving wellbeing? Is measuring wellbeing most important or is educating for it? In this chapter I will try to engage with some of these issues. I suggest that teachers should welcome the education for wellbeing policy agenda, but not in an unqualified way.

Main findings

Sen on capability, being well off, wellbeing and agency

Amartya Sen, the economist and philosopher, has undoubtedly influenced the OECD's mission to measure wellbeing. The OECD suggests that conceptually their framework for measuring wellbeing is partly based upon Sen's capabilities approach to understanding wellbeing (OECD, 2015). Sen first introduced the idea of 'capability' in a 1979 lecture called *Equality of What?* There he argued that the diversity of human capabilities was not fairly taken into account in (then dominant) theories of justice. Sen thus put forward 'capability' as a more egalitarian principle of justice than utility. What was needed he maintained is 'some notion of basic capabilities: a person being able to do certain basic things' (Sen, 1979, p. 218). Sen suggested that equality requires consideration not only of human desire or need but also capability – of what people are actually able to do in their context. In the second of his Dewey lectures five years later, called *Wellbeing, Agency and Freedom*, Sen further remarked that it is useful to distinguish between being 'well off' on the one hand and 'being well' on the other. The well off person is financially well off. They own riches, assets and other material possessions and have money abundant enough to acquire further riches, assets, goods and possessions. They are as Sen puts it 'opulent' and are likely to have opportunities to enhance their opulence in the future. Wellbeing in contrast is less focused on riches, possessions and wealth. Instead it is more akin to a personal capability – of how able a person is to function well in their life. For Sen (1984) wellbeing occurs when a person does things that contribute to their wellbeing. As such wellbeing is an achievement. However, Sen stresses that wellbeing is also concerned with things a person has not yet achieved but is nonetheless capable of. Some persons have greater capacity for future wellbeing than others and this capacity influences their current wellbeing. Being well off may help a given person to be well, but being well off in no way guarantees personal wellbeing.

While the goods of being well off are in a vital sense external to a person, the goods of wellbeing are in a vital sense part of that person. Sen suggests that wellbeing will often by embodied necessity vary from person to person. He takes the example of the difference between *consumption of food* and *being well-nourished*. One person with high metabolism may be undernourished yet consume much more food than another person who is amply nourished. As wellbeing is experienced (or not) at the personal level, there is undoubtedly a subjective aspect to it. However, for Sen, wellbeing is not essentially about being well off, nor for that matter is wellbeing essentially about subjectively felt happiness, desire or utility. In his later work especially, Sen emphasises that the essence of wellbeing revolves around human capability (Saito, 2003; Nussbaum, 2011). However, in his Dewey lectures Sen emphasised that the wellbeing aspect of a person ought to be distinguished from the agency aspect of a person. Indeed, he insisted that people may have desires, goals and values unrelated to wellbeing. He stated that people 'have aspects other than wellbeing ... There are goals other than wellbeing and values other than goals' (Sen, 1984, p. 186). While agency freedom is concerned with the freedom a person has to achieve whatever goals they regard as important, wellbeing freedom is always concerned to achieve the particular goal of wellbeing. Wellbeing freedom, and doings related to it, are thus much more specific than agency freedom and any doings related to it. Indeed, he suggested that while people may often in their actions and decisions aim at wellbeing sometimes they will not. Being free means being free to act in ways that are contrary to our wellbeing or that of others (Sen, 1984).

Sen makes three key conceptual distinctions in his Dewey lectures then: between being well-off, being well and having agency. For Sen, people are *well off* when they have monetary goods or opportunity to get further monetary goods. In contrast to this they have *wellbeing* when they do act in ways that aid their wellbeing or when they can. They finally have *agency* when they have the freedom to act in ways important to them. However, if his capability concept of wellbeing is to be properly understood, Sen's Dewey lectures need to be viewed in light of his wider critique of traditional welfare economics and utilitarianism. From the 1970s onwards Sen and others such as Nussbaum (2011) sought to highlight the inadequacy of mainstream welfare economics which tended to regard individuals and states as having wellbeing if they had a high GDP. However, for Sen and Nussbaum such traditional *income and commodity* accounts of wellbeing are fundamentally incomplete. For them there is much more to wellbeing than affluence and economic growth alone. Sen points out that a 'person's wellbeing is not really a matter of how rich he or she is' (1985, p. 28). However, utility-based accounts of wellbeing (understood as satisfaction of desire preferences) are inadequate too. Sen is skeptical of desire satisfaction and utility-based accounts of wellbeing because people can have desires that run contrary to the demands of justice (Saito, 2003). Chief Executive Officers (CEOs) can desire and come to believe that they deserve to paid hundreds of times more than other employees in their company on the one hand while people in poverty can habituate themselves to not desire what they know to be unobtainable on the other. In such circumstances neither the desires of the CEO nor the impoverished person would provide sufficient motivation for actions that aim at just change. Sen thus defends the merits of a capabilities approach as it represents a more socially just way of evaluating human wellbeing. Nussbaum is another well-known advocate of the capabilities approach.

Nussbaum on creating capabilities

> What are capabilities? They are the answer to the question, 'What is this person able to do and be?'
>
> *(Nussbaum, 2011, p. 20)*

Like Sen, Nussbaum believes that a capabilities approach to the evaluation of human wellbeing should be endorsed as it provides a more socially just alternative to utility or GDP approaches. Nussbaum indeed defines the capabilities approach as 'an approach to quality of life assessment and to theorizing about social justice' (Nussbaum, 2011, p. 18). For Nussbaum (and for that matter Sen), assessments of wellbeing should specifically seek to tackle entrenched injustice and inequality.

Here, the core question to ask when comparing quality of life and justice in different societies becomes not, 'how rich is each person, region or country' or 'how satisfied are different people with their lives' but 'what is each person able to do and be in their life'? Nussbaum's capabilities approach calls for a focus on understanding the overall capabilities each person has the opportunity to develop in their context, and not only on their affluence or capacity to satisfy desires. Nussbaum suggests there are three different types of capability; basic, internal and combined. *Combined capabilities* are the sum total of capabilities that each person has developed or has the opportunity to develop. They represent the overall range of possible choices and actions that each person can take in their specific context. In contrast to this, *internal capabilities* are achieved states of persons. They are the specific things that people can do. Here it is worth stressing that the capabilities each person has opportunity to develop or has developed may evolve over time – they are fluid rather than fixed states.

Finally, there are *basic capabilities*. These are the innate faculties of each person that render later development of capability possible. As fluid states, capabilities are educable. However, whether a person will have the freedom to translate their basic capabilities into internal and combined ones depends upon the particular context and time they find themselves in. Sometimes personal, institutional and/or cultural circumstances will greatly restrict opportunities for capability development. Nussbaum takes the example of Vasanti to explain how capabilities might emerge when previously they could not. Vasanti is an Indian woman who lacked many opportunities to develop her capabilities while in an abusive marriage. She was not employed so was financially dependent on her husband who beat her in the knowledge (consciously or otherwise) that she was dependent on him and so less likely to leave him. She was not literate, which in turn affected her employment prospects. However, with the support of her family and a women's organisation, Vasanti left her abusive husband and found that opportunities to develop her capabilities increased over time. She became able to set up her own sewing business, and pay back the loan she needed to set up the business. She enrolled on an education programme and she became more socially and politically active in her community. She started to turn her basic capabilities into internal and combined ones. As she did this her wellbeing improved.

Nussbaum insists that there are ten specific central capabilities that political orders must ensure for all citizens if their region or country is to be considered minimally just. These are:

1. *Life.* Being able to live to the end of human life of normal length; not dying prematurely.
2. *Bodily Health.* Being able to have good health … to be adequately nourished, to have adequate shelter.
3. *Bodily Integrity.* Being able to move freely from place to place; to be secure against violent assault, including sexual assault and domestic violence; having opportunities for sexual satisfaction and for choice in matters of reproduction.

4. *Senses, imagination and thought.* Being able to use the senses to imagine, think and reason – and to do these things in a truly human way, a way informed by an adequate education, including but by no means limited to literacy and basic mathematical and scientific training.

5. *Emotions.* Being able to have attachments to things and people outside ourselves; to love those who love and care for us … to experience longing, gratitude and justified anger. Not having one's emotional development blighted by fear and anxiety.

6. *Practical Reason.* Being able to form a conception of the good and to engage in critical reflection about the planning of one's life.

7. *Affiliation.* (A) Being able to live with and towards others, to recognize and show concern for other human beings, to engage in various forms of social interaction; to be able to imagine the situation of another … (B) being able to be treated as a dignified being whose worth is equal to that of others. This entails provisions of non-discrimination on the basis of race, sex, sexual orientation, ethnicity, caste, national origin.

8. *Other species.* Being able to live with concern for and in relation to animals, plants and the world of nature.

9. *Play.* Being able to laugh, to play, to enjoy recreational activities.

10. *Control over one's environment.* (A) Political. Being able to participate politically in political choices that govern one's life … (B) Material. Being able to hold property … and having property rights on an equal basis with others … In work, being able to work as a human being, exercising practical reason and entering into meaningful relationships of mutual recognition with other workers.

(Nussbaum, 2011, p. 33–34)

For Nussbaum full justice will not be delivered if one capability is achieved at the expense of another. Though all ten central capabilities are important then, Nussbaum argues that two are 'architectonic' in that they 'pervade' the rest – *practical reason* and *affiliation.* According to Nussbaum, all persons should be afforded the opportunity to plan and live their lives in freely chosen ways. This capability is one of practical reason, and practical reason is needed in all the other capabilities too. People should be free to plan their leisure for example and they should be able to choose who they socialise with and when. Similarly, if people are not able to form caring relationships with others, and for others, if they are not able to affiliate with others in loving ways, then their capacity to achieve other capabilities will be greatly restricted. In compiling this list Nussbaum wants to raise expectations about what it means to live life well. She especially wants to challenge nations and regions across the globe to take action to support the development of central capabilities for all persons. Here she feels that central capabilities need to be aspirational but not so utopian as to be unrealistic and unfeasible.

In this respect, she concedes that her list is only a proposal whose specific merits can and should be contested and debated and whose specific contents may need to be amended in different regions and countries to take into account prevailing local, cultural and/or religious values, interests and needs. However, she maintains that this list nonetheless represents a minimum threshold of capability entitlements that all citizens across the world should enjoy. This is perhaps the most controversial aspect of her thesis – as Nussbaum is well aware. Nussbaum acknowledges that some may interpret her formulation of universal norms of capability entitlement for all as wanting to impose Western, imperialist values on other countries and regions. However, Nussbaum does not regard these central capabilities as inherently Western. Indeed, she points out that the capabilities approach was in no small part developed by an Indian (Sen), in India. She also points out that the capabilities approach has close links to the human rights movement, the architects of which came from diverse countries including France, China and Egypt. She also suggests it is not imperialist to call for action that enhances the dignity of each person. Imperialism often hinged on Westerners treating non-Westerners with little or no dignity (Nussbaum, 2011). However, such indignity is precisely what her capabilities approach seeks to challenge. She maintains that if a person is denied the opportunity to develop capabilities in any of these ten areas, then their dignity as a person is not being respected (Nussbaum, 2011). Nussbaum suggests that the importance that she places on human dignity renders her account different to that of Sen's. There are though other important differences between the capabilities approaches endorsed by Sen and Nussbaum, perhaps especially in respect to the issue of measurement.

Measuring and comparing wellbeing capabilities, or creating them?

> The earliest and still most common use of the Capabilities Approach is to supply a new account of the right way to compare and rank development achievements. When nations or regions compare with one another for ranking in the global development 'marketplace', trying to show that they offer a better quality of life than other nations do, or than they themselves used to do, the Capabilities Approach provides a new account of the right way to make such comparisons.
>
> *(Nussbaum, 2011, p. 69)*

In *Creating Capabilities: The Human Development Approach* Nussbaum explains how her capabilities approach to human development in places differs to the approach provided by Sen. Nussbaum regards Sen's account as unduly open ended about the minimum capability entitlements all persons should have. Unlike Nussbaum, Sen does not specify a threshold level of capability entitlements that all persons in the world should enjoy. Nussbaum considers Sen to be too permissive in respect to the issue of freedom as well. She is critical of the distinction Sen makes between wellbeing and agency freedom and regards this as a needless remnant of utilitarianism in Sen's essentially non-utilitarian project. She maintains that Sen does not do enough to challenge orthodox, politically powerful views about human freedom. As she puts it: 'some freedoms limit others … The freedom of industry to pollute the

environment limits the freedom of citizens to enjoy an unpolluted environment ...
Sen ... says nothing to limit ... such conflicts' (Nussbaum, 2011, p. 71). Indeed, it
is partly because some choices and actions limit others that Nussbaum insists that
none of the ten capabilities that she delineates should be pursued to the expense
of others. Nussbaum thus considers her theory to be more *normative* and less *comparative* than Sen's. Like Sen, Nussbaum believes that capability evaluations should
inform public policy so that they can 'improve the quality of life for all people as
defined by their capabilities' (Nussbaum, 2011, p. 19).

However, for Nussbaum, capabilities primarily pertain to individual persons
and only derivatively to groups. Nussbaum therefore deliberately refrains from
using her capabilities approach to provide comprehensive and comparative assessments of the quality of life for different groups of persons. This is in contrast to
Sen who has asserted that capabilities can provide the foundation for a comprehensive, comparative quality of life assessment for groups of persons in nations
and regions. For Nussbaum the emphasis should be on *creating* wellbeing capabilities for all – not on *measuring and comparing* them. For Nussbaum (2011) the
capabilities approach is not so much a means of measurement for comparison but
rather a way of ensuring that minimal social justice capability entitlements are
worked towards in practice and enshrined in constitutional law internationally
for all citizens. Nussbaum thus implies that while both her and Sen bring moral
philosophy into development economics, her capabilities approach is primarily
normative whereas Sen's is primarily *comparative*. Nussbaum does, like Sen, think
that measuring capabilities can help to bring about action that creates capabilities.
However, she cautions against over-reliance upon statistical measurement when
assessing capability. Some capabilities might be best understood through qualitative and narrative research (Nussbaum, 2011). At a more fundamental level she
also suggests that measurement is important, but only in so far as it supports the
creation of actual wellbeing capabilities. Measurement and comparison of wellbeing capability are not in themselves good. They are only good if they support the
creation of actual wellbeing capabilities. In this respect, education is at the core of
Nussbaum's approach to creating capabilities.

Education and creating capabilities

> At the heart of the Capabilities approach since its inception has been the
> importance of education. Education ... forms people's existing capacities into developed internal capabilities ... This formation is valuable in
> itself ... it is also pivotal to the development of many other human capabilities:
> a 'fertile functioning' of the highest importance in addressing disadvantage
> and inequality.
>
> *(Nussbaum, 2011, p. 152)*

Nussbaum argues that people who have received even a basic education greatly
enhance their capabilities. They will have higher chances of employment, better

options for social and political participation as well as heightened access to leisure opportunities. Nussbaum follows Adam Smith in believing that deprivation of education takes an 'inestimable toll' on the wellbeing of people and on their capacity to achieve things in later life. Indeed, she argues that compulsory schooling in the early years is justified precisely because it will enhance the capabilities of people in adulthood. Here she stresses that it is important not to confine education to the development of literacy, scientific and numeracy skills alone. A good education will be sensitive to the local context and culture of students. Importantly Nussbaum suggests that teachers should pay attention to how both curriculum content and pedagogy can help in the development of central human capabilities. In this respect, Nussbaum questions a current tendency evident in many national school systems: to focus on fostering 'marketable' skills. Such a narrow focus, borne out of short-term anxieties for profit, reduces opportunities for the development of critical thinking and engagement with the humanities (Nussbaum, 2011). However, for Nussbaum, education properly conceived will attend to more than economic needs. It will be concerned with human development in its fullness. It should strive to promote social justice within countries and across the globe. Here it is interesting to compare Nussbaum's thinking on education with that encouraged by the OECD. As we have seen, for Nussbaum, education should create diverse capabilities for all. Education is not just about developing marketable skills in young persons so that the needs of the market economy can be met.

The OECD encourages a rather different view of education – one that appears to be centrally about the development of marketable skills in young people. Countries can after all only become members of the OECD if they are committed to the needs of the market economy (Sellar and Lingard, 2013). Via tools like the Programme for International Student Assessment (PISA), the OECD has become a key player in promoting the outcome- and exam-orientated vision of education that is all too common today, in Europe and elsewhere (Sellar and Lingard, 2013; Grek, 2014). Grek suggests that the OECD is now a 'powerhouse' in education policy terms: a powerhouse that has been only too happy to generate and share data about the performance of national school systems. Unfortunately, 'because of the OECD, assessing education is often presently simplistically as an empirical problem open to quantification' (Grek, 2014, p. 278). Not everything that is educationally valuable is open to numeric quantification, yet the OECD's measurement of the educational aspect of wellbeing looks like it will be based upon such simplistic assessments. They assert that when evaluating the wellbeing dimension of education, the focus is not on inputs and outputs but on *outcomes* – on skills and competencies achieved by persons in education (OECD, 2015). However, the two indicators that the OECD uses to measure the wellbeing aspect of education are the percentage of the adult population (15–64 years) holding at least an upper second-class degree and the PISA reading test taken by 15-year-olds (OECD, 2011). Quite how these indicators represent *outcomes* rather than *outputs* is not clear. What does seem clear is that the OECD intend on continuing their policy of collecting data on the performance of education systems globally through programmes like PISA. It is positive that more nuanced concepts of wellbeing are beginning to figure in policy discourses (see Chapter 3). However, the collection of statistics about educational outcomes will not by itself help in the creation of wellbeing capabilities. Nussbaum's capability framework is notably different to the OECD's then. The OECD only seems interested in collecting statistical data about wellbeing and education. Nussbaum in contrast believes education should focus on the creation of wellbeing capabilities and she insists that some capabilities cannot be properly understood in statistical terms.

Three pedagogies for wellbeing: Measurement, subjective or capabilities approaches

My sympathy for Nussbaum's views about wellbeing and education over those perpetuated by the OECD are probably by now clear. However, that does not mean that I regard the OECD's mission of measurement of student and school performance and wider human wellbeing as wholly unhelpful and without warrant. I do think schools should help learners develop marketable skills in literacy, numeracy and science. As Nussbaum points out, even a successful basic education can greatly aid in the development of human capability. Knowing which national and regional school systems might need support to provide such basic education better would seem important from a social justice point of view. However, as Nussbaum also points out, there is more to education than developing marketable skills in the same way that there is more to human wellbeing than GDP alone. How might teachers in schools support learners to be well then? It is my view that teachers (and schools) will only be able to help learners to 'be well' if both teachers and students are clear about the sort of wellbeing they aspire to achieve. Here, I think we can draw a distinction between schooling for *real* and *pseudo* wellbeing. In the case of real wellbeing, teachers in schools focus on supporting students to develop diverse capabilities. In the case of real wellbeing, children and young persons are treated with dignity and encouraged to think about the shape and direction of their own lives with a focus on their long-term wellbeing and that of others. When learner wellbeing is real, it is integral to many, if not all, aspects of school experience.

In the case of pseudo wellbeing, a more limited perspective of wellbeing is adopted. Wellbeing is held to be an add-on to and by-product of examination success. However, a focus on exams in schools in this way may do little other than provide information for wellbeing indexes such as those developed by the OECD. Students with pseudo wellbeing might be encouraged to reflect upon and gratify their own desires but there is no need to show active concern for the wellbeing of others. Nor are they supported to develop what Nussbaum calls practical reason – the capacity to reflectively shape the direction of one's life with an eye on the common good. I do not think there is a specific formula that teachers can adopt in order to promote real wellbeing in schools. I do nonetheless think it is important that teachers reflect upon how their activities can support the development of genuine, rather than pseudo, student wellbeing. At the moment a *measurement model* arguably prevails in education policy and, as a consequence, in many schools. Here, teacher-led instruction in examinable bodies of knowledge and skills are regarded as the best way to promote wellbeing. However, the problem with this model is that it encourages a narrow fixation on test scores and outcomes. How might teachers challenge such tendencies in practice? One possibility might be for them to aim to instill a love of learning in all students during their schooling. For if students do often find themselves immersed in their school experiences they may be more likely to develop and sustain a capacity to learn throughout the length of life. A positive disposition towards learning can after all greatly aid long-term wellbeing. No doubt many teachers already try to inspire their students and not just prepare them for exams. However, the more recent policy tendency to value examinable knowledge most highly perhaps encourages teachers to neglect the need for schooling to be an absorbing, whole-hearted affair that encourages students to love learning. Of course most teachers know all too well that knowledge and skills are not just valuable on account of the enhanced employment prospects that they may offer when packaged up in a qualification.

Knowledge can also illuminate and enrich the human predicament beyond the workplace. There is also more to education than the acquisition of knowledge or the desire for it though. Another way in which schools might help young persons to be well is by helping them to learn how to satisfy their own interests and desires. This might be called a *subjective model* of teaching for wellbeing. Here, the curriculum is built up from the current interests and desires of learners. A premium is placed upon supporting young persons to learn how to satisfy their own subjective wellbeing preferences. An advantage of this model is that it encourages young people to go after what they want in life and reflect upon their desires and values. John White is perhaps the most well-known exponent of such a subjective theory of wellbeing and schooling. White suggests that schools should centrally aim to promote the wellbeing of students. Learners are well, he suggests, when they are able to pursue activities that they regard as worthwhile, in a whole-hearted way, and when they allow others to do the same (White, 2011). White has though been criticised for endorsing an unduly desire-focused story about education and wellbeing (Marples, 1999). However, White (1999) insists this mud does not stick to his later work, where he emphasises that people learn to desire and value what they do through social interactions with others. de Ruyter (2015) is probably therefore right to suggest that White's account of wellbeing and schooling contains aspects of objectivity, and is *intersubjective* rather than subjective in nature. This is an important distinction as in purely subjective theories of wellbeing, young people may not learn to care about the needs and interests of others or wider societal injustices. In *subjective* accounts of wellbeing, persons are well when they feel content with their lives. They feel that they have fulfilled their desires – but this might just mean desiring to be well-off and feeling satisfied when they become well-off. In contrast to this, in *objective* theories (such as that developed by Nussbaum) persons are well when they are able to develop their natural capabilities, when they are able to attain goods that are in some crucial way identifiably good for all people (de Ruyter, 2015).[1]

De Ruyter speculates that there are similarities between White's views and Nussbaum's. This may be so as they do both defend the value of liberal education while considering certain basic needs like food, shelter and safety to be necessary for human wellbeing. However, *capabilities* are to the fore in Nussbaum's framework rather than *desires*. In a *capabilities model,* teaching for wellbeing is a matter of ensuring that all young persons have opportunity to develop ten central capabilities. Teaching to develop diverse wellbeing capabilities is much more than teaching to the test. Teachers committed to a capabilities approach will need to help students learn how to affiliate with each other in caring ways. They will need to give all students room to think about long-term life-goals and not just the satisfaction of short-term desires. Teaching to create capabilities will almost certainly mean different things in different places however. In some regions of the world educators might be first and foremost concerned to ensure that learners get access to a basic education. In many regions a key task facing teachers committed to a capabilities approach will be to help young persons learn how to actively care more about the demands of justice than the needs of the market economy. The enormity of the challenge to create central capabilities for all should not be underestimated. It is easy to mouth such words of aspiration – it is another to live them in practice in our increasingly globalised market society. As MacIntyre (2013) has observed, today young people are generally habituated into desiring what the market economy needs them to desire – they are schooled with concern for the common good minimally, if at all. Thus teachers committed to fostering real wellbeing in students might need to spend a good deal of time asking learners if the needs of the market economy really should have such influence over human desires and actions. Fairly obviously, schools will not be able to tackle such wellbeing challenges alone. However, aiming to create diverse student capabilities at school, and encouraging students to take an active concern for the basic wellbeing entitlements of others might represent one way in which teachers can challenge entrenched injustices while also supporting the children in their care to be well.

Future directions

In this chapter I have considered the role of the OECD in the agenda to promote wellbeing as an aim of schooling. I have also considered in depth the work of Sen and Nussbaum on the capabilities approach. I have suggested that the capabilities approach to human wellbeing advanced by Nussbaum has several advantages over the multi-faceted model favoured by the OECD. The stress from the OECD is on *measuring and comparing* wellbeing competences of groups of persons where such competences are generally measured by statistics alone. This is in contrast to Nussbaum, who is not opposed to wellbeing measurement but nonetheless believes the focus should be placed on *creating wellbeing capabilities for all persons*. Here Nussbaum suggests that some human capabilities are best understood through qualitative and narrative research rather than statistics and numbers. Given the OECD seem thoroughly committed to collecting statistics about wellbeing there is arguably a real need for research on wellbeing and education that employs narrative and qualitative methodologies. Such research could compliment the statistical work being conducted by the OECD. However, there is also a need for further research that critically interrogates the role of the OECD in measuring wellbeing. I have tried to contribute to this research need in this chapter. In this chapter I have also suggested that teachers need to do more than promote pseudo wellbeing in schools. There is more to educating for wellbeing than fostering marketable skills in the same way that there is more to human wellbeing than being well-off.

This is not to say there should be no measurement in schools, or of schools, or no fostering of marketable skills in schools. Of course there should. However, if teachers want to promote genuine rather than pseudo wellbeing, a balance of different pedagogies will need to be adopted, where the fostering of wellbeing capabilities in all is nonetheless vital. In this respect there is arguably an urgent need for narrative and qualitative research about how schools are trying to create wellbeing capabilities in learners and about the sorts of wellbeing capabilities they are creating. As schools are now expected to promote wellbeing, it only seems fair to conclude by asking if at least some of the time and money being expended on measuring wellbeing would be better spent on creating student capabilities in schools. If the lion's share of time and funding goes on measuring wellbeing rather than creating wellbeing capabilities, this might be a concrete indicator of how serious the OECD (and those they influence) really is about creating better policies for better lives. How much more statistical data on wellbeing needs to be collected before action for real change is taken? In my view it is not so much *data* about wellbeing injustices that is lacking but a *will* for real change on the part of the powerful. In some instances, the obsessive gathering of wellbeing statistics on a large scale might even serve as a smokescreen for inaction – inaction which ill-serves those most dispossessed of wellbeing. Whether well intended or not, measuring wellbeing is no substitute for developing it.

Summary of key points

- There is more to educating for wellbeing than fostering marketable skills – in the same way that there is more to human wellbeing than being well off.
- The OECD mostly seems interested in *compiling statistics on wellbeing.*
- Nussbaum believes focus should be placed on *creating wellbeing capabilities for all persons*. Education is at the core of this.
- Teachers should reflect upon how their activities can support the development of *real* rather than *pseudo* student wellbeing.
- There is a need for further research on wellbeing and education that employs narrative and qualitative methodologies.

Reflective tasks

- Compare the ten central capabilities of Nussbaum with the 11 wellbeing measurements favoured by the OECD. What are the strengths and weaknesses of each list? Which list is more overtly committed to the promotion of social justice? Are any aspects of wellbeing especially important for you? Why?
- What do you think the difference between an objective and subjective account of schooling for wellbeing is? What pedagogy for wellbeing do you think is most *educational* and why?
- Imagine you are a class teacher committed to wellbeing. How would this be evident in your classroom practices? Give precise examples. Provide further examples of how wellbeing might feature in your discussions about school priorities with a range of professional colleagues.

Key texts

Nussbaum, M. (2011). *Creating Capabilities: The Human Development Approach*. London: Harvard University Press.

Organisation for Economic Cooperation and Development. (2015). *How's Life: 2015? Measuring Wellbeing*. Paris: OECD.

Sen, A, (1984). Wellbeing, Agency and Freedom: The Dewey Lectures, *The Journal of Philosophy, 82*(4), 169–221.

Note

1   Kristjánsson (2016) offers a slightly different description of the differences between subjective and objective accounts of wellbeing, one that can perhaps shed light on how the OECD (2015) understands wellbeing. He suggests that in a *subjective* account the criteria used to assess wellbeing are restricted to self-reports on psychological states experienced by the agent whose wellbeing is being evaluated. In contrast to this, the criteria used to assess *objective* wellbeing have to do with objective features of the agent's life – things that are external to the agent but relate to how they do or are able to live their life. Here, the feelings an agent has about their wellbeing need not come into it.

References

Crown Copyright. (2003). *Every Child Matters*. London: The Stationary Office.

de Ruyter, D. (2015). 'Wellbeing and education'. In J. Suissa, C. Winstanley & R. Marples (Eds.), *Education, Philosophy and Wellbeing, New Perspectives on the Work of John White*, (pp. 84–98). London: Routledge.

Grek, S. (2014). OECD as a Site of Coproduction: European Education Governance and the New Politics of 'Policy Mobilization', *Critical Policy Studies, 8*(3), 266–281.

Kristjánsson, K. (2016). Recent Work on Flourishing as the Aim of Education: A Critical Review, *British Journal of Educational Studies*, in press. Retrieved from http://www.tandfonline.com/doi/full/10.1080/00071005.2016.1182115

MacIntyre, A. (2013). 'How Aristotelianism can become revolutionary: Ethics, resistance and Utopia'. In P. Blackledge & K. Knight (Eds.), *Virtue and Politics: Alasdair MacIntyre's Revolutionary Aristotelianism*, (pp. 11–19). Indiana: University of Notre Dame Press.

Marples, R. (1999). 'Wellbeing as an aim of education'. In R. Marples (Ed.), *The Aims of Education*, (pp. 133–144). London: Routledge.

Organisation for Economic Cooperation and Development. (2011). *OECD Compendium of Wellbeing Indicators*. Paris: OECD.

Saito, M. (2003). Amartya Sen's Capability Approach to Education: A Critical Exploration, *Journal of Philosophy of Education*, *37*(1), 17–33.

Sellar, S., & Lingard, B. (2013). 'PISA and the expanding role of the OECD in global educational governance'. In H.D. Meyer & A. Benavot (Eds.), *PISA, Power and Policy: The Emergence of Global Educational Governance*, (pp. 185–206). Oxford: Symposium.

Sen, A. (1979). *Equality of What?* The Tanner Lecture on Human Values, Delivered at Stanford University, May 1979. Retrieved from http://tannerlectures.utah.edu/_documents/a-to-z/s/sen80.pdf

Sen, A. (1985). *Commodities and Capabilities*. North Holland: Oxford University Press.

White, J. (1999). 'In defence of liberal aims in education'. In R. Marples (Ed.), *The Aims of Education*, (pp. 185–200). London: Routledge.

White, J. (2011). *Exploring Wellbeing in Schools*. London: Routledge.

7

THE TEACHER-IN-TRAINING PERSPECTIVE

Preparing teachers to incorporate wellbeing into learning and teaching

Monica Porciani

Introduction

The newness of wellbeing to curricula is likely to create a tension between teachers seeking greater pedagogical guidance on wellbeing, while national curriculum organisations expect teachers to take on greater responsibility for wellbeing more immediately (Porciani, 2013). Similarly, Dewhirst *et al.* (2014) have raised concerns about how educational policies often insufficiently support wider public health priorities. The challenges exist elsewhere in Europe where a wide range of policy initiatives have been introduced to improve HWB and tackle related inequalities. For example, The *European Child and Adolescent Health Strategy* (2015–2020) have a vision for the European region which requires greater investment in children and young people. A key aim is for children and adolescents to 'develop the confidence and skills to make informed choices and decisions, and develop positive relationships' (WHO, 2014, p. 10). The strategy advises that their guiding principles will help lay good foundations in the drive to improve child wellbeing. These are: adopting a life-course approach, adopting an evidence-informed approach, promoting strong partnerships and intersectoral collaboration and adopting a rights-based approach (WHO, 2014, p. 4). Young *et al.* (2014) conclude that the evidence for the effectiveness of health promotion in schools is clearly established and requires a strong commitment to teacher training and to health and education sectors working in partnership to 'build trust and capacity' (p. 140).

The Scottish Government has been at the forefront of creating a strategic framework which includes the WHO's 'guiding principles' as a cornerstone of the policy landscape e.g. *Curriculum for Excellence* (CFE) (2009), *Getting It Right for Every Child* (GIRFEC) (Scottish Executive, 2006) and *Better Relationships, Better Learning, Better Behaviour* (Scottish Government, 2013). In 2013, an evaluation of the impact of HWB as a core area of Scotland's CFE found that secondary school programmes still concentrated too much on one-off events and health days (Education Scotland, 2013). A major challenge identified was for initial teacher education (ITE) programmes to ensure that student teachers are well prepared to confidently contribute to teaching, learning and behavioural change in HWB. An internal audit developed by Education Scotland to assist ITE providers' reviews on how they can address and integrate core aspects of HWB into ITE programmes demonstrates the complexity of this challenge. The audit included policy directives, pupil entitlements and a wide range of issues such as nurture, attachment, inclusion, equality, food education, physical activity, outdoor learning and sustainable development education, all of which are now considered fundamental to school HWB. Given that the vast majority of secondary teachers in the UK undertake their teacher training in a one-year postgraduate course, there is a pressing need for ITE programmes to find innovative ways of providing meaningful HWB learning and to highlight the benefits of career-long professional learning and development in this area. Thus, teacher education programmes need to be viewed as a starting point to lay the foundations and develop mechanisms which help student teachers identify their own learning skills, competencies and needs in order to support their start in teaching. This chapter aims to explore how secondary school teachers can be better prepared by reviewing research and theory and by considering some of the implications for their practice. The chapter presents some recent innovations and flexible ways of learning, using digital technologies, external partners and school placement to develop teacher agency and competency in HWB.

Main findings

Background

In the past, school health programmes were primarily concerned with improving public health and preventing infectious diseases by improving hygiene. Nowadays, health promotion has been widely developed as a core school activity, encompassing holistic and multi-faceted models and approaches. Dewhirst *et al.* (2014) point out that UK teachers are integral to the wider public health improvement workforce, and are therefore expected to help deliver national public health priorities. More recently a rapid expansion of the teaching role and remit has placed even greater demands on teachers trying to manage competing priorities. The media often reports a profession under pressure from an ever-increasing workload, while under the added burden to improve exam results, while also implementing a raft of policies and guidelines. Therefore, it is no surprise to learn that health promotion is often poorly addressed and has a low status in UK secondary schools. At primary school level, Formby and Wolstenholme (2012) suggest there is clearer progress towards health promotion, and more time is devoted to the priority within the curriculum. In comparison, secondary schools have been slow to integrate HWB into the curriculum, with research highlighting the low status afforded to PSHE in secondary schools in England and the reasons for this being the case. For instance,

Formby and Wolstenholme (2012) note that school leadership often does not value personal, social, health and economic (PSHE) education, nor considers it to be fundamental to the school's main purpose, i.e. improving academic attainment.

Similar findings have also emerged in Scotland, where despite the introduction of CFE in 2010, a consultation by Education Scotland (2013) evaluating practice in aspects of HWB indicated that progress had not been consistent across all sectors. The report suggested that not all secondary teachers felt comfortable working in this area of the curriculum, either because they were unclear about their role or unsure how to implement aspects of the curriculum. More worryingly, some newly qualified teachers commented that they did not feel adequately supported during their ITE programme and were not sufficiently prepared to confidently teach HWB (Education Scotland, 2013). The main issue seems to be one of inconsistency, with some newly qualified teachers feeling well prepared to address HWB, while others felt insufficient teaching time had been allocated to effectively address the issues requiring review. The report points out that in secondary schools, there remains too much emphasis on one-off HWB events with 'insufficient opportunities for follow up' (Education Scotland, 2013, p. 23). This correlates with research in England which highlights that PSHE lessons routinely rely on tutor/form group time or drop-down days rather than integrating PSHE with day-to-day school learning and teaching (Formby and Wolstenholme, 2012). Similarly, a report by Ofsted (2013, p. 6) also concluded that PSHE was not 'yet good enough in a sizeable proportion of schools'. In the UK therefore many secondary teachers currently feel poorly prepared to engage effectively with HWB and unable to embed HWB into their learning and teaching. The report also highlights the need to provide adequate training and support in subject specific areas such as teaching sensitive or controversial issues (Ofsted, 2013). Typically subjects that are closely aligned to health such as home economics, physical education and biology, have assumed a bigger role and responsibility for delivering health promotion. A major challenge for ITE is to ensure that *all* secondary teachers feel competent and have the knowledge, skills and confidence to teach HWB education and take an active role promoting young people's health. This chapter considers how to position and frame HWB, or PSHE in teacher education, by examining teacher education frameworks in Scotland and how these can be integrated more cohesively into a School of Education's ITE programme.

Developing effective teacher education for health and wellbeing

In 2011, Professor Graham Donaldson made a series of recommendations to improve teacher education and the quality of teaching in Scotland (Scottish Government, 2011). The five-year evaluation of the impact of these recommendations highlights several strengths in ITE. Black *et al.* (2016) confirm the contribution of newly qualified teachers to the shift in the culture of professional learning that had taken place and also note positive developments in ITE programmes which have ingrained in teachers from the start of their training that they should be self-reflective, keen to engage in professional dialogue and share practice and work collaboratively and be willing to try new teaching approaches. Just over four-fifths (81%) of probationers interviewed responded that they found the pedagogical approaches to learning and teaching the most useful aspect of their ITE. However, this did not apply to HWB with teachers-in-training commenting that HWB had not been given the same priority or covered in as much depth as literacy or numeracy, with fewer opportunities to incorporate HWB into teaching and learning. One student teacher interviewed noted that 'Considering it's given the same weight as literacy and numeracy in policy there's very little on it compared to either of those' (Black *et al.*, 2016, p. 28) and overall only half (50%) of newly qualified teachers found the provision of HWB in their ITE course to be very useful or useful.

In the UK, it appears that secondary teachers are often inadequately prepared to address the wider aspects of PSHE, particularly those issues which are linked to public health priorities. For example, in Scotland and England, Chief Medical Officers' annual reports routinely publish key health priorities and risk factors (NHS Scotland, 2016; Department of Health, 2014). The reports highlight lifestyle and behavioural risks such as high alcohol consumption, poor sexual wellbeing, drug abuse and tobacco consumption as being key concerns for young people's health. Yet a survey of ITE providers in England claims that these topics were often rarely covered, indicating that future teachers may well be poorly prepared to tackle these issues as part of the wider public health workforce (Dewhirst *et al.*, 2014). Related research has shown that this often leads to secondary teachers lacking confidence in tackling challenging or sensitive issues such as sexual health and relationship education (SHRE) (Formby and Wolstenholme, 2012; Ofsted, 2013).

In Scotland, like many other European countries, ITE is grounded in university-based schools of education and informed by practice in schools. Recent reports argue that, despite some of the constraints of University courses, these courses remain the most effective and efficient vehicle for good-quality learning and lead towards having a reflective and enquiring teaching force (Scottish Government, 2011; OECD, 2015). However, Black et al. (2016), in their review of teacher education, acknowledge that improvements need to be implemented to ensure that HWB is properly incorporated, and more explicitly referenced.

A related study by Flaschberger (2013, p. 219) in Austria highlights that there has been 'little research that focuses on an analysis of teacher education or training' for school health promotion. The study identifies that many ITE programmes only offer modules which are explicitly called 'health', 'health education' or 'health promotion' as optional modules. The study identified factors such as timetable demands, competing subjects and time constraints as barriers for ITE providers. As University systems tend to be based around modular structures, integration across courses or between modules can be problematic. Darling-Hammond (2006, p. 300) suggests that to create stronger and more effective teacher education programmes there needs to be 'tight coherence and integration among courses and between course work and clinical work in schools, extensive and intensely supervised clinical work integrated with course work using pedagogies that link theory and practice'. This requires more explicit referencing of HWB within ITE, and for course structures to present greater coherence between practitioner-based reflective practice, theory-based learning on campus and school-based placement practice.

Learning and teaching approaches

It is not only the structures that need to be coherent, but also the content and knowledge base. As a starting point, student teachers require a solid knowledge base of issues identified as health priorities. A research brief for the Scottish Parliament acknowledges that 'the most effective teachers have deep knowledge of the subjects they teach' and that the 'quality of instruction' also has a significant impact on student outcomes' (Marcus, 2016, p. 13). It is evident that ITE can play a role, developing teachers who are 'educators of the whole person as well as subject experts' and, according to Young *et al.* (2014, p. 130), 'attitudes and knowledge are key factors in their intention to work with health-related content'. With these intentions in mind, students should be encouraged to identify generic teaching skills and assess how these might be applied to addressing individual HWB topics. A research study in the Netherlands demonstrated that knowledge and skills can be transferred across different health domains when they share 'common factors'. Peter's (2012) study of a transfer-orientated programme showed that knowledge and skills gained in one health domain such as safe sex or smoking behaviour had a positive effect on health behaviours in other domains. This could be promising for ITE course designers as it may offer a solution on how to capitalise on specific health classes or topic-based approaches and apply the knowledge and skills gained more widely. Young *et al.* (2014) stress that links across and between subjects should be explored to make better connections both to the wider life of the school and real-life connections. For instance, some of the life skills and health competencies such as critical reflection, peer support, negotiation and assertiveness skills may be shared across a range of subject domains. Similarly, Thorburn (2014, p. 206) has argued that there needs to be greater 'philosophical clarity on well-being values and by the development of pedagogical models which highlight how effective learning could take place'.

Incorporating health and wellbeing into ITE programmes: Implications for future practice

High levels of professional autonomy and collaboration are the hallmark of high-performing educational systems around the world (Schleicher, 2012; Scottish Government, 2016). Schleicher's review for the OECD on how to build a high-quality teaching profession highlights the importance of encouraging strong collaborative approaches to support pupil-teacher relationships and ultimately, a positive school culture. Scotland tends to allow teachers to have relatively high levels of autonomy over how they teach and to take responsibility for their professional development. The OECD considers that Scotland is at the forefront of developing professional learning and acknowledges the progress made since the introduction of new professional standards claiming that the GTCS (the professional body for regulating teachers) have designed core standards which are supportive of high quality professional judgements (OECD, 2015).

Professional standards in teaching for HWB

Black *et al.* (2016), in their evaluation of improvements in ITE, claim that new professional standards for teacher registration, developed by the *General Teaching Council for Scotland* (GTCS), have been a catalyst for change and improvement in professional learning. The GTCS suite of Professional Standards introduced a set of core professional values which encompass a commitment to improve and promote HWB within changing and complex social contexts (GTCS, 2012). The new framework includes standards for student teachers to ensure that all new teachers will develop as enquiring professionals with expertise in teaching HWB (see Table 7.1). The suite of revised standards aims to provide student teachers with clear guidance on the competencies and benchmarks they need to achieve full registration. This set of core professional values is central to the continuing development of the education profession, regardless of a teacher's experience or career stage.

This single set of standards guides the process from student teacher to probationer, and then onwards to full teacher registration. For the first time in Scotland, ITE providers have a baseline for HWB that addresses professional competence in three distinct aspects: professional values, knowledge and understanding and skills and abilities. Alongside HWB, a commitment to 'Learning for Sustainability' (LfS) has been embedded into the standards as a core aspect. Developing a whole

TABLE 7.1 General Teaching Council for Scotland: Standards for student teachers

---

2.1.4 Have knowledge and understanding of contexts for learning to fulfil their responsibilities in literacy, numeracy, health and wellbeing and interdisciplinary learning. http://www.gtcs.org.uk/professional-standards/the-standards/the-standards.aspx

Professional actions student teachers:

1. Know how to promote and support the cognitive, emotional, social and physical wellbeing of all learners in their care, and show commitment to raising these learners' expectations of themselves.
2. Know how to apply knowledge and understanding of areas of the curriculum which contribute to personal and social development and health and wellbeing.
3. Have knowledge and understanding of current guidance on the use of digital technologies in schools and know how to use digital technologies to enhance teaching and learning.
4. Know and understand the content of the curriculum in relation to literacy, numeracy and health and wellbeing as set out in national guidance.
5. Know and understand the methods and underlying theories for effective teaching of literacy, numeracy and health and wellbeing, and select the most appropriate methods to meet all learners' needs.
6. Have knowledge and understanding of current educational priorities such as learning for sustainability.

(GTCS, 2012, pp. 8–9).

school commitment helps the school to take decisions which are compatible with a sustainable future (GTCS, 2012). LfS is a new and dynamic feature but as the OECD (2015) cautions, without much consideration or evidence on how to move some of these bold and inspiring principles from theory into practice. That said, for ITE providers the standards provide a good foundation to develop courses that provide a consistent set of core standards for teachers.

Case Study: HWB programme in a Scottish School of Education

In 2012, a review of ITE programmes at the University of Strathclyde provided an opportunity to review HWB and consider how it could be re-positioned to improve student learning and satisfy key policy drivers and imperatives. A key focus was feedback from an aspect review of ITE, carried out by HMIe (2010) which noted that almost a quarter of newly qualified teachers reported not being well prepared to teach the aspects of HWB which are the responsibility of all teachers, and furthermore that the development of this strand is not yet 'systematically embedded into the learning of all students' (p. 23). The challenge for the School of Education (SoE) was to develop a model or approaches which could embed HWB more cohesively into core course structures, while also providing greater flexibility for student teachers to identify their own learning needs and plan their own professional learning journey from undergraduate level through to master's level study.

Feedback and recommendations from the Aspect Review (HMIe, 2010) of teacher education (Scottish Government, 2011), and the GTCS professional standards (GTCS, 2012) provided the impetus for the realignment of HWB. CFE and GIRFEC were the main policy drivers which shaped the design and content. Rather than tailoring a programme to address all the 'Experiences and Outcomes' (Learning and Teaching Scotland, 2009) associated with the HWB strand of CFE, the aim was to ensure that physical, social and mental health were embedded throughout the course. A flexible model was developed which offers both undergraduate (four years) and postgraduate (one year) programmes as an introduction to HWB and identifies key core competencies, skills and knowledge in relation to professional standards. In addition, a range of option modules allow students to build on the foundational knowledge base and undertake more specialised courses and modules. For the student, option modules have the added benefit of allowing them to identify their own learning needs, skills and strengths, which can build their expertise in a specific area or address a gap in their core skills. For the SoE, this provides an opportunity to utilise the expertise of staff more effectively, and to develop innovative pathways and partnerships, often working with other departments or developing blended-learning courses online. The pathway described in Table 7.2 illustrates some of

TABLE 7.2 Core competencies and skills: Context and principles of health promotion in Initial Teacher Education

Core Principles	Brief content description with links to professional standards or resources
1. Attitudes, values and beliefs	'*Critically examining personal and professional attitudes and beliefs and challenging assumptions*' (GTCS, 2012, p. 4). Exploration of own personal values and beliefs about health is a good starting point for student learning: '*What does being healthy mean to you*' in 'Promoting Health' provides a good starter activity (Scriven, 2010, p. 4).
2. School health promotion – principles, models, evidence	Historical context and development of the European Network of Health Promoting Schools since the Jakarta Convention. Principles and evidence for school health promotion: see SHE Factsheet 2 (2013).
3. Health intelligence	National data sets and surveys highlight trends in youth health, challenges and priorities requiring further action (see Chapter 8 for more information on surveys).
4. Health needs assessment	Assessing health needs at national, local and community level, including information and data on health inequalities and the needs of vulnerable children. Public health information for Scotland including a wide range of profile tools are available from '*The Scottish Public Health Observatory*' (ScotPHO). http://www.scotpho.org.uk/comparative-health/profiles/online-profiles-tool
5. Health policy and legislation	'*Develop an understanding of current, relevant legislation and guidance such as … GIRFEC*' (GTCS, 2012, p.10). The policy framework is complex, and legislation now includes the Children and Young People (Scotland) Act (2014) with the GIRFEC model of wellbeing enshrined in law – for more information see Chapter 8.
6. Public health approaches	'*Read and analyse a range of appropriate educational and research literature*' (GTCS, 2012 p. 18). Health interventions, whole school approaches and partnerships for health improvement. Current issues and emerging theories such as asset-based approaches versus a more directed public health model. Briefing Paper 10 (Glasgow Centre for Population Health) – provides an analysis of current research on asset-based approaches in practice – for more information see Further reading below or discussion in Chapter 3.
7. Effective Interventions	'*Use what they have learned from reading and research to challenge and inform practice*'(GTCS, 2012, p. 18). Using the evidence base to plan effective interventions – promoting social and emotional wellbeing is fundamental and therefore a good starting point – see Promoting Health in Schools: From Evidence to Action (IUHPE, 2010).

the core skills and competencies which the programme has identified at introductory level, and provides a link to professional standards, tools and resources which support learning and development. Thereafter, the option module on 'Protecting Scotland's Children' is elaborated on in more specific detail (Table 7.3).

Protecting Scotland's children: Option module

Child protection policies and safeguarding procedures have been identified as pre-requisite core skills for pre-service teachers (see Chapter 8 for a fuller analysis), and ensuring child safety is one of the key *SHANARRI* indicators for children and young people (Scottish Government, 2008). This is a central aspect of Scottish Government policy as reflected in *Getting It Right for Every Child* (Scottish Government, 2008), *Better Relationships, Better Learning, Better Behaviour* (Scottish Government, 2013) and the Children and Young People (Scotland) Act 2014 (Scottish Government, 2014). The GTCS professional

TABLE 7.3 Protecting Scotland's children: Module outcomes and workshop approaches

Tutorial classes will provide experiential learning opportunities and participatory methods such as group work, role play and problem solving.	'*Understanding the Children's Hearing System*' **Role Play** – case studies. Students plan for attending a children's hearing. Use assessment tools. Explore resources and materials that support children's voice and participation. **Resources:** '*All About Me*' form http://www.scra.gov.uk/children/	Students learn about their statutory role in child protection Better understanding of legal system and process Rights of the child are fully understood and respected Multi-agency working and using common assessment tools
Critically analyse the relationship between child protection concepts, theories and policies and implementation in national and local programme	Violence reduction as a public health approach – exploring WHO model Children and Young People's health profiles – examine indicators and outcomes 'No Knives Better Lives' primary prevention programme http://noknivesbetterlives.com/ Violence Reduction Unit http://www.actiononviolence.org.uk/	Public health data Public health approach Knowledge of causes and consequences of violence, policy interventions and advocacy

standards for teacher registration have an expectation that student teachers will be able to 'provide a safe and secure environment; have a working knowledge of the teacher's contractual, pastoral and legal responsibilities; including strategies for understanding and preventing bullying' (GTCS, 2012, pp. 7, 11 and 17). Rapid societal change, particularly in the last twenty years, has changed the landscape of childhood, with body image and the influence of the media and technology, the high rate of teenage pregnancies and the sexualisation of childhood emerging as concerns, seem to have a negative impact (for a fuller analysis see Chapter 8).

So, how can student teachers' efficacy and ability to understand their statutory duties and develop their pastoral role be better supported? First, students need to feel competent and know how to protect and promote children and young people's wellbeing; while at the same time knowing how to address key public health challenges. Second, in addition, students need to develop confidence using experiential-learning strategies with young people who allow them to practise negotiating risky behaviours and applying their skills to real-life situations. This could include applying safety settings to social networking sites or developing assertiveness skills to handle peer pressure. The module entitled 'Protecting Scotland's Children' was launched to try and embed the 'guiding principles' in *The European Child and Adolescent Health Strategy* (WHO, 2014) into a coherent programme – linking global strategy with the local context. The programme was ambitious in intending to develop a working knowledge and engagement with child protection legislation and policy and provide practical experiential opportunities for students to identify and address the needs of vulnerable groups of young people. Furthermore, the module considered universal and targeted-support models and approaches. This involved student teachers taking part in scenarios and role-play activities based on real-life situations with the module overall emphasising the importance of understanding the role of protective factors in supporting young people to address their risk-taking behaviours. In addition, the module was designed to overcome some of the earlier-identified shortcomings of ITE programmes, such as weak partnerships between national and local organisations, linking campus learning with school-based placement, working in collaborative groups and using public health models and interventions to address issues such as substance misuse, teenage pregnancy, violence reduction and online safety.

Future directions

If ITE providers are to address the needs of a twenty-first-century teaching workforce, they should consider how to position HWB/PSHE within courses in order to improve course integration. Although Scotland has made significant progress in the last decade, with HWB now a core responsibility of all teachers, this has not necessarily been embraced by all secondary teachers. Furthermore, many probationary teachers claim their ITE course did not adequately cover this area. In response, Education Scotland has been working with ITE providers to develop a collaborative approach between institutions and to establish a common framework for ITE. Institutions have shown a commitment to this new approach by meeting regularly, sharing ideas and resources, and creating an online community network. Secondary teachers-in-training need to work collaboratively, experience interdisciplinary approaches that help make connections between subjects and engage with professional learning opportunities online or via social networking sites. Digital technology is having an impact as well and can help advance early career professional development. Teacher-led innovations, such as the recent 'Pedagoo.org', have helped connect and energise professional learning. For HWB this is encouraging, and will likely be enhanced in the future with the introduction of 'Massive Open Online Courses' (MOOCs) in many universities.

Summary of key findings

- In secondary schools, there is an over-reliance on one-off health days and events with little chance for follow-up.
- Secondary teachers report that they have not received effective guidance or preparation to teach PSHE/HWB as part of their ITE.
- ITE institutions need to prepare teachers to be effective in promoting HWB/PSHE in secondary schools.
- The most effective teachers are self-reflective, engage in professional dialogue, share their practice and work in collaboration.
- Early career development is increasingly supported by online tools and resources.

Reflective tasks

- What are your own values and beliefs about health and is it a priority for you?
- Have you used any public health profiling tools to assess the health needs of your own school community?
- To what extent has HWB/PSHE been addressed in your ITE and are there models or approaches that you have used effectively?
- What are your key skills and competencies in HWB?
- Have you used a portfolio or self-reflection tool to build your skill set e.g. seeking out information on health policies or pedagogical approaches?
- How might you develop a way forward for your personal development in HWB/PSHE e.g. to what extent have you used technology to facilitate your learning?

Further readings

Glasgow Centre for Population Health. (2012). *Putting asset based approaches into practice: identification, mobilisation and measurement of assets*. Briefing Paper 10, Concepts Series. Retrieved from http://www.gcph.co.uk/publications/362_concepts_series_10-putting_ asset_based_approaches_into_practice

Pedagoo. http://www.pedagoo.org/

PSHE Association. https://www.pshe-association.org.uk/

Schools for Health in Europe (SHE). (2013). Factsheet 2. *School health promotion: evidence for effective action*. Retrieved from http://www.schools-for-health.eu/uploads/files/SHE-Factsheet_2_School%20health%20promotion_Evidence.pdf

Scriven, A. (2010). *Promoting Health: A Practical Guide* (6th ed.). London: Elsevier Ltd.

References

Black, C., Bowen, L., Murray, L., & Zubairi, S.S. (2016). *Evaluation of the Impact of the Implementation of Teaching Scotland's Future*. Edinburgh: The Scottish Government.

Darling-Hammond, L. (2006). Constructing 21st-Century Teacher Education. *Journal of Teacher Education, 57*(3), 300–314.

Department of Health. (2014). Chief Medical Officer's annual report. Retrieved from: https://www.gov.uk/government/publications/chief-medical-officer-annual-report

Dewhirst, S., Pickett, K., Speller, V., Shepherd, J., Byrne, J., Almond, P., Grace, M., Hartwell, D., & Roderick, P. (2014). Are Trainee Teachers Being Adequately Prepared to Promote the Health and Well-being of School Children? A Survey of Current Practice, *Journal of Public Health, 36*(3), 467–475.

Education Scotland. (2013). Health and wellbeing: The responsibility of all 3–18. Retrieved from http://www.educationscotland.gov.uk/Images/HealthandWellbeing3to18_tcm4-814360.pdf

Flaschberger, E. (2013). Initial Teacher Education for School Health Promotion in Austria. *Health Education, 113*(3), 216–231.

Formby, E., & Wolstenholme, C. (2012). 'If there's going to be a subject that you don't have to do …' Findings from a Mapping Study of PSHE Education in English Secondary Schools, *Pastoral Care in Education, 30*(1), 5–18.

General Teaching Council for Scotland. (2012). *The Standards for Registration: Mandatory Requirements for Registration with the General Teaching Council for Scotland*. Edinburgh: GTC Scotland.

HMIe. (2010). Report on the aspect review of initial teacher education. Retrieved from http://dera.ioe.ac.uk/2286/1/arite.pdf

International Union for Health Promotion and Education (IUHPE). (2010). Promoting health in schools: From evidence to action. France: IUHPE. Retrieved from http://www. iuhpe.org/images/PUBLICATIONS/THEMATIC/HPS/Evidence-Action_ENG.pdf

Learning and Teaching Scotland. (2009). Health and wellbeing outcomes. Retrieved from http://www.ltscotland.org.uk/curriculumforexcellence/healthandwellbeing/index.asp

Marcus, G. (2016). *Closing the Attainment Gap: What Schools Can Do?* SPICe Briefing 16/68. Edinburgh: The Scottish Parliament.

NHS Scotland. (2016). Chief Medical Officer's annual report: Realistic medicine. Edinburgh: The Scottish Government. Retrieved from http://www.gov.scot/Resource/0049/00492520.pdf

Ofsted. (2013). Not yet good enough: Personal, social, health and economic education in schools. Retrieved from https://www.gov.uk/government/uploads/system/uploads/

attachment_data/file/370027/Not_yet_good_enough_personal__social__health_and_economic_education_in_schools.pdf

Organisation for Economic Co-operation and Development. (2015). Improving schools in Scotland: An OECD perspective. Retrieved from http://www.oecd.org/education/school/Improving-Schools-in-Scotland-An-OECD-Perspective.pdf

Peters, L. (2012). Searching for similarities: Transfer-orientated learning in health education at secondary school schools. University of Amsterdam. Retrieved from http://dare.uva.nl/document/2/146091

Porciani, M. (2013). 'Health and wellbeing in secondary education'. In: T.G.K. Bryce, W.H. Humes, D. Gillies, & A. Kennedy (Eds.), *Scottish Education* (pp. 567–572). Edinburgh: University of Edinburgh Press.

Schleicher, A. (Ed.) (2012). Preparing teachers and developing school leaders for the 21st century: Lessons from around the world. OECD Publishing. Retrieved from http://dx.doi.org/10.1787/9789264174559-en

Scottish Executive. (2006). *Getting it Right for Every Child Implementation Plan.* Edinburgh: Scottish Executive.

Scottish Government. (2008). Getting it right for every child: A guide to getting it right for every child. Edinburgh: Scottish Government. Retrieved from http://www.gov.scot/Resource/Doc/238985/0065813.pdf

Scottish Government. (2011). *Teaching Scotland's Future: Report of a Review of Teacher Education in Scotland.* Edinburgh: Scottish Government.

Scottish Government. (2013). Better relationships, better learning, better behaviour. Edinburgh: Scottish Government. Retrieved from www.gov.scot/Publications/2013/03/7388

Scottish Government. (2014). The Children and Young People (Scotland) Act. Edinburgh: The Scottish Government.

Scottish Government. (2016). *National Improvement Framework for Scottish Education: Achieving Excellence and Equity.* Edinburgh: Scottish Government.

Thorburn, M. (2014). Educating for Well-being in Scotland: Policy and Philosophy; Pitfalls and Possibilities, *Oxford Review of Education, 40*(2), 206–222.

WHO (World Health Organization). (2014). *Investing in children: The European child and adolescent health strategy.* Copenhagen: World Health Organisation Regional Office for Europe, Copenhagen. Retrieved from http://www.euro.who.int/__data/assets/pdf_file/0010/253729/64wd12e_InvestCAHstrategy_140440.pdf?ua=1

Young, I., St Leger, L., & Buijs, G. (2014). 'Evidence for effective action on health promoting schools: Background paper of SHE factsheet on evidence'. In G. Buijs., K. Dadaczynski., A. Sculz., & T.Vilaca (Eds.), *Equity, Education and Health: Learning from Practice* (pp. 122–140). Utrecht: CBO.

8

THE PASTORAL PERSPECTIVE

Handling sensitive issues

Monica Porciani

Introduction

The chapter provides insight and direction to teachers on how to develop their pastoral role and remit. The initial discussion is influenced by findings from large-scale surveys of young people, their concerns and emerging behaviours. The chapter then discusses international evidence that suggests that health outcomes improve when schools adopt multi-faceted approaches which embrace and address social and emotional interactions. School culture, peer relationships and the social learning environment are well documented as influential factors which promote social inclusion, increase emotional wellbeing and help reduce health risk behaviours (St. Leger, Young, Blanchard and Perry, 2010).

This process and the range of factors which impact on how young people think, feel and behave are then examined from a national (Scottish) experience where health and wellbeing has become a responsibility of all teachers and a core standard for professional registration. Teachers in Scotland must develop an understanding of, and empathy for, positive mental, social, emotional and physical wellbeing. This includes being able to address some of the more sensitive issues, which learners identify as important, such as sexual health, peer pressure and body image. These issues are often difficult to address and consequently, the role of the teacher in contemporary schooling is now much more complex. In brief, teachers now require specific knowledge of evidence-based health interventions and pedagogical approaches which address health issues affecting young people.

Within the broad area of teachers' pastoral perspective on handling sensitive issues, a recent European survey of *Health Behaviour in School-aged Children* (HBSC) indicated that gender differences have increased significantly in the last few years (Inchley *et al.*, 2016). This study provides crucial information on the cultural norms and social context of young people and their relationships with family, school and peers. These findings are used to inform the *Report Card* series published by UNICEF. In 2007, *Report Card* 7 (UNICEF, 2007) examined child wellbeing in rich countries and provided a sharp 'wake-up call' to the UK when it was bottom of the 'league table'. By 2011, matters had improved with *Report Card 11* (UNICEF, 2011) showing that the UK had moved up to 16th out of 29 of the world's wealthiest nations. However, this improvement was not consistent across all areas. Despite a fall in consumption rates for alcohol, tobacco and cannabis, alcohol abuse and teenage pregnancy were still exceptionally high with the teenage pregnancy rate one of the highest in Western Europe. Improving sexual health is therefore a key priority for public health policy. The evidence reviewed for this chapter suggests that schools should be doing better to address this issue.

In summary, the main objective of the chapter is to help teaching staff gain confidence and to develop a better understanding of how to sensitively address difficult areas of health and wellbeing. The chapter does not dwell on describing structures of pastoral support or the role and remit of teaching staff involved. The focus instead is to establish basic principles and to highlight approaches which are considered effective in building solid foundations between teachers and learners. Finally, the chapter considers how digital technology and the media can be harnessed to promote health and wellbeing in the future.

Main findings

What are young people telling us?

The latest HBSC survey advises that there have been a number of improvements and changes in youth health in recent years. In most European countries, 80% of children report an above-average rate of life satisfaction with risk-taking behaviors, such as alcohol and tobacco use, falling steadily. However, the report also warns that gender and socio-economic differences now play a bigger role in determining health outcomes for young people (Inchley *et al.*, 2016). Data from the UK suggests that despite two decades of trying to tackle poverty and health inequalities the problems remain and may even be increasing. Adolescents from less affluent backgrounds tend to have poorer health and life satisfaction, and experience less support from family and friends. A similar study by The Children's Society (2015) found similar findings, noting a growing concern about the widening gap in wellbeing gender differences compared to five years ago with a sharp rise in young girls feeling unhappy or having a poor self-image. Girls told researchers that they felt 'ugly or worthless'. On the other hand, for boys, these emotions remained stable and unchanged.

From the two large-scale research studies a complex profile is emerging of how teenage girls are growing up in the UK, particularly those from less-affluent backgrounds. Changes in family relations and an increase in perceived pressure and stress from school work may all be significant factors in the steady increase in psychosocial health complaints reported by just over half of teenage girls (51% in the

UK at age 15). Furthermore, findings suggest that while obesity in young girls has stabilised in recent years, more than two-thirds consider themselves 'too fat' (43% of girls at age 15). Inchley *et al.* (2016) report that the gender gap is now at the widest it has been for the last two decades, with young girls less likely to report 'good looks' compared to boys. This finding correlates with the most common reasons for children and young people contacting the national charity ChildLine. *Under Pressure: The ChildLine Review* – published to cover 2013/14, (NSPCC, 2014) presents a first-hand account of how young people feel about their lives. Four principal concerns were: family relationships, low self-esteem, unhappiness and self-harm. The review also highlighted a significant increase in counselling for eating disorders, with demand from girls outnumbering boys 11 to 1. Conversely, negative lifestyle behaviours and risk-taking are more prevalent in boys, increasing as they move from puberty into adolescence (NSPCC, 2014).

The growing trend in the rates of anxiety and depression in general have been widely discussed and acknowledged in a number of research studies. Wilkinson and Pickett (2010) found a substantial increase in disorders, such as anxiety and depression, in countries which have much higher rates of inequality. They conclude that 'the rising trend across so many studies is unmistakable' and argue that by the 1980s the 'average American child was more anxious than child psychiatric patients in the 1950s' (2010, p. 33–34). Their evidence also points to increased rates of anxiety and depression in adolescents being closely associated with behavioural problems, such as youth crime and substance misuse (Wilkinson and Pickett, 2010).

It is therefore important that educators understand the gender norms and cultural expectations which influence behaviour. As such, educators need to question why this might be happening and what are the underlying factors contributing to gender differences influencing subjective wellbeing. Why, for instance, do girls seem to suffer disproportionately from low self-esteem in comparison to boys? What is evident from the wider research base and the ChildLine review is that this can no longer be dismissed as hormonal changes in adolescence or simply just part of growing up. The evidence is clear; gender and inequality play a much bigger role than previously understood and merit further analysis.

Understanding the socio-cultural context: Social media, advertising and celebrities

The advertising industry and the media have long been linked to lifestyle choices and it is well known that teenagers are more vulnerable than adults to the influences of the media. The advertising and marketing industry targets girls and boys with very different messages and images, and through a vast network of communications channels. Overwhelmingly, girls learn to focus on how they look. Appearance is very important, and their value and self-worth are linked to their sense of identity and appearance. Images of women with the same 'slim' body types, often digitally altered, can result in young women feeling disempowered and unhappy with their looks. The writer and film maker, Jean Kilbourne, began her exploration of the connection between advertising and key public health issues over forty years ago. She researched violence against women, eating disorders and addictions. In the documentary film *Miss Representation* she states that 'girls end up measuring themselves against an impossible standard, and feel themselves wanting as a result, and boys, they get the message that this is what matters most' (Kilbourne, 2011). Likewise, in the *Girls' Attitude Survey*, 33% of 11–16 year old girls admitted to comparing themselves to celebrities most of the time (Girlguiding, 2016).

The European *Alliance for Childhood* (AFC) was formed in 2006 with the aim of improving the 'quality of childhood in Europe'. The group produced a series of publications which identify trends that are harmful to children. The fifth volume, published in 2014, includes a chapter examining the impact of marketing on children. The review provides a good starting point for educators interested in learning more about these issues as it makes some interesting points about the ubiquitous nature of marketing and advertising to children and the increasingly sophisticated mobile technology 'ingeniously designed to convince them that their happiness is tied directly to what they buy' (Linn, 2014, p. 119). Furthermore, the review suggests a causal link between commercialism and public health and social problems. It results in greater pressure and stress on family life, and promotion of materialistic values linked to depression and low self-esteem. Another phenomenon, debated, is the *sexualisation* of mainstream culture in the last few decades. A major concern is that advertising images and slogans have become increasingly sexualised and disproportionately target young girls. The research links increased sexualisation with some of the 'most pressing mental health problems, such as body dissatisfaction, eating disorders and poor sexual health' (Linn, 2014, p. 131).

Is social media consumption creating an epidemic of youth isolation and unhappiness?

Research, by the University of Essex, found that consumption of social media can occupy every waking hour, and that there were negative associations between increased screen-based media (SBM) exposure, social-networking site (SNS) use and adolescent wellbeing. Negative impacts include isolation, loneliness, cyber-bullying, reduced physical activity and sleep disturbance. Following the findings, the researchers called for a clear UK policy response targeted at tackling the negative consequences of excessive social media consumption on the wellbeing of adolescents (Cameron and Lloyd, 2015). Some of the proposed responses are considered later in the chapter to evaluate how schools and teachers might counteract and redress these negative effects. The rapid expansion and widespread use of mobile technology has had a seismic and long-term impact on the social interactions and behavior of teenagers. Concern for young men is associated with an increase in consumption of pornography, due to easy access to material on the internet. The messages they receive and the media in general give them an inadequate preparation for real life.

The manner in which girls now interact online has been captured yearly since 2009 by the *Girls' Attitude Survey* and shows that the posting of 'selfies' and regular 'updates of their status' on SMS stimulates an overly judgemental culture. As a result, teenage girls are often fearful of how their looks are perceived and rated by their peers (Girlguiding, 2016). Whereas for boys, the evidence suggests that the messages they receive about how they should act, behave and feel can have a profound and detrimental effect on their mental and sexual health in later life (Cameron and Lloyd, 2015; Sex Education Forum, 2006).

The social environment and wider cultural influences are clearly exerting considerable pressure on the health and mental wellbeing of young people. A cross-national study in 2011 that explored the relationship between wellbeing and cultural values found that countries with the highest levels of advertising to children have the lowest rankings on the UNICEF child-wellbeing scale (Kasser, 2011). Education, if it is to play a serious role improving young people's health and wellbeing, cannot afford to ignore the cultural climate of childhood. Educators must understand how advertising and the media shape how young people think, feel and behave. Linn's (2014, p. 136) review concludes that 'children have a right to grow up, without being undermined by commercial interests. It's up to us to protect that right'.

Prevention programmes will also be undermined if they do not consider the impact that culture and technology are having on children and young people. Teachers and school leaders should be encouraged to consider how these are affecting young people – disempowering them and making them unhappy – and what schools can do to effectively redress this balance and create an environment where young people can flourish?

Policy for preventative education and pastoral support: Balancing competing demands

Being 'safe' is one of the eight domains of child wellbeing that the Scottish Government wishes to promote: 'Children and young People should be protected from abuse, neglect or harm'. This is a central aspect of the policy, *Getting It Right for Every Child* (Scottish Government, 2008) and the Children and Young People (Scotland) Act, 2014 (Scottish Government, 2014a), and is intended to provide a strong foundation for working with children and young people, by placing them at the heart of planning and service provision, ensuring their rights are respected across the public sector. A principal pillar of the legislation is the creation of a new role called the 'Named Person'. It is envisaged that for secondary pupils the 'Named Person' will be a member of the school staff, such as a guidance/pupil support teacher. While all teachers have a statutory role to protect children, and are obliged to raise concerns they may have about a young person, it will be the role of the 'Named Person' to monitor and manage issues that may arise and help families access services, provide information and support, and discuss and address concerns with other agencies (Kidner, 2013). In seeking to improve outcomes for children this new agenda places two competing demands on teachers: protect and promote the wellbeing of all children and young people, and address the needs of the most vulnerable, at risk or challenged young people. The principles of GIRFEC, such as early intervention, integrated support, implementing child protection procedures and developing a children's plan might be considered as welcome additions to child protection provision. However, there is the potential to create tension. Therefore, when implementing this new model of wellbeing, teachers need to ensure services and support are clearly 'signposted' and available to everyone. Teachers must also safeguard and protect children at risk, and be proactive in identifying appropriate interventions to support them. This is now a significant part of many teachers' professional remit e.g. the latest survey of Scottish school-aged children highlights that just 30% of pupils aged between 11 and 15 receive a high level of teacher support (Currie *et al.*, 2015).

In recent years there has been a proliferation of national guidance documents, frameworks and policies to address these concerns. The Organisation for Economic Co-operation and Development (OECD) report on *Improving Schools in Scotland* (OECD, 2015) provides an external evaluation of Scotland's Curriculum for Excellence (CFE) and makes specific comment on the proliferation of documentation and guidance, which they suggest could be simplified. The *National Guidance for Child Protection* (Scottish Government, 2014b) is a prime example, running to a total of 188 pages covering all aspects of protecting children and safeguarding them from harm. Therefore, has the policy framework become too complex, and lost sight of the original objectives? In 2004, *The Children's Charter* was launched and listed a set of thirteen statements based on the views of young people (Scottish Executive, 2004). The views were collated from young people who were in need of care or protection and reflected what they wanted most from the professionals in charge. The Scottish Executive responded with a set of 'pledges' stating how they would bring about reform and address the demands of the young people. As a starting point the children and young people stated that they would like professionals who care for them to take time to: get to know us, speak with us, listen to us and involve us (Scottish Executive, 2004).

The promise by the Scottish Government (2014a) to the young people of Scotland clearly states what they can expect: a school culture where teachers will listen, take their views into consideration and involve them. It also presents a path for teachers to develop their own pastoral roles and build good relationships as it makes sense that young people will look for, and seek support from, adults whom they trust and in whose company they feel comfortable. The more connected young people feel to school, the greater their emotional wellbeing. The health promoting school approach, which has been in place for the last thirty years, makes specific reference to the quality of relationships and how connected they are, 'the social environment of the school is a combination of the quality of the relationships among and between staff and students' (St. Leger *et al.*, 2010, p. 4). The evidence also highlights those whole school policies which create a positive social learning environment by fostering open and honest relationships can at the same time help to reduce health risk behaviours. In addition, guidance on preventative education suggests that policy needs to move away from tackling single issues in a 'siloed' approach and focus on developing 'integrated, multiple risk behaviour approaches which recognise that risk behaviours tend to co-occur' (Scottish Government, 2013, p. 7). For instance, we know that in today's world young people under the influence of alcohol are far more likely to take more risks, such as unprotected sex. The new dimension to this equation is that their behaviour is now often recorded, and perhaps posted online, leading to far greater reputational and self-awareness consequences than for previous generations.

Research on earlier drug education programmes in secondary schools found that the use of participatory methods and increasing opportunities for discussion enhanced pupils' experiences (Lowden and Quinn, 2004; NHS Health Scotland, 2009). Evidence suggests that classroom-based approaches rooted in the principles of best practice can reduce harm from risky behaviour. At a pedagogical level, many of the life skills and competencies required, such as critical reflection, debate and discussion, are common to addressing a range of health-risk behaviours. A recent review of effective prevention education produced by the PSHE Association (2016) states that teachers need to deploy a mixture of teaching approaches ranging from instructional through to more interactive learning strategies. This review highlights that 'there is a particular emphasis across the literature on an active skills-based approach, albeit one which incorporates a mix of strategies as part of this approach' (PSHE, 2016, p. 7). Schools should promote skills-based practice using a range of techniques so that pupils get a chance to develop their decision-making skills, learn how to negotiate and become more assertive. Herbert and Lohrmann (2011), identified that the most effective health education curricula include strategies such as role play, co-operation, group work and use of interactive technology. Above all, teachers need to engage young people by making learning relevant to their everyday lives. In order to do this effectively, they need to be well informed about current news, social trends and research, and of the wider impact of socio-cultural factors highlighted earlier in the chapter. Promoting a climate of respect, trust and support is particularly relevant when discussing sensitive health-related issues, and will be further considered in the next section of the chapter.

Addressing sensitive issues at school

In Scottish education, the context for delivering sexual health and relationship education now has a more coherent infrastructure now in place. However, the actual delivery of sex education in Scottish schools by teaching staff has been described as somewhat 'patchy and inconsistent' (Buston, Wight and Scott, 2001). One issue is that too many teachers lack the confidence to address aspects of sexual health and relationship education in the classroom, and often choose to either leave it to the end of the school year or ignore it completely. Other teachers, however, are comfortable discussing issues as and when they come up. The report asserts that it as a sensitive subject, with 'no statutory training or examinations to work towards' it is often given low priority in an increasingly overcrowded curriculum (Buston et al., 2001, p. 353). The Scottish Health and Relationship Education (SHRE) training and resource pack provides a national programme (aimed at 13–16 year olds) for practitioners to access (NHS Health Scotland, 2014). It offers comprehensive and cohesive support and guidance on legal, social and moral issues i.e. the very issues teachers often 'dread' or which make them anxious e.g. disclosure of sexual abuse, addressing faith perspectives, acknowledging young people's sexual relationships and sexual identity and handling parental objections.

According to research there are a number of crucial factors which help ease teacher discomfort and facilitate the engagement of young people more effectively. Research in Scottish schools concluded that teachers need to be able to stay 'in control' of the class, consider the gender dynamics, organise class groupings sensitively and 'eliminate hurtful humour while maintaining a light-hearted and approachable manner' (Buston et al., 2002 p. 317). In this study, almost three-quarters of the young people interviewed said they felt uncomfortable in the classroom. Creating the right environment, where young people feel safe and secure, was a prime factor in reducing 'pupil discomfort'. How can this translate into effective classroom practice? The following points have been taken from the SHRE guidelines (NHS Health Scotland, 2014) and offer some fundamental steps for practitioners to create the 'right atmosphere':

- be open to a wide range of opinions and encourage diversity of opinion;
- listen and encourage students to listen to one another;
- be prepared to explore feelings, attitudes and skills as well as information,
- maintain a sense of humour and have fun;
- spend time forming a group agreement with the class about behaviour at the start;
- establish what language is acceptable.

(NHS Health Scotland, 2014, pp. 1–2)

Given that many teachers have very limited personal experience of SHRE, this may not be as straightforward as the guidance suggests. Student teachers and teachers frequently mention that: in their own school experience this was either never talked about or poorly covered, it was not adequately addressed in their own initial teacher education and initial teacher education does not prioritise or assess student teacher competency to deliver SHRE. In this light, student teachers have often commented that they have been asked to leave the room while on placement when a classroom teacher is addressing sensitive issues or teaching SHRE. It would be hard to imagine this happening for any other area of the curriculum and only serves to reinforce the idea that teaching SHRE is difficult and uncomfortable.

How can teachers become more confident sexual health educators?

Research indicates that teachers are more effective and confident in their role if they receive high-quality training, resources and support. Furthermore, effective programmes should provide a developmental approach and be sensitive to the age, stage and differing needs of learners (Nation *et al.*, 2003; Kirby and Laris, 2009). To that end, many of the health boards in Scotland have produced their own programmes in partnership with local education authorities. NHS Lanarkshire is one such example and has developed a comprehensive programme covering early years through to secondary school stage, including additional support needs (ASN). The programme is designed to provide a progressive, step-by-step approach across a range of topics with online support (NHS Lanarkshire, 2014). For example, their Relationships, Sexual Health and Parenthood (RSHP) Framework for Secondary Schools was designed and developed in collaboration with teachers and pupils and promotes strategies which meet the relevant CFE strands and at the same time addresses local needs and resourcing issues (NHS Lanarkshire, 2014). An important aspect showcased in this programme is a focus on gender-sensitive approaches and in particular, the needs of boys as they go through puberty; an area that many teachers struggle to address. This interactive approach provides a simple yet flexible approach for practitioners to incorporate into their classroom practice. Advice from research would suggest teachers need to be more sensitive to the needs of boys when delivering SHRE as their discomfort during lessons can lead to disruptive behaviour. This is in keeping with earlier research which suggests that teachers need to create an 'atmosphere where boys feel able to take the lessons seriously without losing face' (Buston *et al.*, 2002, p. 332). The Sex Education Forum published a factsheet: *Boys and Young Men: Effective Sex and Relationship Education in Schools* (Sex Education Forum, 2006) which provides an evidence-based approach or 'route map' to help boys and young men navigate through this difficult period of adolescence (needs of boys, concepts of masculinity, participation, rights-based approaches) and provides a counter-balance to some of the more insidious influences, such as pornography.

Another consideration for teachers is ensuring sensitivity to the specific needs and experiences of young people, especially when issues are being discussed in class. In particular, teachers need to be aware that young people may disclose abuse or discuss confidential information. If so, they need to be prepared to act accordingly. A working knowledge of school guidelines and policies on confidentiality and safeguarding are essential pre-requisites to delivering personal and social education (as earlier discussed in Chapter 7). Given the widespread media coverage of child sexual abuse, it is likely that young people may want to discuss these issues with each other in class. A briefing paper entitled *It's My Body: Calls to ChildLine Scotland About Sexual Health and Wellbeing* highlighted a wide range of concerns that children and young people have about their sexual health (Newall and Lewis, 2007). The concerns varied from those looking for some simple explanations about 'normal' development to those seeking more detailed advice and support on sexual abuse matters. The recommendations in this briefing paper are important for school-policy makers and pastoral-support teams looking to integrate whole school approaches with providing effective support. In particular, the recommendations stress the need to provide access to 'confidential spaces that enable children and young people to disclose concerns at their own pace ... since the fear of not being believed appears to be a major barrier to disclosing sexual abuse' (Newall and Lewis, 2007, p. 4).

The publication of this paper also coincided with a new digital technological age and the launch of social networking (as discussed earlier in this chapter). Phenomena such as online grooming, cyberbullying and sexting very quickly entered into common discourse. In 2014, the National Society for the Prevention of Cruelty to Children (NSPCC) reported a 168% increase in the number of young people receiving counselling services related to online sexual abuse (NSPCC, 2014). National organisations which support young people, such as ChildLine, immediately began to see a link between cyberbullying and the sharp rise in the reporting of mental health problems – with self-harm and substance misuse being disclosed as coping strategies.

How can educators effectively promote positive health?

A review of *Substance Misuse Education* stressed the importance of developing appropriate life skills that realistically help young people to assess risk and minimise harm (NHS Health Scotland, 2009). Furthermore, a meta-analysis of the evidence for effective health promotion highlighted that whole-school approaches which are *interactive* and focus on *life skills* are more effective at addressing risk-taking behaviour (St. Leger *et al.*, 2010). Increasingly, protective assets such as friendships, peer relationships and building connections with the wider school community help young people to cope and become more resilient. Schools can do this more effectively if they work in collaboration with key stakeholders and the voluntary sector. For instance, Fast Forward, an Edinburgh-based charity (http://www.fastforward. org.uk/about-us.html) funded through central government to develop prevention approaches with young people, has had a high degree of success training teachers to use informal group-work approaches. This is helping teachers gain wider skills and become more confident with aspects of experiential learning such as role play, drama and peer-education programmes which use a social norms approach. Their work is innovative and youth-led and many of the resources and training materials have been developed by young people who have first-hand experience of the issues. Most of the concerns encountered by teachers come through unreal expectations that they need to be 'experts' in areas such as substance use in order to address this and other risk-taking behaviours effectively. While basic-knowledge training for staff is useful, the approach that Fast Forward often takes with teaching staff is to encourage them to become 'co-learners' with pupils and to use their skills as educators to guide that process of discovery. Fast Forward often demonstrates this through the use of games and exercises that encourage decision making, testing out of values and attitudes and which encourage staff to 'learn by doing'.

Peer education

Since the early 1960s, interest in peer education has gained widespread currency as an effective way to work with, engage and empower young people to take action. The momentum to develop school-based peer-education programmes was triggered in the 1990s with the emergence of issues such as HIV/AIDS, increased rates of sexually transmitted infections (STIs) and lifestyle behaviours such as rising drug use.

Peers play an important role for adolescents in the transition to adulthood and studies such as the HBSC survey (Inchley *et al.*, 2016) show that the peer group assumes increasing prominence as young people move away from dependency on their families for support. Young people have a tendency to talk to their peers about most issues, including discussion of sensitive matters such as reproductive health and risk-taking behaviour. Furthermore, evidence indicates that peers can be a stabilising influence and offer a safety net or help to regulate standards of behaviour. For instance, studies show that young people who believe their peers are practising safer sex are also more likely to do so (Department of Health, 2002).

Research over the last twenty years confirms that peer-education programmes can have a significant effect on attitudes, cultural norms, knowledge, behaviours and health outcomes, when used to complement traditional classroom-based approaches. For example, the Joint United Nations Programme on HIV/AIDS states that concepts of peer education can offer 'an approach, a communication channel, a methodology, a philosophy and a strategy' (UNICEF, 1999, p. 5). As a behaviour-change model, peer education draws on a number of well-known behaviour theories including 'social learning theory' (Bandura, 1986) with its emphasis on the role influential peers can play in eliciting behaviour change among their peers. Additionally, the design and philosophy of many school-based peer-education programmes have been influenced by Brazilian educationalist Paolo Freire and his theory of 'participatory education' (Freire, 1970). Freire's theory advocates that people are more likely to effect change and be empowered when they are invited to participate in the process as equal partners. Empowerment in the Freirean sense results through the full participation of the people affected by a given problem or health condition (UNICEF, 1999).

In the UK, peer education has increasingly been used to explore issues that are difficult to address in the classroom, such as sexual health and illegal drugs. It is considered to be more effective as the young people involved often have first-hand experience of the issues being addressed and are seen to provide a more credible source of information than say perhaps, teaching staff. As well as addressing a topic or issue and imparting knowledge, peer-education approaches develop a wide range of social competencies and skills, which can in turn lead to increased self-esteem for the peer educators. Overall, peer-education approaches address many of the features highlighted as good practice by St. Leger *et al.* (2010) in their review of the evidence for effective health promotion practice including:

- *Inclusion*: peer-education approaches benefit all young people by reaching out to those who are often excluded from the mainstream such as black and ethnic minority groups.
- *Collaboration*: in partnership with organisations, third-sector providers and issue-based self-help groups can help create effective partnerships with teaching staff and pupils, between teaching staff groups and between schools and local community groups.
- *Pupil Voice*: allow young people to give their views, ask questions and talk on a level about sensitive issues that they might not feel comfortable discussing with a member of school staff.

- *Empowerment*: involve pupils as active participants in the planning, implementation and evaluation stages of a programme, as role models for change and after as peer educators.

Peer education in Scotland has been widely developed through informal youth-work settings and in schools. The Scottish Peer Education Network (SPEN) is a national network set up and funded to develop and support projects across the country by providing resources, training manuals and toolkits as well as free consultations and advice. More recently, the national body Education Scotland has endorsed peer education as an effective learning and teaching strategy to address health and wellbeing issues. Together, SPEN and Education Scotland have produced a short video on peer education to show how this can work in a Scottish secondary school. The video also highlights (https://www.youtube.com/watch?v=alqHm8o HMC8&feature=youtu.be) how peer-education programmes can be implemented and the facilitation skills required when managing this type of programme. The role of the pupil support teacher (lead teacher for pastoral care) in the film demonstrates a whole school approach and the project management skills required, e.g. training and deployment of peer educators, liaison with the voluntary-sector partners and overall day-to-day management of the programme.

Future directions

James Steyer, Professor of Civil Rights at Stanford University and founder of the media education programme Common Sense Media (Steyer, 2012), believes that media education can assist teachers to raise awareness of issues, through debate, discussion and critical reflection. Multimedia programmes are emerging which tackle many of the issues discussed in this chapter. Helping to harness young people's energies and interests in new and vigorous ways can lead to activism and self-empowerment. The Miss Representation Project is a prime example with a documentary film of the same name relaunched to include accompanying media-literacy resources, social-action campaigns and a vibrant social media presence. National children's charities seem to agree that engaging young people in this way builds their sense of self-esteem and improves their life satisfaction. Similarly, digital technologies offer fresh opportunities and approaches to address issues. They can be used by teachers to react to new issues as they emerge or to build up a toolkit of ideas and resources which help children stay safe online. Alternatively, they offer a new platform for professional discourse and enquiry where teachers can join an online community or link more effectively with partner agencies.

Summary of key findings

- A working knowledge of child protection policies and safeguarding procedures are essential prerequisite core skills for all teachers.
- Building strong relationships with young people to ensure the 'pledges' in the Children's Charter work in practice.

- Health and wellbeing programmes need to be sensitive to the needs of boys and girls and develop more gender – focused approaches.
- Providing opportunities for young people to critically reflect on various issues including media literacy and media education should be an integral part of health and wellbeing programmes.
- Ensure children's rights are promoted and protected and where possible the views and opinions of young people are taken seriously.
- Peer-education programmes are effective and involve young people more actively in planning and delivery as equal partners. Above all, they can build the social assets of the school community.

Reflective tasks

- How do you plan to identify your own professional development needs to support young people?
- To what extent are you sensitive to the needs of boys and girls in your class – perhaps your subject specialism appeals to boys or girls differently? If so how can you address this?
- Which strategies help you to create a positive social learning environment: how do you communicate this to learners?
- Remember, like most relationships in life you can't go on and talk about the 'things that really matter' until you feel safe and secure in the relationship.
- Can you identify your own strengths and weaknesses – or comfort levels discussing SHRE?
- What experience do you have of partnership working – and how can you further develop this?

Further readings

Bradshaw, J. (2016). *The Well-being of Children in the UK* (4th ed). Bristol: The Policy Press.
Common Sense Media. https://www.commonsensemedia.org/
Scottish Peer Education Network. http://spen.org.uk
Steyer, J.P. (2012). *Talking Back to Facebook*. New York: Simon and Schuster.
Stuckler, D., & Sanjay, B. (2014). *The Body Economic: Eight Experiments in Economic Recovery from Iceland to Greece*. London: Penguin.
The Representation Project. http://therepresentationproject.org/film/miss-representation/

References

Bandura, A. (1986). *Social Foundations of Thought and Action: A Social Cognitive Theory*. Englewood Cliffs: Prentice-Hall.
Buston K., Wight D. & Scott S. (2001) Difficulty & Diversity: The Context & Practice of Sex Education, *British Journal of Sociology of Education*, 22(3) 353–368.
Cameron, G., & Lloyd, J. (2015). Screened out: Meeting the challenge of technology and young people's wellbeing. Retrieved from http://strategicsociety.org.uk/wp-content/

uploads/2015/10/Screened-Out-Meeting-the-challenge-of-technology-and-young-peoples-wellbeing.pdf

Currie, C., Van der Sluijs, W., Whitehead, R., Currie, D., Rhodes, G., Neville, F., & Inchley, J. (2015). *HBSC 2014: Survey in Scotland National Report*. Child and Adolescent Health Research Unit (CAHRU), University of St Andrews.

Department of Health. (2002). *Involving Young People in Peer Education: A Guide to Establishing Sex and Relationship Education Projects*. London: Department of Health.

Freire P. (1970). *Pedagogy of the Oppressed*. New York: Seabury Press.

Girlguiding. (2016). Girl's attitudes survey. The final report. Retrieved from https://www.girlguiding.org.uk/social-action-advocacy-and-campaigns/research/girls-attitudes-survey/

Herbert, P.C., & Lohrmann, D.K. (2011). It's All in the Delivery! An Analysis of Instructional Strategies from Effective Health Education Curricula, *Journal of School Health*, *81*, 258–264.

Inchley, J., Currie, D., Young, T., Samdal, O., Torsheim, T., Auguston, L., & Barnekow, V. (2016). 'Growing up unequal: Gender and socioeconomic differences in young people's health and well-being'. *Health Behaviour in School-aged Children (HBSC) Study: International Report from the 2013/2014 Survey*. Copenhagen: WHO.

Kasser, T. (2011). Cultural Values and the Well-being of Future Generations: A Cross-National Study, *Journal of Cross-Cultural Psychology*, *42*(2), 206–215.

Kidner, C. (2013). Children and Young People (Scotland) Bill. SPICe Briefing 13/38. Edinburgh: The Scottish Parliament.

Kilbourne, J. (2011). Miss Representation. The Representation Project, Retrieved from http://therepresentationproject.org/

Kirby, D., & Laris, B.A. (2009). Effective Curriculum-based Sex and STD/HIV Education Programs for Adolescents, *Child Development Perspectives*, *3*(1), 21–29.

Linn, S. (2014). 'Marketing to children in the 21st century: A review of its breadth and impact and a call to advocates for children to take action'. In: Matthes, M., Pulkkinen, L., Pinto. L.M., & Clouder. C. (Eds.), *Improving the Quality of Childhood in Europe* (pp. 119–137). Belgium: Alliance for Childhood European Network Foundation.

Lowden, K., & Quinn, J. (2004). *Evaluation of the Scotland Against Drugs Education Sector Initiative Training*. SCRE: University of Glasgow.

Nation, M., Crusto, C., Wandersman, A., Kumpfer, K. L., Seybolt, D., Morrisey-Kane, E., & Davino, K. (2003). What Works in Prevention: Principles of Effective Prevention Programmes, *American Psychologist*, *58*(6/7), 449–456.

Newall, E., & Lewis, R. (2007). It's my body: Calls to ChildLine Scotland about sexual health and wellbeing. Centre for Research in Family Relationships: University of Edinburgh. Retrieved from http://www.gov.scot/Publications/2007/02/13111657/13

NHS Health Scotland. (2009). *School-Based Substance Misuse Education: A Review of Resources*. Edinburgh: NHS Health Scotland.

NHS Health Scotland. (2014). *Sexual Health and Relationship Education*. SHRE Appendices. Edinburgh: NHS Health Scotland.

NHS Lanarkshire. (2014). RSHP Secondary School Framework. NHS Lanarkshire. Retrieved from http://www.lanarkshiresexualhealth.org/resources/?did=146

NSPCC. (2014). Under pressure: ChildLine review. Retrieved from https://www.nspcc.org.uk/globalassets/documents/annual-reports/childline-review-under-pressure.pdf

Organisation for Economic Co-operation and Development. (2015). Improving schools in Scotland: An OECD perspective. Retrieved from http://www.oecd.org/education/school/Improving- Schools-in-Scotland-An-OECD-Perspective.pdf

PSHE Association. (2016). Key principles of effective prevention education. Retrieved from https://www.pshe-association.org.uk/curriculum-and-resources/resources/key-principles-effective-prevention-education

Scottish Executive. (2004). *Protecting Children and Young People: The Charter.* Edinburgh: The Scottish Executive.

Scottish Government. (2008). *Getting it Right for Every Child.* Edinburgh: The Scottish Government.

Scottish Government. (2013). *Supporting Young People's Health and Wellbeing: A Summary of Scottish Government Policy.* Edinburgh: The Scottish Government.

Scottish Government. (2014a). The Children and Young People (Scotland) Act. Edinburgh: The Scottish Government.

Scottish Government. (2014b). *National Guidance for Child Protection in Scotland.* Edinburgh: The Scottish Government.

Sex Education Forum. (2006). Boys and young men: Effective sex and relationship education in schools: Factsheet 35. Retrieved from http://sexeducationforum.org.uk/resources/resources-a-z.aspx

St. Leger, L., Young, I., Blanchard, C., & Perry, M. (2010). Promoting health in schools from evidence to action. France: International Union for Health Promotion and Education (IUHPE). Retrieved from http://www.iuhpe.org/images/PUBLICATIONS/THEMATIC/HPS/Evidence-Action_ENG.pdf

Steyer, J. (2012). Common sense media. Retrieved from https://en.wikipedia.org/wiki/Jim_Steyer

The Children's Society. (2015). *The Good Childhood Report 2015.* London: The Children's Society.

UNICEF. (1999). *Peer Education and HIV/AIDS: Concepts, Uses and Challenges.* Switzerland: UNAIDS.

UNICEF. (2007). *Child Poverty in Perspective: An Overview of Child Well-being in Rich Countries.* Report Card 7. United Kingdom: UNICEF.

UNICEF. (2011). *Child Well-being in Rich Countries: A Comparative Overview.* Report Card 11. United Kingdom: UNICEF.

Wilkinson, R., & Pickett K. (2010). *The Spirit Level: Why Equality is Better for Everyone.* London: Penguin.

PART IV

Practice perspectives on wellbeing

9

LITERACY, LANGUAGE AND WELLBEING

Vivienne Smith and Sue Ellis

Introduction

'We have always known by intuition that reading is valuable' (Nikolajeva, 2012).

Ask any committed reader, and he or she will tell you that reading is good for you. People who choose to read do so for many reasons: to escape from the humdrum reality of their daily lives, to relax, to imagine, to explore new worlds, new people, new ideas, new ways of being. Readers, quite simply, find reading worthwhile. It is only recently, however, that research evidence has enabled us to relate that 'worthwhileness' to emotional and social wellbeing. Some of this evidence comes from studies of adult mental health. Billington (2015) shows that those who read for pleasure report fewer feelings of stress and depression and Dowrick *et al.* (2012) tell us that being part of a reading programme can help reduce depressive symptoms in sufferers. There is even evidence (Billington *et al.*, 2013) that dementia can be alleviated in those who read. This sounds impressive, but if it is to be seen as relevant to *children's* reading and wellbeing, we need to delve beyond the surface relationship of cause and effect and ask why this is happening. What is it about reading and what readers do that lifts mood and opens possibilities to wider thinking?

The aim of this chapter is to explore some of the ways that reading actually makes a difference to wellbeing. We do this by showing how texts can change the way readers think about themselves and how texts that challenge readers' thinking can help them think about the world they live in differently and understand people, and the motivation of people, better. We look at the way reading is taught in schools. We look first at the conversations that children have *around* texts in school, and consider whether these advantage some children more than others. We look at the way the teaching of reading is organised and ask teachers to remember the social and emotional implications of what they do and how their practices impact on reading identity. Finally, we highlight the importance of seeing reading as social practice and show how an emphasis on this will enhance the social, emotional and intellectual wellbeing of pupils.

Main ideas

Reading

A first and obvious answer to the question: 'How does reading contribute to well-being?' might be that reading is relaxing. As readers engage in story, their minds shift from the concerns of their day-to-day lives to the different places, different times or different people in the story. Reading, in effect, creates a mini break in the mind, an escape from real life. Mihaly Csikszentmihalyi called this state 'flow' (Nakamura and Csikszentmihalyi, 2014). It is a state where the reader becomes so engrossed in reading that they put aside their sense of time, space and other people. The poet and writer Jack Ousbey draws our attention to how another writer, John Gardner describes this in a 1977 novel *October Light*:

> The real world lost weight and the print on the pages gave way to images, an alternative reality more charged than mere life, more ghostly yet nearer, suffused with a curious importance and manageability ... By degrees, without knowing she was doing it, she gave in to the illusion, the comforting security of her vantage point, until whenever she looked up from her page to rest her eyes, it seemed that the door, the walls, the dresser, the heavy onyx clock had no more substance than a plate-glass reflection; what was real and enduring was the adventure flickering on the wall of her brain, a phantom world filled with its own queer laws and character.

Because readers invest in this intellectual and emotional engagement, it would be wrong to think of reading as the cognitive equivalent of basking on a sun lounger. Reading is not an absence of activity. In fact, it is the presence of mental activity, of thinking, as a person reads that makes reading especially powerful in terms of wellbeing. For while a good story might take the reader away from his or her own worries, it is very likely to take that reader into somebody else's. This is a good thing. By engaging with another person's experience, the reader learns how fictional characters cope with danger, with worry, or with fear, for example, and by reading about these, his or her own repertoire for coping with these emotions and with difficult situations develops.

Seen in this way, reading achieves two purposes. First, it helps the reader make sense of his or her own experience. The young child who reads a picture book such as Maurice Sendak's *Where the Wild Things Are*, (1963) sees the main character, Max, get sent to bed as a result of his naughtiness. The reader recognises first his or her own experiences of naughtiness and the emotions that go with it, and second that others have experienced these emotions too. There is learning here about the reader's place in the world, about human experience and, perhaps the most important of all, the beginnings of empathy – the ability of one person to 'think' into the mind of another. In terms of wellbeing this is important because people who can empathise are developing emotional intelligence. They understand the motivation and emotions of others.

Nikolajeva (2012) acknowledges the wonder of this. It *is* truly astonishing that fictional characters – inventions of an author's imagination and realised only through marks on a page – can have power in developing a person's ability to recognise emotional states and to empathise with real people and real situations: but there is now tangible evidence to show that they do, and that reading is perhaps even more powerful than life in this respect. Cognitive scientists Kidd and Castano (2013) studied the responses of adult readers to a variety of texts: non-fiction, popular fiction and literary fiction. They found that reading any fiction positively impacted upon the ability to recognise and infer thoughts and emotions, what psychologists call 'theory of mind'. This was so for all readers, but for those readers who read challenging, literary fiction, the changes were long lasting. The researchers suggest that literary texts changed not just *what* readers thought about people and situations, but fundamentally changed *how* they thought, that is, it changed the approach they took in their thinking. They were more open to understanding the complexity of motivation and the social and political implications of what they read.

This is an important idea, and it has a number of implications. If reading is so powerful that it can change the patterns of thought in adults, then we need to ask what might it do for children, whose patterns of thinking are not yet established. We need to ask too about texts. Kidd and Castano show that texts matter: texts that challenged readers' thinking were more effective than easy 'holiday reads' in developing long-lasting understandings of others.

The question then becomes, what is the equivalent of literary fiction for a 9-year-old? Is it a reading scheme? Is it a book such as *The Diary of a Wimpy Kid* (Kinney, 2008) or *Captain Underpants* (Pilkey, 2000)? What do we need to know about texts to help us decide? And then, how do we balance a need to entertain and motivate with the need to develop emotional literacy? Finally we need to ask, what are the effects of any of this?

Paterson (2009) provides one empirical answer to the question of the effects of reading on children. His review of the evidence from longitudinal studies into civic values shows that young people who report reading for pleasure at the age of 14 years grow into adults who are more likely to contribute to society than not: that is, they vote more, volunteer more and play an active part in their communities. Reading, it seems, is good for the wellbeing of society itself!

The earlier questions about what constitutes quality fiction for young children seem to be much more problematic. It is not clear that the features that mark quality adult fiction are important in the same way for children's fiction, not least because children's minds are different: they are still, by definition, in a state of development. Nikolajava's work on cognitive literary theory continues to ask how children who are still grappling with the complexity of decoding engage with the demands of texts that challenge them emotionally and cognitively (2014).

We do know that experienced and committed readers of fiction think that genre matters. They know that different types of story provide different rewards for the reader: the satisfaction of a neatly solved whodunit, the vicarious thrill of an adventure story, the rosy glow of light romance. In children's literature, genre is just as important, and as with adult readers, different genres afford different experiences for child readers. Some of these genres seem to be especially useful in encouraging emotional wellbeing in young readers.

Fairy tales provide a good place to begin, for, though to us in the twenty-first century, they seem to be a natural, and perhaps anodyne, starting place for children's engagement with literature, they have at times been at the cutting edge of thinking and controversy. Back in the late eighteenth century, for example, Sarah Trimmer, educationalist and writer herself, disapproved of them. She found them irrational, and of questionable morality. She thought they were likely 'excite an unregulated sensibility' in the child reader. Concerns about the moral wellbeing of children who might be influenced by fairy tales persisted into the twentieth century, albeit on rather different grounds from Trimmer. Zipes, for example, (1999) considers the versions of the tales made popular by Disney. He is concerned by the *lack* of moral ambiguity they display: the stereotyped gender roles, the supremacy of cleanliness and housework, the unproblematic 'happy-ever-after through marriage' endings. What sort of expectations for real life do these certainties set up in young readers' thinking, he wonders.

Bettelheim (1976) gives another perspective. A Freudian psychologist, he was interested in how the underlying themes of fairy tales spoke to the unconscious needs of readers as they negotiated their roles and relationships in the family. Tales of good mothers and wicked step-mothers, for instance, helped children accommodate the inevitability of their own mothers becoming angry with them at times, and stories such as Jack and the Beanstalk showed that even the youngest and most powerless of people can outwit authority. According to Bettelheim, fairy tales were *necessary* for the psychological health of children.

There is still another way in which fairy tales contribute to children's wellbeing: they show children that there are alternative ways of being and thinking. The child who reads fairy tales 'buys into' a world where animals talk, where beans turn out to be magic and where christening gifts are prophecies. It is not that the child actually believes any of this, rather, he or she takes on a different sort of logic, and accepts, for the duration of the story, a set of assumptions about how the world works that are different from those he or she lives by. This is important and prompts two tangible cognitive benefits. First, taking on a different system of logic encourages alternative paths of thinking. The child who is able to think divergently can be creative and the connection between creativity and wellbeing is well established (Barnes, 2015; Burnard and Dragovic, 2015). Second, this thinking is important because it allows children to perceive that those assumptions on which their moral compass is set *might not* be the only ones, or indeed, the best.

Jan Mark's novel for older children, *Riding Tycho* (2005) illustrates this process rather well. This is the story of Demeter, a girl who lives in a remote, bleak, island community with her mother and brother. As the novel begins, the reader has no thought that Demeter's world is different from our own: so much is the same. There is a village and a school, a community sustained by fishing and craftwork and a family where the usual sorts of sibling and parental relationships can be played out. It looks like social realism, of a geographically remote kind. Then the reader learns more. There is a prison on the neighbouring island, and though drowning is the most likely outcome of escape attempts, these attempts happen, regularly. Political prisoners are billeted in households in the village and harsh rules regulate their lives. The reader is not told why, or what these people have done, but the idea begins to develop that the political system underlying this society must be different from our own.

Gradually, more emerges. The reader discovers that in Demeter's village, school is different. Boys learn navigation and seamanship, and girls learn knitting. For girls, knitting is more important than reading and although Demeter is already a better reader than her teacher, this counts as nothing. The status of boys and girls is different. In every respect, in this community, boys are superior to girls. Brothers can boss, bully and strike their sisters, and where there is no father, their mothers too. This is not only accepted behaviour, it is expected. Most interestingly, everybody knows one indisputable truth: women are physically unable to swim.

Eventually the reader realises that this is actually science fiction. The action takes place on an earth-like planet where the seas have no tides and most importantly to the plot, there are no birds or insects. It is because a political prisoner tries to explain the concept of flight to Demeter that the denouement of the novel comes about. Demeter is the focaliser of *Riding Tycho*. It is through her eyes that the reader sees this world. What happens to Demeter is that she gradually learns to question the assumptions and the unfairness that govern her life and, as she does so, she takes the reader with her. It is a small step for the intelligent reader to ask the obvious question: so what are the assumptions that my society relies on? Are they fair and are they grounded in truth? The reader who asks these questions is developing a political conscience.

Talking about texts

It is also clear that the socio-emotional context for reading is likely to matter for young children as much as the nature of the text. Young children learn to read and make meaning in negotiation with an adult who guides and scaffolds the interpretation. The research question that matters in this context is not 'what makes a literary text' but 'what makes a literary *conversation* about a text'. What we learn from children and parents reading books together is that the ways that different communities regard texts, and how they talk about them, is socially determined. Heath (1983), in her seminal work *Ways with Words* points out that whereas many middle-class communities see reading as a source of relaxation and enjoyment, and texts as artefacts to be discussed, disputed, explained and elaborated, other communities see different purposes (or little purpose at all) in reading and have normalised having different kinds of conversation, or no conversation at all, about texts. For teachers and others who work with young people, this means recognising that the sorts of conversations about books that happen in classrooms are likely to be more familiar to some children than others and that work needs to be done to make talk about stories accessible to those who are less familiar. The adult behaviours that are helpful here are scaffolding, inviting children to contribute, listening carefully to what children say, prompting them to tell more, and generally being clear that everyone's opinions matter and should be taken seriously. Teachers need to show that they value children's responses because doing so builds self-esteem, and helps children think of themselves as people with good ideas. The 'talk skills' that develop as a result of such interactions build confidence and identity, resilience and growth mindsets. This is both socially and emotionally important.

Patterns of talk and implications for learning

Oral language abilities affect how children participate in the learning and social activities in class and often how they are regarded by teachers and other children. This in turn affects their social and emotional wellbeing because the ways that children are positioned by others impacts on how they feel about themselves and about school. The more general linguistic and behavioural traits promoted by middle-class parenting have been well documented by researchers such as Lareau (2011) and Wells (1986). Lareau looked at families with children aged ten and followed them up years later, talking to some when they were adults aged up to 21 years. In her study of the 10-year-olds, she found that the logic of middle-class parenting was one of 'concerted cultivation'. It engendered a strong sense of entitlement in the children – entitlement to have their opinions heard, to expect adult assistance and co-operation, and generally to be able to organise their world in ways that suit them. Middle-class adults expected their 10-year-old children to take centre-floor in conversations, to give extended answers, to interrupt and to disagree. The adults adopted conversational styles that trained their children to do this, often answering a child's questions with more questions, requiring extended reasoning and coaching their children on how to engage with other adults and new situations, rehearsing what they might say and how they might speak. Children from working class and poor families on the other hand had experienced a 'natural growth' logic of parenting. In these families there was a stronger division between adult and children's lives which, although it made the children more independent and better at organising their time, did not breed a sense of entitlement. Conversations between parents and children in working class and poor families tended to be shorter and more focused. The children were more respectful of adult opinions and less likely to challenge or interrupt. Lareau argues that these conversational differences are just one example of how the sense of middle-class confidence and entitlement positions children to do well in school and get the most from their teachers. It links to classroom research showing that confident middle-class pupils take more than their fair share of talk time in school, improving their talk skills even further (Martlew et al., 2010). It also links to ethnographic classroom research showing that middle-class five- and six-year-olds are more assertive in ensuring teachers' help with their work (Calarco, 2011).

The ability to communicate clearly and precisely in school confers a general learning advantage because strong oral language skills allow learners to recall, compare, explain and elaborate. This helps to ensure that children have a positive experience of learning, of school, and that others – school staff and pupils – see them in a positive light. Promoting oral language development is not just about individual skills, however; progress is affected by the collective skills of the class because children learn from each other. Martlew *et al.* (2010) found that children in classrooms with many high-poverty pupils tended to have less individual and collective linguistic resources upon which to draw. The children spent less time talking to each other than children in mixed- or middle-class classrooms and the researchers recommended that it is particularly important that the adults in high-poverty classrooms provide overt modelling and adopt collaborative conversational styles and that they structure collaborative tasks in ways that require children to talk to each other. These recommendations build on the work of Wells (1986), studying children aged 18 months to 7 years, who found that children who developed strong language skills tended to have parents who adopted a collaborative style of talk. These parents followed the conversational agenda of the child and built on the child's choice of topics and comments. In schools, he found that very few teachers adopted this conversational style; most expected young children to follow the adult's conversational agenda. For teachers and others working with children and young people therefore, the message is that literary experiences, quality of talk and narrative matter. Impacts are long-term and more than advantage learning; they help to regulate and develop emotional, empathy and theory of mind.

Learning to read and the impact on wellbeing

Given what is now well-accepted evidence that the structure of the brain changes according to how it is used (Goswami, 2016), this may not seem so surprising. The neuropsychological evidence is certainly strong enough to encourage all those who work with children and young people to direct their attention to both *what* children read and *how* reading is framed and taught. For many children, early experiences in learning to read appear to be effortless; successful, playful affairs that offer social, emotional and linguistic riches. Ousbey (2002) describes how his granddaughter, Jenny, weaves reading and rhyme through her play, her imagination and her relationships in ways that are fluid and informal. He writes that she engages in literary play situations so that the language seemed to have 'entered the echo chamber of the head', where without conscious effort it was held available in its entirety, alongside but separate from all the other units of story language (Ousbey, 2002, p. 30). For other children, however, learning to read is a less joyful, more disjointed, disconnected and altogether a more socially and psychologically dangerous experience. Stanovich (1986) describes how schools and the 'literacy' curriculum can make certain skills both highly visible and highly desirable whilst keeping others hidden.

For Stanovich, the mastery of phonics was one such visible practice. Marie Clay (1985; 1991) identified another in the way that schools identify reading attainment groups and book levels without differentiating the nature of instruction. Stanovich (1986) pointed out that those who experienced early success entered an upward spiral in which their early advantage bred confidence, further practice opportunities, development and mastery. Their school experience of literacy formed a virtuous circle which contributed to positive reader identities. However, those who took just a few weeks longer to 'catch on' entered a downward spiral and became less and less confident. They read more slowly and falteringly, were offered (and took) fewer opportunities to read, and consequently got less practice. As the difference between the fluent and less fluent became more salient, those who were less fluent began to actively avoid reading, getting even less practice, which further slowed their progress. Teachers often attempt to deal with this divergence in progress by organising children into reading groups, which makes the differences even more visible and can often enshrine attainment differences, affect friendship and work patterns and reinforce low esteem. Marie Clay (1991) notes that those who are already beginning to struggle may need a different approach but are instead asked to do the same tasks as their more successful peers – only later, more slowly and less successfully.

And there are important socio-emotional side effects of this sort of organisation that teachers sometimes overlook. It is true that seen through one lens, putting children into reading groups that reflect their cognitive skills at a particular point in time makes sense; it allows teachers to tailor instruction and resources to meet children's needs. However, seen with a different lens, such overt positioning of young children can have detrimental effects and damage self-esteem: everyone knows who is in the 'bottom group'. There is strong evidence that developing a positive learner identity is an important influence on learning (Dweck, 2000; Lamb, 2011). It affects a child's confidence and sense of self, their willingness to 'have a go' at new tasks, and to persist with challenging tasks. It can also affect their friendship groups. With this lens, being five or six months into the first year of school and finding oneself in the 'bottom group' for reading is not a positive start to a child's school career, their view of schooling, of reading or of themselves. Teachers and parents need to be more aware of this.

Community: The importance of belonging

Reading is often portrayed as a solitary activity but is however fundamentally social in nature. What children choose to read is often determined by the interests of their social group and reflects the image that they want to portray to others. We can all remember children who would wander round clutching a huge tome of a book – one that they couldn't actually read – because they wanted to 'look like a reader' to others. Fostering reading as a social activity in the classroom requires a fine balance between teaching structures or interference and allowing sufficient social space for children to find or create their own reading communities. Moss and McDonald (2004) used library-borrowing records to show that, in classrooms where teachers afforded children the social and intellectual space to choose their own books and networks, there was clear evidence of children talking about books, swapping books and developing their own reader identities. They had intrinsic social motivation for reading and their membership of a particular friendship group in the class was signalled by their reading choices. In classes where the teacher had strong views about what was appropriate for particular children and exercised tight control of what children should read – by prescribing the type of books (genre) and the amount of time they had to finish a book, reading was seen less as a self-directed pleasure and more of a chore. It was not part of the social fabric of the classroom and pupils lacked genuine engagement. The message for teachers is that, in creating reading communities pedagogical attention needs to focus on developing a healthy classroom 'ecology for reading', too much control can stunt development just as much as too little control, and that it is important to recognise when 'the sum may be greater than the parts'.

Central to forming a healthy reading ecology in class, therefore, is an empathetic understanding of the social dynamics around reading, the effect of this on how children feel about themselves as readers and how it affects the choices they make. In an earlier ethnographic study, Moss (2000) observed how social status with peers affected book choices. In particular she noted that boys who were struggling readers tended to select non-fiction books as reading material. She interpreted this, not as boys having a natural preference for non-fiction (skilled boy readers preferred fiction), but as boys trying to protect their social status within the class. Selecting a novel would broadcast (through the larger print, fewer words per page, the greater number of pictures) that the child was a low-status, struggling reader. The design principles of non-fiction texts make acceptable the existence of illustrations and fewer words per page, making reading competence much harder to gauge. What this illustrates more than anything else is how important status is to children: their emotional wellbeing depends on it. Teachers need to remember this and consider it as they shape the reading curriculum for the children in their class.

Future directions

We began this chapter by suggesting that reading is never a passive activity and that the texts we read have a real effect on our thinking about ourselves and our society. They contribute to wellbeing by helping us to understand the world and to act in it. We ended by suggesting that the way we teach reading matters too. Practices that forefront the emotional and social needs of children as well as their developing cognitive abilities are more likely to be successful than those that do not, because they build self-esteem, reading identity and growth mind-sets. In designing a literacy curriculum for wellbeing, we need to think about whether we are teaching the reader or the text. We need to think about whether we teach reading skills or a person who is going to become an engaged reader. Dilemmas such as these are serious and fundamental in every curricular area. We have illustrated them in terms of literacy, but we could equally have chosen science, physical education, mathematics or any other area. How teachers choose to teach determines the opportunities we give our pupils but also the opportunities they take up. These choices can create the spaces that allow our pupils to exercise their agency and grow, or they can constrain and limit what pupils become. We need to make sure the spaces we allow for pupils to grow are big enough, and we need to understand how the nature of the space shapes how and what children become. It is, quite simply, as important as that.

Summary of key findings

- Reading is not just about relaxation. The real benefits in terms of reading and wellbeing come through the thinking we do around the texts we read.
- Challenging texts are more likely to encourage this sort of thinking than others.
- Conversations around tests are important, because they are where children learn to think about texts. Teachers need to make sure that *all* children are included in them and that their voices are heard.
- Reading in school is a highly visible social practice: how children think of themselves as readers and how they think others see them as readers really matters.
- Practices that forefront the emotional and social needs of children as well as their developing cognitive abilities are more likely to be successful in encouraging readers than those that do not, because they build self-esteem, reading identity and growth mind-sets.

Reflective tasks

- How do texts feature in the curriculum? Are they places where children practice reading skills, or are they places where children learn to think, reflect and wonder?
- Does the range of texts available to children challenge them to think emotionally, socially and politically? What do teachers need to know about children's literature to enable them to answer this question? How and when are they able to learn it?
- Who talks most in the classroom? Whose opinions matter? How do children, already disadvantaged by socio-economic status, and who perhaps have fewer books at home than others, and different home talk practices, learn to engage confidently in literary conversations?
- How does the curriculum and the way it is implemented position children as readers? To what extent does an emphasis on cognitive skills obscure the social and emotional aspects that make reading worthwhile and life-changing?

Further readings

Goodwin, P. (Ed.) (2008). *Understanding Children's Books: A Guide for Education Professionals.* London: Sage.
The Reading Agency et al. (2016). *Reading Outcomes Framework Toolkit*, London: The Reading Agency.

References

Barnes, J. (2015). 'Creativity and promoting wellbeing in children and young people through education'. In: S. Clift & P.M. Camic (Eds.), *Oxford Textbook of Creative Arts, Health, and Wellbeing: International Perspectives on Practice, Policy and Research* (pp. 201–210). Oxford: Oxford University Press.

Bettelheim, B. (1976). *The Uses of Enchantment: The Meaning and Importance of Fairy Tales.* London: Thames & Hudson.

Billington, J. (2015). Reading between the lines: The benefits of reading for pleasure. Retrieved from http://www.thereader.org.uk/media/118690/The_Benefits_of_Reading_for_Pleasure.pdf

Billington, J., Carroll, J., Davis, P., Healey, C., & Kinderman, P. (2013). A Literature-Based Intervention for Older People Living with Dementia, *Perspectives in Public Health, 133*(3), 165–173.

Burnard, P., & Dragovic, T. (2015). Collaborative Creativity in Instrumental Group Music Learning as a Site for Enhancing Pupil Wellbeing, *Cambridge Journal of Education, 45*(3), 371–392.

Calarco, J.M. (2011). 'I need help!' Social Class and Children's Help-Seeking in Elementary School, *American Sociological Review, 76*(6), 862–882.

Clay, M.M. (1985). *Reading: The Patterning of Complex Behaviour.* Auckland: Heinemann.

Clay, M.M. (1991). *Becoming Literate: The Construction of Inner Control.* Auckland, New Zealand: Heinemann.

Dowrick, C., Billington, J., Robinson, J., Hamer, A., & Williams, C. (2012). Get into Reading as an Intervention for Common Mental Health Problems: Exploring Catalysts for Change, *Medical Humanities, 38*(1), 15–20.

Dweck, C.S. (2000). *Self-Theories: Their Role in Motivation, Personality, and Development.* Abingdon: Routledge Psychology Press.

Goswami, U. (2016). Educational Neuroscience: Neural Structure-Mapping and the Promise of Oscillations, *Current Opinion in Behavioral Sciences, 10*(1), 89–96.

Heath, S.B. (1983). *Ways with Words: Language, Life and Work in Communities and Classrooms.* Cambridge: Cambridge University Press.

Kidd, D.C. & Castano, E. (2013). Reading Literary Fiction Improves Theory of Mind, *Science, 342,* 377–380.

Kinney, J. (2008). *Diary of a Wimpy Kid.* London: Puffin.

Lamb, T.E. (2011). Fragile Identities: Exploring Learner Identity, Learner Autonomy and Motivation Through Young Learners' Voices, *The Canadian Journal of Applied Linguistics, 14*(2), 68.

Lareau, A. (2011). *Unequal Childhoods: Class, Race, and Family Life.* Berkeley: University of California Press.

Mark, J. (2005). *Riding Tycho.* London: Macmillan.

Martlew, J., Ellis, S., Stephen, C., & Ellis, J. (2010). Teacher and Child Talk in Active Learning and Whole-Class Contexts: Some Implications for Children from Economically Less Advantaged Home Backgrounds, *Literacy, 44*(1), 12–19.

Moss, G. (2000). Raising Boys' Attainment in Reading: Some Principles for Intervention, *Reading, 34*(3), 101–106.

Moss, G. (2001). To Work or Play? Junior Age Non-Fiction as Objects of Design, *Reading, 35*(3), 106–110.

Moss, G. & McDonald, J.W. (2004). The Borrowers: Library Records as Unobtrusive Measures of Children's Reading Preferences, *Journal of Research in Reading, 27*(4), 401–412.

Nakamura, J., & Csikszentmihalyi, M. (2014). 'The concept of flow'. In M. Csikszentmihalyi (Ed.). *Flow and the Foundations of Positive Psychology: The Collected Works of Mihaly Csikszentmihalyi* (pp. 239–263). Amsterdam: Springer.

Nikolajeva, M. (2012). Reading Other People's Minds Through Words and Image, *Children's Literature in Education, 43*(3), 273–291.

Nikolajeva, M. (2014). *Reading for Learning: Cognitive Approaches to Children's Literature.* Amsterdam: John Benjamins Publishing.

Ousbey, J. (2002). 'Reading and the imagination'. In M. Coles, & C. Harrison. (Eds.), *The Reading for Real Handbook* (27–36). London: Routledge. Available online http://booksforkeeps.co.uk

Pilkey, D. (2000). *The Adventures of Captain Underpants.* London: Scholastic Children's Books.

Sendak, M. (1963). *Where the Wild Things Are.* New York: Harper.

Stanovich, K.E. (1986). Matthew Effects in Reading: Some Consequences of Individual Differences in the Acquisition of Literacy, *Reading Research Quarterly, 21*(4), 360–407.

Wells, G. (1986). *The Meaning Makers: Children Learning Language and Using Language to Learn.* London: Heinemann.

Zipes, J.D. (1999) *When Dreams Come True: Classical Fairy Stories and Their Tradition,* Psychology Press: London.

10

WELLBEING/WELFARE, SCHOOLING AND SOCIAL JUSTICE

Caring relationships with students, parents and community

Maeve O'Brien

Introduction

While strongly supportive of the view that schools should be concerned with student wellbeing and aim to foster and teach for *and* about wellbeing, the chapter begins on a somewhat cautious note around the possibilities and challenges to a 'wellbeing project' in schools today. My concern is around the relation between the reproduction of inequality in society through schooling and how this affects holistic wellbeing and welfare for particular groups of students. In other words, this chapter seeks to explore the relation between wellbeing in the context of schooling, and the social and economic inequalities that compromise wellbeing in the broader social world. Traditionally, schooling has been more concerned with cultural and knowledge production than with wellbeing, and I argue that this is a powerful reason why we cannot ignore the processes of schooling itself, and how unequal resources possessed by families translate into different material and social consequences for students, which in turn affect their flourishing and welfare. What I wish to spell out here is the role that schooling has consistently played in maintaining hierarchical societal relations and socio-cultural inequalities both through formal and informal relations of production (e.g. formal and informal/hidden curricula) in schools (Bourdieu, 1984; Baker, Lynch, Cantillon and Walsh, 2004). Given the role of schooling in social and economic reproduction, it would be disingenuous to discuss wellbeing and schooling without contextualising schooling as a significant means of production of valued cultural capital. How schooling can advantage/disadvantage groups and individuals relative to participation and the acquisition of capital is a matter that needs to be teased out in relation to this newer 'wellbeing' role for schools. In doing so, we can better understand the possibilities and limits of teaching and of supporting something we can call wellbeing. In other words, there is a need to name an inherent tension between the new assigned wellbeing role of schools, and their role in the social reproduction of inequality, which can act as an obstacle to being well. It is within this broader societal and socio-economic context that we need to think about a wellbeing curriculum. Some educators might argue that the school and a traditional curriculum are not the appropriate space in which to expect transformations of equality and social justice, what we think of as 'welfare wellbeing' to come about (Baker *et al.*, 2004, see also MacAllister Chapter 6 on these distinctions).

A tension that is prevalent in the wellbeing literature (noted by other authors in this book), and in the politics around wellbeing interventions, is between individualised psychological conceptions of wellbeing (subjective wellbeing), and how they sit often at odds with, or as if unconcerned or disconnected from, challenges around collective, welfare wellbeing of society (welfarist approaches, also alluded to in Chapter 2 by Thorburn; O'Brien, 2008a). These may seem rather obvious problems, but they reflect not just particular disciplinary approaches to wellbeing, but also political/ideological perspectives around the good of the individual and the good of society (see Cassidy, Chapter 1). In responding to recent demands and trends for a wellbeing curriculum in schools, some critiques of *schooling for wellbeing* and wellbeing curricula have focused on this issue of wellbeing definition, and the problem of conceptual pluralism. These question how teachers can teach for or about wellbeing when it is understood interchangeably as individual flourishing, development, mental health, happiness or quality of life.

My concern in this chapter recognises these challenges and confusions around wellbeing schooling, but it focuses more precisely on the damage that can ensue from assumptions that underlie the demand to *universally* teach for 'wellbeing,' and especially in the context of increasingly economically and culturally divided societies. One might ask, (as my own students have), how to approach the issue of wellbeing with students who come from socio-economic contexts where even basic needs for human flourishing such as housing, a safe environment and nutrition are not properly met. Even in the field of family therapy, practitioners recognise that it is impossible to help and support mental health without recognising the effects of inequality and injustice on wellbeing. Sutherland, Couture, Gaete Silva, Strong, Lamarre and Hardt (2016) argue that effective therapy needs to have a concern with social justice:

> A social justice orientation in therapy involves critical analysis of the sociocultural context of clients' lives and concerns (Kosutic and McDowell, 2008). While encompassing systemic thinking, such an orientation also includes an analysis of systems of oppression.
>
> *(ibid., pp. 76–99)*

While it is not traditionally within the remit of schools to solve problems of material deprivation in any immediate or direct way, a tension quickly arises as to how wellbeing and flourishing in the fullest sense, and for all, can be genuinely fostered through schooling. This is a very real issue as institutional values and norms within schools themselves have systematically reproduced inequalities in the socio-cultural order, including material inequalities, to the detriment of the wellbeing of marginalised groups and individuals.

In response to this problem, I explore why it is important for teachers to develop an informed understanding around inequalities and their relation to individual and societal wellbeing. Informed social understandings around the *systemic* causes of inequalities improve the possibilities for engaging in real wellbeing work in schools. Drawing on interdisciplinary wellbeing and care scholarship, my own experiences in schools and marginalised communities, and more recently, from teaching and researching with teacher education students, I explore the pressing wellbeing challenges for these school communities. Despite the struggles and the serious obstacles encountered by teachers in this rugged terrain where wellbeing needs tending, I argue that relational caring and meaningful dialogue can take us some distance towards working with a wellbeing curriculum and a relational justice approach to human flourishing.

The chapter begins with a consideration of material inequality and its relation to wellbeing, and then explores the relationship between wellbeing and other forms of inequality. In seeking some solution and means of grappling with wellbeing and justice problems, it shifts gear to focus explicitly on the significance of affective life and relationship, to discuss how care and the caring dimensions of teaching can enable the development of greater justice and equality, 'welfare wellbeing' with our students and the broader community.

Main findings

The relationship between material inequality and wellbeing/welfare

As I have suggested already, it is rather unhelpful and some argue impossible to abstract wellbeing and being well from context, whether understood as a psychological construct, or a skill set that can be fostered and taught, without including reference to the lives of students in particular contexts. And for some groups and individuals, the contextualisation of wellbeing and being well requires meeting their pressing material needs as a fundamental dimension of wellbeing development. This unavoidable reality sets parameters around what teachers and schools can do for students' wellbeing in the absence of basic material goods and services. Research on wellbeing from welfarist perspectives strongly indicates that our basic material needs should be met and are not trivial to our overall wellbeing.[1] Wilkinson and Pickett's acclaimed book, *Spirit Level* (2011), reveals that large-scale material inequalities within societies while problematic in themselves are also seriously damaging to subjective wellbeing, in respect of our mental and physical health, to issues around identity, our morale and self-esteem. Equality and human-development disciplines all broadly agree that we cannot dismiss or ignore the problem of gross material inequality in thinking about schooling as a context for development. This gross inequality is problematic in itself, but it also seriously affects other aspects of flourishing/wellbeing/welfare for individuals and groups, including their educational experiences. Young people who experience consistent poverty and live in areas of high social disadvantage have been shown to drop out of school earlier, to have poorer physical and mental health, and to be at risk of bullying by their peers. In an Irish in-depth report on families living in consistent poverty pre the recent economic recession (Daly and Leonard, 2001), young people reported that one of the main reasons they dropped out of school was because they felt that teachers were not interested in them or didn't like them, and because they were bullied by peers. Moreover, young people who are living in homes without consistent poverty, but where there is 'low family affluence' find themselves struggling to participate and stay in school and to engage in social activities with peers (National Economic and Social Council, 2009). Nic Gabhainn and Sixsmith's (2006) work with children and young adolescents, developing child wellbeing indicators, also shows the significance of material welfare to young people's assessment of quality of life, not for the sake of having wealth and money per se, but because it enables families to live in decent housing and participate in society. What emerges from this literature suggests that adults and children experience poor levels of 'welfare' and 'happiness' when their material lives are compromised relative to others in their society.

Socio-cultural inequality, wellbeing and schooling

This section of the chapter seeks to explore the relation between identity inequalities (cultural), wellbeing and schooling. In his book *Wasted*, Furedi (2009) following Arendt's conception of natality and education, argues for the separation of schooling from the pressing concerns of politics and public life and he suggests that schools should not be used as places 'where the unresolved issues of public life can be pursued … where problems that are avoided in the domain of politics appear as a subject for the school curriculum' (Furedi p. 51). The argument that schools should not be given over to political fads or programmes of social engineering seems wise, and it does seem responsible to question public discourses around wellbeing and how they are translated into the space of education. It is undoubtedly important to recognise political agendas that shape our understandings of wellbeing, and to critique normalising and uni-dimensional paradigms of wellbeing that can be marginalising for teachers, children and their parents, and that act against the enabling of wellbeing in particular local contexts (Sen, 1993). Cognisant of the tensions between political/public agendas for wellbeing, and the very real injustices and oppressions experienced by individuals and groups in society, I argue that it is nonetheless important to explore some 'wellbeing space' within schools that is about some real objective good and development (see Thorburn, Chapter 2). To suggest that wellbeing as an aim of education lies outside the scope of schooling entirely as I think Furedi does, would be to reduce educational aims and processes in a very radical way. We may argue that schools cannot solve problems of 'illbeing' and inequality directly, but that does not mean that we should eschew any consideration of what is good, or give up on the idea of wellbeing development through education. So, while taking Furedi's critique seriously, I argue that school communities have a responsibility, as do teachers, for thinking about and acting for wellbeing in the context of schooling, at both formal and informal levels.

However, the issue of grossly unequal resources and the marginalisation of students of certain classes and communities still blocks our way on the path towards wellbeing work in schools. The relationship between school achievement, material success and status in the socio-cultural context is well rehearsed. Despite investment, research and interventions to tackle 'educational disadvantage' for more than half a century, the problem of educational inequalities in participation and outcomes persists in relation to classed and socio-cultural identities. Moreover, it is difficult to see how these can be eradicated through education when the economic and cultural inequalities in the larger societal context in which schooling occurs continue to intensify (Baker *et al.* 2004) and polarise rich and poor, oppressor and oppressed. The link between educational achievement and success within the labour market, though changed somewhat in recent years, has broadly endured,[2] and higher educational credentials are often necessary for access to even the most entry-level positions in the labour market. This persistent economic and social reality has tended to focus the minds of teachers, parents and students more narrowly on the challenges of how to compete and obtain legitimated forms of academic/cultural capitals, and sometimes at the expense of realising areas of learning and development that are relevant to discovering and pursuing other meaningful life goals.

The demands of the knowledge economy too may present a challenge for universal wellbeing development as it demands students have particular sets of cognitive skills and technical knowledge and yet research has borne out time and again that the kinds of knowledge and skills taught in schools are more easily acquired by those who are cultural insiders. That a great deal of the energies of students in their formative years are trained and honed on obtaining points and grades as capital, in order to proceed to the next level of education or to enter the job market seems hugely wasteful of their creativity and developmental possibilities for flourishing. The relationship between our classed, cultural and gendered habitus[3] and the resources we possess to make our way through the educational field is significant for teaching for wellbeing, and for developing a wellbeing curriculum. From an equality perspective, we know that if school culture and curricula do not recognise our social identities and habitus, if we have little say in our schooling and feel devalued, then engagement becomes irrelevant for us, and we may exercise our agency to leave or to resist these processes of misrecognition[4] in ways that compromise the possibilities of educational success.

The problem of what is most recognised and valued in schools is core in working and teaching for wellbeing. Richard Pring confronts this significant issue of value differences and wellbeing in his introduction to *The International Research Handbook on Values Education and Student Wellbeing* (2010). He suggests that differences in values are indicative of significant differences in understandings around what it is to be fully human, of human flourishing and of wellbeing. He advises that education and curricula that seek to support student wellbeing cannot easily dismiss the kinds of tensions that are inherent across different value systems, and how they are expressed in particular approaches to wellbeing. Values may un/wittingly shape teachers' understandings, pedagogies and curricula, and versions of wellbeing that are privileged over others. Models of subjective wellbeing that focus on individual skills, esteem and engagement can be worthwhile for individual students (Waters, 2011) but in the context of intensification of performativity, and where academic success is a top value, then some students will find it challenging to engage in learning that is meaningful for them relative to their own goals (what MacAllister has termed pseudo-wellbeing, see Chapter 6).

Using the language of Sen's (1993) influential capability approach[5] to wellbeing, we could argue that the global performativity agenda has increasing potential to narrow our freedoms to achieve our own valued functionings within the formal education system and school curriculum. From an equality perspective we might further suggest that this process of thinning and narrowing has had more detrimental consequences for some classes and groups in society without access to valued resources/capitals, because they must rely so heavily on the educational system to provide opportunities for their development and success.

It is evident that one of the main weaknesses in educational policy in relation to inequality and the problem of wellbeing is that it has been approached from a liberal, rational justice perspective; a perspective which has framed equal opportunity policy since the second half of the twentieth century (Baker *et al.*, 2004). It is apparent from critique and research that the advantages that accrue to students from families and social contexts that are rich in economic and dominant forms of social and cultural capitals are difficult to confer systematically upon students from less privileged and culturally recognised contexts. Redistribution through the current school system is not effective or even possible for many reasons.[6] Thus we are faced with a 'limit situation' (see Freire's *Pedagogy of the Oppressed*, 1972), schools and the school curriculum can go only some of the distance in working towards wellbeing for all students.

Responding to injustice and inequality with an ethic of care

When we become aware of the limit situation in relation to inequality and wellbeing, as educators we can unmask the *rhetoric* of universal-welfare wellbeing, and how politicians and others may shift responsibility for wellbeing onto educators and schools (see again Ecclestone and Hayes, 2009). Understanding this tendency to *use* schools, as instruments for the creation of social stability and liberal redistributive justice, enables us as educators, to refocus on the real good of education, on what is possible, and on the complexity and specificity entailed in working towards real wellbeing with students in awareness of their particular contexts and identities. One of the big ideas that underpin this book is an overarching concern that schooling today can, despite these challenges, still offer or in some cases create, a space where individual meaning goals of students[7] (O'Brien and O'Shea, 2016) can be supported and recognised without a radical dismantling of the entire schooling system. Taking this premise as a guide, I now explore how this might be possible in schools and communities where students and parents have been traditionally distanced or marginalised. In grappling with the issue of gross inequality, poor welfare and the problem of redistribution and schooling, I turn to the work of feminist care theorists and educators in the later part of the twentieth century. This scholarship argues that an overemphasis on traditional rational justice and liberal equality in educational and social systems has been generally silent or blind to the significance of the affective/emotional dimension of life for our wellbeing and flourishing, and particularly within the so-called public space. Within a radical-care perspective, it is these subjective, textured experiences, and supportive and rich relationships that are fundamental to our development as humans and to the development of society (Noddings, 1999; Gilligan, 1982; Tronto, 2010; Nussbaum, 2000; Kittay, 1999). Care theorists argue that a political and social system that recognises the importance of interdependent caring would tackle these enduring issues of inequality,[8] because care, when taken seriously, can have a revolutionary effect on how we view social institutions and processes of education. Putting care at the heart of institutional life necessitates 'other orientation', empathy and connectedness, and a valuing of the effort and work of care. The consequences of valuing of care and relationship are that self-interestedness and self-serving time and energies have to be moderated and educated, in order to meet basic affective and material needs of all.

Even if we are not committed to a revolution of social institutions through care, I want to argue here for the potential of caring relationality *within schools*, to nurture students' development and wellbeing, and as a way of engaging with justice that enriches more traditional perspectives on opportunities to flourish. In the introduction to *Justice and Caring*, Nell Noddings (1999) poses the question as to whether justice and care orientations can work together, and if they can produce a more satisfactory solution to problems of students' flourishing than could be wrought by one of these approaches alone. She suggests that justice is often regarded as important as a perspective to more general approaches to schooling policy, but 'that care is essential in refining and implementing it' (ibid., p. 1). Thinkers such as Noddings, Kittay, Nussbaum, Gilligan and Lynch acknowledge our universal and inalienable need for care throughout the life span, and argue that this reality should inform how we conceptualise what it is to be human and to be well. Moreover, care theory broadly suggests that we need to understand emotional and rational dimensions of our being as related rather than dichotomised as emotional *or* cognitive, and to thus challenge the current dominant understanding of the adult human as an autonomous, rational economic maximiser. Care theory's conceptualisations of the human subject have profound implications for education, in terms of recognition of the significance of our affective development, and in challenging the traditional emphasis on academic achievement as wellbeing development (see Soutter *et al.*, 2012 on the prevailing emphasis on the academic at second level despite attempts to teach for wellbeing).

Within this care frame/paradigm, we begin to shift from traditional rationalistic justice paradigms and to understand how emotional development and ethical development work hand-in-hand with the development of care thinking. Empathy for example is a capacity that assists our decision-making capacities and our ability to reach out to another being in ways that mere reason *alone* cannot support. My argument for care in the context of wellbeing schooling is based on a philosophical view of the human as caring, and that includes the richness of our human inter-dependencies and our vulnerabilities. This challenges individualistic or positivistic accounts of human development and argues for human interconnectedness as a basic condition of human life. Kittay's (1999) view is that we cannot flourish as humans if we do not take interconnection *and* dependent relationships as funda-mental to the human condition and development. In education and human devel-opment, we must therefore engage with and understand the principles and politics around caring and relationality, so as to scaffold a wellbeing approach that is just and inclusive, and that enables wellbeing learning. A commitment to an ethos of caring relationality can assist teachers and school leaders to think 'carefully' about identity and wellbeing in relation to individuals and groups of students, and to respond meaningfully to their particular expressed needs.[9] Research has borne out that if our basic needs for care and affection are not met or where we suffer from neglect and harm, learning is severely compromised.[10] Drawing on feminist care theory, I suggest a conceptualisation of wellbeing that recognises it as a process of over time, as non-linear, and that fundamentally recognises our need for relation-ship and emotional interconnection in our individual struggles, and for a commit-ment to justice and equality. This wellbeing draws upon an ethics that is based in and develops from relationality.

The social ecology of care and wellbeing: Parents, students and wellbeing development

Lynch (1989) suggests that it is often more in the absence of care and relationship that we notice its significance for our development and human flourishing. Taking this as a starting point, I wish to consider how teachers and professionals working in education might understand care and its relation to wellbeing. Research and theory inform us that our views of care and relationship as professionals may be framed by our own understandings and positionings within the social world (Lareau and Horvat, 1999; Freire, 1972). We may judge parental care and engagement by our own personal and professional standards and against what is normatively excellent and optimal for development in educational discourses, and particularly as under-stood within the powerful discourses of psychology. While this is understandable, it may however reinforce limited understandings of how care and educational support work can be carried out by families and communities, day-to-day, where mate-rial and cultural, and consequently affective (emotional) resources, are consistently over-stretched. Research suggests (Reay, 1998; O'Brien, 2008b) that where material resources (capitals) are constrained and cultural/educational resources are basic, that parental knowledge of the educational system and its workings are limited, and in turn this leads to educational care that does not line up with a predominantly middle-class standard of expectation by teachers and schools. Moreover, the energies required to do educational support work and care at home may be radically reduced because of more pressing life needs; to find work, to deal with medical issues and in just feeding the family and paying bills to survive from day-to-day. Writing in the second half of the twentieth century, the French sociologist and anthropologist, Pierre Bourdieu, was acutely aware of the kinds of 'horizons of expectation' of working-class families, that were necessarily focused on daily living, rather than long-term investments in education, what he termed the 'choice of the necessary'.

Today, in the aftermath of a European economic crisis and its effects, many are struggling to keep their homes and jobs, and even the traditional middle-classes feel the pressures of job insecurity on a grander scale than previously. Research indicates that despite the newer economic challenges faced by middle-class parents, that these groups still possess valuable cultural and social capitals. They often have 'insider knowledge' of the educational system and the requisite social and cultural resources to support and encourage their children to take part in schooling and to reap the benefits that accrue to educational success (O'Brien, 2008b; Vincent and Martin, 2002; Observer Newspaper, 2016). Not alone do these classes of parents have cultural resources, but the educational-care work they seek to enact for their children can draw on their cultural knowledge to support 'the best' routes and trajectories in the education and economic 'fields', even in harsh times. The education support work/effort of working-class parents often compares starkly with the focused engagement of middle-class families, and teachers and professionals often unwittingly read this as an absence of interest and care in their children's education. Building on Reay's work in the UK, and from my own research and work with marginalised mothers in Ireland, I argue that the emotional capital that translates care into effective actions to support children's schooling, and particularly at second level, is over-stretched and dissipated among the marginalised, lone parents and the poor (Reay, 1998; O'Brien, 2008b). Research suggests that mothers/parents[11] regardless of class and social positioning care deeply about their children's education. But how they translate care into schooling support may be limited relative to other pressing concerns of the family, and those who are struggling economically and socially often cannot match the emotional capital that middle–class insiders have developed because of their accumulation of *social and cultural resources* and indeed their access to economic capitals.

Mothers' accounts of their engagement with schools to support their children's wellbeing at transition to second level (O'Brien, 2008b) highlight the particular and indeed often heart-breaking struggles to ensure the child's happiness, and how that care intersects with the demands of the educational system. Teachers' own care and professional awareness (Noddings, 2010), their critical understandings of these familial challenges (Freire, 1972), and their attunement to child and parental needs (Gilligan, 1995), can at least help teachers to create a more welcoming environment that is less judgemental of family practices and more supportive family/school relationships, so the young person does not immediately experience emotional and cultural dissonance that leads to alienation. Educational/community interventions that recognise the significance of relationship, particularly where there is distance between home and school in values and practices, can support the development of a caring relationship between home and school that can enhance wellbeing. This of course is easy to say, but in reality will present many learnings for parents and educators. Nevertheless, it has been demonstrated time and again in research that the relationships between school staff, with their students and with parents are crucial to engagement and success, but all the more so in areas of socio-economic and cultural disadvantage (Cohen, 2006).

This may seem to be a very different sort of discourse regarding the role of the school in supporting and teaching for wellbeing, but I argue that it is this *informal curriculum of relationality*, and broader dialogue with the main responsible actors in a young person's life, that creates the conditions for working towards students' wellbeing in the holistic and real sense of the term. Across the West since the latter half of the twentieth century, school programmes and interventions have sought to tackle educational disadvantage and many have failed to equalise outcomes and participation. They failed in part because interventions were underpinned by a deficit view of the poor, the working-classes and the socially and culturally marginalised. They were seen to be in need of fixing with middle-class educational values and knowledge. The great South American educator Paulo Freire challenged this view of the 'oppressed' as deficient and less rational. His work has inspired other radical educationalists and has had considerable influence in community development education though not as much on school systems in the West as they continue their business of social reproduction. Freire's philosophy of education *as* development, flourishing and humanisation is also based in the view of education as relational and dialogical, and in pedagogy that problematises hierarchies and inequality in the world. A school that seeks to support student wellbeing has to commit to dialogue with its students and parents, around values, needs and desires, in order to name our world. Freire, care theorists and educationalists concerned with our full development and the matter of inequality argue for deep engagement and reflection on self in order to respond ethically and with care towards another. In her recent work on care and care ethics in a globalised world, Noddings (2010) suggests that caring and the development of the capacity for empathy is a way forward in preparing students for ethical citizenship and to tackle gross injustice. Biesta (2016) too (discussed in Chapter 4) has expressed concerns around the individualisation of emotional education for wellbeing that neglects a notion of a collective good and of ethical citizenship. These are not easily resolved matters at the level of policy or school practices because they are concerned with prioritisation and contestation around values. Even in awareness of these tensions and complexities, at a fundamental level, creating the space for genuine dialogue and relationship is a way forward for schools in this joint endeavour for wellbeing that respects individuals, their own needs and a collective good grounded in social justice.

Future directions

Teacher education, wellbeing and social justice

It is clear that there is a great deal to be done to support wellbeing for all students in the fullest sense, and particularly in relation to students who are challenged in their schooling because of injustice and inequalities in the wider social world. Teachers and schools are assigned a tremendous responsibility if they are to take student wellbeing seriously, and indeed this is problematic for schools when their work is not supported by radical changes in wider society. My concern therefore, is how to prepare students in their initial teacher education around these wellbeing demands that they will be expected to meet as they enter the school system.

Working recently with a seminar of fourth year BEd students in an Irish University, I employed a dialogical approach to explore the significance of wellbeing and care for them as early career professionals. Drawing on our care and wellbeing dialogues, one of the key concerns that emerged from collective and individual reflections was in relation to their own self-care and wellbeing. Students broadly agreed that this was their first explicit encounter with debates on the significance of caring and wellbeing for them as young professionals, and how this related to the dialogical relational dimensions of teaching. These young teachers expressed strong messages from the social world reflecting a lack of value for self and other care, and moreover, how it has been seen as natural and gendered:

Jenny: Looking after yourself is seen as a weakness.
Marie: I never thought about my own care and myself, it's always been about pleasing others.
Helen: Caring for yourself is seen as selfish but care for yourself is important.
Joan: My father says 'what are you getting stressed about re school placement, sure you're only minding children.

The student dialogues, their care reflections and the artefacts they produced during this module are rich and informative, but unfortunately the detail of these will have to remain the subject matter of another paper. I do want to say however, that I am in debt to the generosity of these young teachers in their hunger for reflection and their commitment to exploring care and its significance for wellbeing. Their capacity to critique and ask personal and professionally relevant questions about care, inequality and gross injustice created a powerful environment for us to face these challenges together, and to draw on key thinkers to shed light on these significant and complex human questions around emotional and relational identities and human flourishing. There were no simple answers to the profound issues considered, but we came away with a strong sense of education as a process of personal and collective development that can aim to create the conditions for wellbeing development in the full sense of the term.

As teachers and schools are increasingly faced with a responsibility for teaching a wellbeing curriculum, and supporting students to be well, and often against a harsh economic landscape where poverty and intense cultural and social upheaval are a reality, they will have to actively engage with the complexities around justice, equality and wellbeing in the communities where they are working. The school cannot work for wellbeing with abstracted learners or in isolation from the context in which students live. Biesta has recently argued that if education is for emancipation, then we must call students as persons, subjects and speakers into dialogue (Biesta, 2016). If we cast them merely as 'learners', we have already conceded they are in deficit and we have metaphorically put an 'L' plate on their backs. We need to see them as already equal, and as human beings rather than reductively cognitively framed as learners. Biestas's argument for seeing and hearing students as equal in the educational process echoes the Freirean conception of teachers' and students' voices as essential in the dialogical encounter. Feminist care discourse too focuses on hearing, voicing, embodying and on relating with students within an ethic of care. The matter of how teachers conceptualise students in the wellbeing space is both a personal and political issue. Our job is to empower students in their own journeys towards wellbeing, not to set the terms and the endpoints for them. Taking care as a frame for wellbeing education necessitates an education that is fluid, responsive, an endeavour that invites persons into relationship and reflection, to speak, feel and name their world. By keeping the relational and personal at the centre of our work we educate for personal wellbeing and take steps in the right direction to creating a good and a just society.

Summary of key findings

- Student wellbeing can only be thought of 'in context' and that includes understanding diversity and inequality in familial and community life.
- Personal wellbeing is shaped by material and socio-cultural contexts and socio-cultural capital.
- Emotional life and care are central to human wellbeing.
- The absence of resources can compromise care and emotional wellbeing.
- Putting care at the centre of life will bring about greater justice and tackle inequalities that hamper wellbeing especially for oppressed groups.
- Education for wellbeing requires that teachers have opportunities in their own education to reflect on care, relationship and wellbeing.
- Problems that are intransigent and reproduced in the wider social context cannot be eradicated by usurping the space of education i.e. social engineering through schooling is not education.
- Wellbeing is about becoming fully human, schools are about persons and not just learners.

Reflective tasks

- Make a case for the significance of teachers' caring for students' wellbeing in education.
- How does inequality compromise wellbeing?
- How can the school challenge inequality and injustice?
- In your view what are the limits to teachers' caring responsibilities?

Notes

1 Allardt's (1993) Having, Loving and Being welfare model which has been adapted for use in schools is based on the explicit premise that to compromise any one dimension of the three-dimensional model of wellbeing compromises overall wellbeing. If having needs i.e. resource needs are not met, then wellbeing is not achievable.
2 Brown, Lauder and Ashton (2011) suggest that educational credentials do not buy job success to the extent they did in the past, a broken promise of the system, but research shows that a degree holder stands a better chance than a non-degree holder of gaining employment.
3 Bourdieu (1977) conceptualises the habitus as a structure of fields of practice and as an organising structure of individual psychology, as sets of practices that are internalised and affect the choices we make in life.
4 Paul Willis' work *Learning to Labour* (1977) is classic in how it demonstrates how working class lads remove themselves from the middle-class norms of schooling and end up in poorly paid jobs.
5 Sen, A.'s (1993) 'Capability Approach' has been very influential in fields of Human Development. His work places capabilities – our individual capacities to achieve valued beings and doings and the freedoms to follow these at the very heart of wellbeing (Sen 1993). Capability and well-being. Nussbaum (2000, p. 156) highlights with specific reference to the capabilities approach these types of challenges we wish to see being taken forward when he notes that we 'need to attend carefully to issues of both pedagogy and content, asking how both the substance of study and the nature of classroom interactions fulfil the aims.
6 Baker, Lynch, Cantillon and Walsh, *Equality from Theory to Action* (2004) argue that the liberal justice model of schooling will fail to redistribute wealth and public goods because it entails an acceptance of hierarchy and gross material differences which are experienced as power and recognition inequalities.
7 O'Brien and O'Shea (2016) discuss the problem of normative accounts of wellbeing and the issue of values, and suggest that students cannot move in the space of wellbeing unless they develop their own meaning goals and not the hand-me-downs of others.
8 Fraser, N. (1994). After the family wage: Gender equity and the welfare state, *Political Theory*, 22(4), 591–618.
9 In her work, Noddings (2015) suggests that teachers often respond, because of pressures in schooling, to students' assumed rather than expressed needs. Assumed needs are what we assume are good for them rather than what they say they need!
10 Feeley, M.'s (2014) research on the concept of learning care explores the challenges to learning experienced by survivors of institutional abuse and how care is required in the successful acquisition of literacy.
11 It is well documented that mothers have been the primary and active education-support workers and carers in families. Fathers, particularly middle-class fathers, help with decision making but it is mothers who do the daily donkey work, see O'Brien (2007).

References

Allardt, E. (1993). 'Having, loving, being: An alternative to the Swedish model of welfare research'. In M. Nussbaum & A. Sen (Eds.), *The Quality of Life* (pp. 88–94). Oxford: Clarendon Press.

Baker, J., Lynch, K., Cantillon, S., & Walsh, J. (2004). *Equality from Theory to Action*. London: Palgrave.

Biesta, G. (2016). 'Learner, student, speaker: Why it matters how we call those we teach'. In M.A. Peters & M. Tesar (Eds.). *Beyond the Philosophy of the Subject: An Educational Philosophy and Theory Post-Structuralist Reader* (pp. 146–159). London: Routledge.

Bourdieu, P. (1977). *Outline of a Theory of Practice*. Cambridge: Cambridge University Press.

Bourdieu, P. (1984). *Distinctions: A Social Critique of the Judgement of Taste*. London: Routledge and Kegan Paul.

Brown, P., Lauder, H., & Ashton, D. (2011). *The Global Auction: The Broken Promises of Education, Jobs and Incomes*. New York: Oxford University Press.

Cohen, J. (2006). Social, Emotional, Ethical and Academic Education: Creating a Climate for Learning, Participation in the Democracy and Well-Being, *Harvard Educational Review*, 76(2), 201–237.

Daly, M., & Leonard, M. (2001). *Against All Odds: Living Life on a Low Income*. Dublin: Combat Poverty Agency.

Ecclestone, K., & Hayes, D. (2009). *The Dangerous Rise of Therapeutic Education*. London: Routledge.

Feeley, M. (2014). *Learning Care Lessons: Literacy, Love, Care and Solidarity*. London: The Tunfell Press.

Fraser, N. (1994). After the Family Wage: Gender Equity and the Welfare State, *Political Theory*, 22(4), 591–618.

Freire, P. (1972). *Pedagogy of the Oppressed*. London: Penguin.

Furedi, F. (2009). *Wasted: Why Education Does Not Educate Anymore*. London: Continuum.

Gilligan, C. (1982). *In a Different Voice: Psychological Theory and Women's Development*. Cambridge Harvard University Press.

Gilligan, C. (1995). Hearing the Difference: Theorizing Connection, *Hypatia*, 10(2), 120–127.

Kittay, E. (1999). *Love's Labor: Essays on Women Equality and Dependency*. New York: Routledge.

Kosutic, I., & McDowell, T. (2008). Diversity and social justice in family therapy literature: A decade review. *Journal of Feminist Family Therapy*, 20(2), 142–165.

Lareau, A. & Horvat, E. (1999). Moments of Social Inclusion and Exclusion Race, Class, and Cultural Capital in Family-School Relationships, *Sociology of Education*, 72(1), 37–53.

Lynch, K. (1989). Solidary Labour: Its Nature and Marginalisation, *Sociological Review*, 37, 1–14.

National Economic and Social Council. (2009). *Well-being Matters in Measuring Social Progress: Beyond GDP*. Dublin: National Economic and Social Council.

Nic Gabhainn, S., & Sixsmith, J. (2006). Children Photographing Well-being: Facilitating Participation in Research, *Children and Society*, 20(4), 249–259.

Noddings, N. (1999). 'Care, justice, and equity. Justice and caring: The search for common ground in education'. In M.S. Katz, N. Noddings & K.A. Strike (Eds.), *Justice and Caring: The Search for Common Ground in Education* (pp. 7–20). Columbia: Teachers College Press.

Noddings, N. (2010). Moral Education in an Age of Globalisation, *Educational Philosophy Theory*, 42(4), 390–395.

Noddings, N. (2015). *The Challenge to Care in Schools*. Columbia: Teachers College Press.

Nussbaum, M. (2000). Women's Capabilities and Social Justice, *Journal of Human Development*, 1(2), 219–247.

O'Brien M. (2007). Mothers' Emotional Care Work in Education and Its Moral Imperative, *Gender and Education, 19*(2), 159–167.

O'Brien, M. (2008a). *Wellbeing and Post-Primary Schooling: A Review of the Literature and Research.* Dublin: National Council for Curriculum and Assessment.

O'Brien, M. (2008b). Gendered Capital: Emotional Capital and Mothers' Care Work in Education, *British Journal of Sociology of Education, 29*(2), 137–148.

O'Brien, M., & O'Shea, A. (2016). *A Human Development (PSP) Framework for Orienting Education and Schools in the Space of Wellbeing.* Dublin: National Council for Curriculum and Assessment.

Observer Newspaper Editorial on Theresa May and Grammar School Policy. (11/9/16). Retrieved from https://www.theguardian.com/commentisfree/2016/sep/09/the-guardian-view-on-theresa-mays-schools-speech-a-divisive-blueprint

Pring, R. (2010). 'Introduction'. In T. Lovat, R. Toomey & N. Clement (Eds.), *International Research Handbook on Values Education and Student Wellbeing* (pp. xix–xxiv). Dordrecht: Springer.

Reay, D. (1998). *Class Work: Mothers' Involvement in Their Children's Primary Schooling.* London: Taylor & Francis.

Sen, A. (1993). 'Capability and well-being'. In M. Nussbaum & A. Sen (Eds.), *The Quality of Life* (pp. 30–53). Oxford: Clarendon Press.

Soutter, A.K., O'Steen, B. & Gilmore, A. (2012). Wellbeing in the New Zealand Curriculum, *Journal of Curriculum Studies, 44*(1), 111–142.

Sutherland, O., Couture, S., Gaete Silva, J., Strong, T., Lamarre, A., & Hardt, L. (2016). Social Justice Oriented Diagnostic Discussions: A Discursive Perspective, *Journal of Feminist Family Therapy, 28*(2–3), 76–99.

Tronto, J. (2010). Creating Caring Institutions: Politics, Plurality, and Purpose, *Ethics and Social Welfare, 4*(2), 158–171.

Vincent, C., & Martin, J. (2002). Class, Culture and Agency: Researching Parental Voice, *Discourse, 23*(1), 108–127.

Wilkinson, R., & Pickett, K. (2011). *The Spirit Level: Why Greater Equality Makes Societies Stronger.* New York: Bloomsbury.

Willis, P. (1977). *Learning to Labour: How Working Class Kids Get Working Class Jobs.* Aldershot: Saxon House.

PART V

Future prospects for wellbeing

11

WELLBEING, OUTDOOR LEARNING AND SUSTAINABLE LIVING

Ina Stan

Introduction

Please begin by reviewing and reflecting upon the following outdoor activity example. The outdoor activity was Blind String Trail. The children were blindfolded, with one hand on the shoulder of the person in front. They had to follow a string through an outdoor obstacle course. The aim of the activity was to introduce them to communication by encouraging them to give short messages to the leader and get them to pass it back like Chinese whispers. This was the group's first activity at the outdoor centre. After the activity, the male teacher engaged the children in discussion:

Tm: Can we all sit down in a nice big circle and I'll join you. You need to concentrate.

       Who can tell me please what you needed to accomplish?

Pg1[1]:   Listening.
Tm: Yeah, listening. Now hands up who thought that they were good at listening?

(All raised their hands up.)

Tm: Yeah, I agree, you were all pretty good. What else do you think we had to do?
Pb: We shout stop.
Tm: We shout stop, what else?
Pb1:   Carry on!
Tm: What else?
Pb2:   Oooh, ooh, you need to say what you felt.

Tm: Yeah, you had to tell everybody what you felt. The idea is that you needed to do it yourselves, but you obviously did it with a bit of help, because it was your first time. The idea of this week is things like that, you've got to think carefully about what you're doing, who you're talking to. Are we all happy now?

Pg: Yeah!

Tm: Well done everybody. Give yourselves a round of applause. That was one of the best, if not the best first time string trails.

(On the way back, two girls were chatting.)

Pg1:   I'm dying here.

Pg2:   I'm sweaty.

(Field notes II, pp. 7–10)

The example above illustrates the importance of not only focusing on the outdoor activity itself, but of also engaging the children in dialogue in order to have an insight into what they have gained from the outdoor experience. Muños (2009) stresses the need for further research to provide a better understanding of the link between children using outdoor spaces and health, and whether there are differences regarding age and gender, as well as the impact of various socio-cultural contexts on health. Assisting teachers to create the conditions for open dialogue with learners could lead to personal growth, and thus contribute to their wellbeing. However, this is actually a lot more skillful and difficult than might be imagined. Therefore, the chapter aims to help in this respect by focusing on some key pedagogical issues that seem to make a difference and which are based on primary research.

It should be noted that the research I have conducted does not deny the noteworthy benefits that being in the outdoors can have on a person's mental and physical wellbeing. Indeed, there are many studies that do just that. For instance, findings suggest improved mental health following exposure to nature and engaging with green spaces, such as forests, can have recuperative benefits (O'Brien *et al.*, 2010). Similarly, the Sustainable Development Commission (2008) found that being in nature is beneficial to one's health. Additionally, many studies evidence the importance of engaging children with the outdoors as part of their learning, as it can contribute significantly to their development (Muños, 2009). Scandinavian countries have long recognised the importance of incorporating outdoor learning (including risky play) in schooling and the significant role this plays in the physical, emotional and intellectual development of children (Sandseter, 2009). It has also been argued that greater creativity and lifelong learning may be achieved by allowing children to have more engagement with the outdoors (Waite *et al.*, 2006). However, Rea and Waite (2009) point out that there is increasingly limited access to the outdoors for primary school children in England, partly due to the rigid curriculum, but also to the risk aversion in British society.

This chapter explores the link between being in the outdoors and wellbeing, focusing specifically on the impact that the outdoors has on children and young people. The chapter draws on primary research and examines the participants' understanding of wellbeing and their perspectives on how engaging with the outdoors impacts on their wellbeing. Different forms of teaching demonstrated in the outdoors are also explored along with an analysis of the importance of the role of the teacher/facilitator in the group while facilitating outdoor activities. In doing so, the chapter examines how, at times, controlling teaching approaches are used and how these approaches can lead to the disempowerment of the learners. Finally, the chapter highlights the importance of taking into account not just how outdoor activities are planned, but also how they are conducted in order for them to be beneficial for children's wellbeing.

Main findings

Chapter 1 highlighted the concept of being well, which goes beyond referring to one's health, but rather looking at wellbeing holistically. In this chapter, I acknowledge this definition of wellbeing and recognise that wellbeing is a complex notion, and that there are multiple understandings of it, hence I will take a holistic view when exploring the link between being in the outdoors and wellbeing.

The outdoors and wellbeing

One of the main benefits that the literature identifies regarding children and young people spending time outdoors is the impact on their physical health, and the potential of addressing negative health issues, such as childhood obesity (Ebberling *et al.*, 2002). Furthermore, the natural elements present in outdoor settings, such as trees and vegetation, rocks and slopes, facilitate active play, which contributes to the physical development of children, especially their motor skills, such as strength, balance and coordination (Fjortoft, 2004). It has been argued that simply being in nature has health benefits in itself; for instance, it was found that children attending nurseries providing extended time in the outdoors experienced less frequency of illness, and higher attendance levels (Fjortoft, 2001). There are also claims that spending time outdoors reduces stress and prevents depression, due to its restorative benefits (Berto, 2005). According to Korpela and Hartig (1996), creating an attachment to place and providing a space that allows young people to spend some quiet time and unwind can contribute to their wellbeing. Being exposed to nature can improve cognitive function (Wells, 2000), develop children's creativity (USDA Forest Service, 2001) and their understanding of risk.

Furthermore, there is evidence to suggest that there are educational benefits (O'Brien and Murray, 2007). Providing well-designed outdoor-learning environments has been shown to be important for children's brain development (Rickinson *et al.*, 2004) and can be beneficial for learning (Downer *et al.*, 2007; Eick, 2012; Jacobi-Vessels, 2013). Moreover, well-planned outdoor learning can limit the amount of environmental stressors (noise, visual overload and crowding). Engaging with the outdoors as part of the curriculum for primary and secondary school children can lead to a better connection with nature, as shown by Tunnicliffe (2008) who explored the use of ponds in teaching biology and science.

Eick's (2012) study showed that connecting the science and literacy curriculum taught in the outdoors impacted positively on standardised test results. Chawla *et al.* (2014) examined the impact of spending time outdoors at school during breaks and lessons for both primary- and secondary-aged children, and found that this improved the children's stress levels, social health and overall wellbeing.

Moreover, Ofsted (the Government quality assurance agency in England and Wales) (2008) investigated the impact of learning outside the classroom by surveying primary and secondary schools across England and found that there was a rise in standards and an improvement in the children's development, personally, socially as well as emotionally, when children participated in learning outside the classroom that was well-planned and well-implemented. Even more importantly, outdoor learning was perceived as more successful when it was integrated as part of the long-term curriculum and related to classroom activities. The report pointed out that the primary schools involved used their buildings, grounds and surrounding area more efficiently and consistently to assist learning than secondary schools. This report demonstrates the value of teaching children outdoors, but also emphasises the importance of having well-structured and well-integrated outdoor activities that are relevant to the school curriculum.

Nevertheless, the time that children can spend outdoors at school has become greatly reduced. This is due to a variety of reasons, e.g. Ernst (2014) investigated teachers' beliefs regarding the use of outdoor spaces and what they perceived as barriers to successful outdoor-learning experiences. Most of the teachers recognised the values of outdoor learning for teaching children about environmental issues, as well as improving their cognitive, social and physical development. Nevertheless, the teachers provided limited opportunities for outdoor learning (approximately once a month) due to lack of access to safe and appropriate outdoor spaces, the need for transportation to appropriate locations, inclement weather and lack of time. A concern for safety has also been identified as one of the barriers which limits children's learning experiences (Humberstone and Stan, 2011). Hence, teachers' approaches can have a significant impact on children's learning experiences in the outdoors, as will be discussed in more depth later.

Participant perspectives on wellbeing

The 'Wellbeing and Outdoor Pedagogies' project (the 'Wellbeing Project') was conducted between 2008 and 2010. This ethnographic study explored teaching and learning in the 'outdoor classroom', examining concepts of risk at primary-school level, body image, wellbeing and participation in outdoor activities. A social constructivist approach was taken in order to allow participants to provide their own perspectives on what wellbeing meant to them.

When asked what the wellbeing of children meant to them, mothers talked about children's happiness, independence and character building, as the quote below shows, where P stands for parent:

Ina: First of all what do you understand by their well-being? [...] What do you think the well-being of a child is?

P4:   If they're happy.

P3:   If they're independent, bring themselves out of themselves.

P5:   It's definitely character building.

P2:   And it gives them a very good memory.

P5:   I think it's the character building, the independence–

P6:   Confidence–

P5:   Yeah, building the confidence and being outdoors and all that fresh air and everything.

(Humberstone and Stan, 2009, p. 27)

All the parents interviewed were very positive about the perceived benefits on their children's wellbeing of the outdoor residential visit. One mother in particular highlighted that it gave children the opportunity to develop their own individuality separate from their other siblings:

Ina: So you think that this visit contributed to their well-being?

Ps: Yeah, yeah.

P3:   I think it makes them feel special as well in their own individual way, I think, 'cause they've not got like brothers and sisters, you know, one's better than the other ....

(Humberstone and Stan, 2009, p. 27)

The contribution of outdoor activities to the wellbeing of the children, both mental and physical, was recognised by all of the parents interviewed, due to the opportunities for increased physical activity, exposure to fresh air and sunshine, as well as the development of communication skills. The parents expressed concern regarding the dominance of technology in their children's life, and the impact this may have on their ability to engage with others, as the extract below illustrates:

P4:   It's good for them.

P6:   They're outside–

P4:   Outside, vitamin D, you know, fresh air and obviously exercise, rather than just sitting indoors.

P2:   I mean there is so much, I mean there's computers and tele, so many things that they can just latch onto now.

P3:   Yeah, I dread to think what's going to be like when he's an adult because there's no communication with anybody–

P2:   That's it, that's the big issue–

P3:   That's the big issue.

(Humberstone and Stan, 2009, p. 27)

Some of the findings in the 'Wellbeing Project' regarding the perceived benefits of being in the outdoors to the wellbeing of children mirror key findings from other studies (e.g. O'Brien and Murray, 2007). For instance, the parents talked about the importance of their children being independent, as this was the first time when they were away from home, their parents and their siblings. This, in turn, was perceived as character building in a holistic way, a way for children to become individuals in their own right and develop their social skills. The parents were not only concerned with the present state of their children, but also with their future and adulthood.

Interviews with the children revealed that although they were anxious about leaving their family and friends for the first time and to go to the residential outdoor centre, the support from parents and siblings helped them overcome their fears[2]:

Ann:	I wasn't really sure if I should go or not, because, at first I wasn't going to go because I didn't really want to leave my mom and dad, but then I wanted to go 'cause I looked, and my mom told me what we were going to be doing, I thought it sounded really fun and I'm glad I went now.
Ina:	What about you Kelly, how did you feel?
Kelly:	I felt excited, because I knew that the activities were really good.
Ina:	Where did you know that the activities were good? Have you been to Greenfield House before?
Pupils:	No. (all together)
Ann:	No, because our moms and dads ... 'cause they ...
Chris:	Our moms and dads told us what we were doing, and my big brother told me about it, 'cause he went back when he was in year four.
Ina:	Right.
Chris:	I was so jealous. I was nervous, and I was nervous before I went, um, and yet I was confused and excited so I looked like this, when I first got off the bus. (He stands up and makes a funny face, they all laugh.)
Ina:	Brilliant. What about you Ken?
Ken:	I was scared, excited and happy.
Charley:	At first it was like: cra-zy!
Ina:	Cra-zy, why was that?
Charley:	'Cause I didn't know ... 'Cause first, I didn't know if I could go or not.
Ina:	So how did you make the decision to go?
Charley:	'Cause my mom told me all the things, everything.
Ina:	Ken, did your parents tell you about what it would be like.
Ken:	It was my brother. 'Cause he'd been before, he said it was really good, he went to another one. 'Cause there were two Greenfield Houses. He went to the other one. And he said it was really really good, he said I should go.
Ina:	What about you Jenny?
Jenny:	Um, well my mom told me all about it, because um, when the coach came, I didn't feel scared or nothing, I just wanted to get on as quick as I could.

(Humberstone and Stan, 2011, pp. 4–5)

The children also revealed that the residential outdoor experience helped them to become more independent and more grown-up, and this is similar to their parents' views. For example, the statements below testify to this:

Jenny: I felt really happy, because I'd never been in a house without my mom. I'm so used to living with my mom.

Chris: I felt pretty happy just to get away from my annoying brother. Oooohooo!!! Freedooom! (Arms up in the air. Ann and Kelly nod in approval.)

Ken: Same as me. (He gives Chris a high five.)

Charley: I did like it 'cause you didn't get that much bossed around.

Ann: I think it helped me because, um, 'cause … to grow up a bit, because my mom said that I should go, then I would get used to going and when I get older I can go on holidays with my friends.

(Humberstone and Stan, 2011, pp. 5–6)

The children further stated that the experience allowed them to develop new friendships and reinforce existing ones, as well as teaching them how to work as a team. This matched the parents' arguments that outdoor residential experiences can enhance the children's social skills:

Kelly: I liked the low ropes because you had to work as a team.

Ann: I liked it 'cause I shared a room with my best friend.

Chris: Yeah, it helped us in our teamwork skills.

Ken: I made, um, when we were having like dinner or lunch and all that, I made a lot more friends at my table while sitting next to and stuff.

Jenny: I thought it helped me in like, um, that I could be on my own and it helped me learn about more teamwork, so I work with the group more.

Chris: It helped me learn more about teamwork and how to interact with your mates.

(Humberstone and Stan, 2011, p. 5)

Thus, the parents' positive views on outdoor learning seem to be aligned with their children's. However, while conducting participant observation at the residential outdoor centre, I was able to see that some of the children who had not been interviewed had a very different outdoor experience, which may have had a less positive impact on their learning and wellbeing.

The 'Wellbeing Project' also sought to include the perspectives of the teachers who accompanied the children at the residential outdoor centre. A strong rapport was built with the teachers (n=3), as they had participated in previous research conducted at the outdoor centre the preceding year. The teachers were interviewed individually, during the residential visit. Two teachers were female class teachers and one male teacher, the head teacher, was called Mr. Harris.

Mr. Harris' understanding of wellbeing was similar to that of the parents, in that he also considered that wellbeing entailed both the physical and mental states of the children, and had the potential to maintain the children's physical and emotional health, as well as develop their social skills. Additionally, Mr. Harris endorsed the view that outdoor learning brings an added dimension to the curriculum:

Mr. Harris: Well, the wellbeing of children probably relates to the physical and mental … state in a healthy way. Certainly the outdoor experience promotes both of these, and it's an added dimension to the curriculum …, absolutely vital.

Ina: In what way?

Mr. Harris: I think not only in terms of teambuilding and that way, in which you promote social skills, but also because they do (it does) seem that exercise and ways in which the activities are promoted at these activity centres have their role in the physical and emotional well-being, … but it's also working as a team … and I think clearly mental wellbeing is very important because the whole thing is stipulated to actually work in a way that minds work together, for the team-building exercises, which is crucial, … we find that really useful.

(Humberstone and Stan, 2009, pp. 27–28)

On a slightly different note, the two classroom teachers, Ms Kent and Ms Grey, placed a greater emphasis on how safety impacts on children's wellbeing. Furthermore, Ms Grey argued that the financial status of the parents has a great influence on children's opportunities for spending time outdoors:

Ms Kent: Well, safety and enjoyment is … the key thing … So, yeah, lots of things outdoors, but being safe and being aware of what's around you as well.

Ms Grey: Well I think … the wellbeing includes obviously protecting them, them being healthy, them having opportunities both in school and outside of school. A lot of it though, … boils down, I think, to the financial side and how much things cost outside of school. And if you're obviously wanting the children to … be more healthy and sort of play more, have more … personality and develop that way, then I think there is going to have to be a big push on how much money goes into it to support parents … And they're going to get big and all around fitness, they're going to develop obviously, … more broader experiences I suppose. But if the parents haven't usually got the money, then it's not going to happen.

(Humberstone and Stan, 2009, p. 28)

This concern for safety on the part of the teachers has been brought up in the Ofsted (2008) report, but also by Ernst (2014), as it can have a serious impact on how teachers engage with the children in the outdoors. The focus on safety may lead to an over-protective approach, which could limit opportunities for social skill development (Humberstone and Stan, 2009).

Approaches to teaching and facilitating in the outdoors

My research revealed that there were two kinds of approaches employed by the teachers/facilitators in the outdoor classroom: controlling approaches and empowering approaches (Stan, 2010a). The controlling approaches are characterised by the use of 'power-on' on the part of the teachers/facilitators in order to deprive the children of 'power-with' (Kreisberg, 1992). This kind of approach entailed engaging in practices that created limited space for dialogue and stifled the children. Empowering approaches were characterised by educational practices which went beyond pursuing intellectual and cognitive outcomes, and which considered the whole prism of human experience, i.e. the social, the emotional, the moral, the creative and the physical, thus creating a space for all of the participants to grow and become 'more fully human' (Robinson, 1994, p. 156).

Controlling approaches

Conventionally, the facilitator conducting the outdoor activity is seen as outside of the group in outdoor education, having either a position of power over the participants (Priest and Gass, 1993; Bendaly, 2000) or being detached and passive (Chapman, 1995). This may stem from the tendency for outdoor education to see learning as individualistic, rather than as socially constructed (Brookes, 2004). In Stan (2009), I argue that most of the definitions of the role of the outdoor facilitators place them outside the group that they facilitate. This is unrealistic since the facilitator has a central role in the outdoor-learning experience. Moreover, Brown (2001) argues that rather than being a 'bystander', the facilitator can be, at times, at the epicentre of power, which entails the exercise of authority (Hayllar, 2005).

Power is also present in formal education, as research on classroom interaction shows (e.g. Delamont, 1983; Pollard, 1985). Delamont (1983) sees power as an integral part of the role of the teachers, as they have control over the children's behaviour and speech. Power is often taken for granted by teachers, but it can be detrimental to the children (Pollard, 1985). Using control as an educational tool has a negative impact on the educational process, as it denies the children opportunities for learning (Stan, 2010b; Stan and Humberstone, 2011).

Some of the teachers/facilitators that participated in my research used order and instructions to impose control over the children. Teachers tended to use them in order to manage stress, by maintaining their authority and independence within the learning environment (Pollard, 1985). Thus, disciplinary and instructional goals were a way for teachers to achieve ends that were suitable for themselves. I observed this on several occasions in the outdoors, where teachers/facilitators took control over the activities, giving specific instructions to the children, and not allowing them to work independently from the adults to solve the group task. Consequently, activities that were described as team building by the outdoor centre were not completed as a team, as the adults were unable to step back and allow the children to work as a team. This can be seen in the example below, where George, one of the facilitators at the centre, is directing the children throughout the task, but becomes frustrated when his use of order and instructions proves ineffective:

George: You guys are useless, useless, you don't talk to each other, you don't listen. I say lift and you pull. You are not working as a team!

(They try again. George guides them.)

George: Girls, you let down, boys, you pull a little! Girls pull yours in! Boys, let yours out!

(They fail again.)

(Stan, 2010a, p. 16)

George also exhibited lack of self-control, while interacting with the children. Robinson (1994) highlights the importance of self-control in groups, as it is conducive to learning, where all participants learn from each other and from themselves, hence becoming empowered. A lack of self-control on the part of a teacher is disempowering and can leave the children demotivated and unwilling to participate in the activity. This happened in this example, as the children started arguing with each other and this impacted negatively on their wellbeing:

Pg1[3]: You need to release yours!
Pb1: No, I don't. (Shouting.)
Pgs: Yes, you do! (Shouting.)
Pb2: Yeah, you do!

(He releases it. … They are still fighting. [They don't seem to be able to work together.][4] George is shaking his head. He shouts at them.)

George: OK, everyone shuuuut up! Shut up! From now on you are not allowed to talk.

(He chooses a girl to direct them. They all get quiet. They listen to the girl. The boy that wouldn't release the string mumbles. [He doesn't seem to agree with her].)

(Stan, 2010a, pp.16–17)

On many occasions, the teachers adopted controlling approaches due to a great concern for the children's safety. Order and instructions were used to minimise the risk to which the children were exposed while participating. Thus, the children were unable to experience their surroundings freely, which limited opportunities for free play. There were several instances where the adults, in an attempt to ensure the children's safety, curbed the children's enthusiasm of being outside in an open space, as can be seen from the examples below:

Gary[5]:	Don't run! It's wet! (to some pupils running in front of us) … Don't run! What did I tell you about running? It's wet grass, wet grass is slippery.
Tm:	These [the checkpoints] are not going to run away, so you can take your time. You don't need to charge like lunatics. We don't want you getting hurt or stung, or anything.

(Stan and Humberstone, 2011, p. 221)

The benefits of free play far outweigh the risks, even more so when they are in an outdoor centre that provides positive risk-taking opportunities, which follow current safety requirements. Therefore the children were never in real danger during their residential outdoor visit.

Empowering approaches

Nevertheless, there were teachers/facilitators at the outdoor centre who did adopt empowering approaches to teaching in the outdoors, by allowing the children to work independently, make their own decisions regarding solving tasks and take ownership of the outdoor classroom. Such practices create a space for the children to feel that the classroom belongs to them too and not just to the teachers (Robinson, 1994). Giving choice in a classroom enables the children to satisfy their need for freedom and power (Glasser, 1990). When the children's needs are met on their own terms, it makes them feel empowered (Robinson, 1994), which inevitably benefits their wellbeing.

For example, Susan, one of the centre facilitators, appeared to be sensitive to the children's needs and was able to achieve a balance between ensuring the children's safety and offering sufficient cognitive and physical challenge to stimulate them. During the activity, even though Susan appeared detached, she seemed interested in the children's interactions. I observed Susan intervening only when needed, and engaging the children in open dialogue and reflective thinking:

Susan:	Ok guys, how did you think you did as a team?
Ps:	Good!
Susan:	From one to five.
Ps:	Four.
Susan:	Ok, you said four. That means that you feel you could improve something. What is that?
Ps:	Communication.
Susan:	What does that entail?
Pbs:	Listening, talking more.
Pgs:	More planning.

(Stan, 2010a, pp. 17–18)

Reflection was an important aspect of the empowering outdoor-learning experience, as it encouraged the children to think about what they have learned, and express their thoughts and feelings. Thorburn in Chapter 2 also highlights the importance of reflection for children's wellbeing. The following example illustrates how a female teacher reviewed the activity with the children and in doing so, identified herself as part of the group, by using pronouns like 'we' and 'us', which shows that she perceived learning as socially constructed, rather than individualistic:

Tf: We learned a lot! I learned a heck of a lot!
Pb1: We worked as a team, it was good!
Pb2: The teamwork slipped up.
Tf: So what happens when the team splits up?
Pb2: We argue and we cannot concentrate!
Tf: What else happened that we didn't like?
Ps: Mocking, arguing.
Ps: Blaming.
Tf: So how does it make us feel when we are blamed?
Pb3: We feel really bad!
Tf: We have to work as a team, we are a team at school, at work, in life!'

(Stan, 2009, pp. 37–38)

Another example that highlights the importance of engaging children in reflection through open dialogue took place after a group of children conducted the low ropes course (an outdoor obstacle course). The facilitator invited the children to evaluate their performance during the activity, asking them to explain and justify their own evaluation:

Lucy: Ok, what I need everybody to do, is to find a twig, maybe a leaf, a stone. Ok, now you're going to hate me, but I want everyone to sit on the floor.

(They all sit in the circle).

Pb1: John,[6] do you want to come in?
J: No, I'm good.
Lucy: Oh, that's very nice (to the child who invited John). I'm going to put this in the middle of our circle. That is our Hex in the middle. What you need to do is to place what you've got, where you think. So if you've been perfect and you don't need to change anything, than put it in the middle. If you think you were ok, but you could improve some things, you can put it a bit further. Then you will have to explain why you put it in there.
Pg1: I did well, but there could be some adjustments.
Lucy: You put it all the way over there, why?
Pg1: I kept on falling off.
Lucy: But other than that, how did you do. I think you did pretty well, 'cause you waited for others. Ahmed, where are you? You're quite in the middle. How did you do? (To another boy).
Pb2: Like my balance was not very good.
Lucy: Where are you?

Pb3:   Where? (He points where he is).

Lucy: So pretty close. Do you know what you did well? (Boy shakes his head.) You don't know. Guys, what did he do well? Did he help you or did he push you?

Pb4:   Yeah!

Lucy: No, he helped you, didn't he? (To another boy). Ok, you're right on top.

Pb5:   Because I did teamwork, I helped everyone.

Lucy: Yeah, you did very well! I agree with you.

Pb5:   I was a team leader.

Pb6:   Good team work!

Pb5:   Yeah, good teamwork, but not so good at balancing.

Pb6:   I kept on falling off.

Pb4:   But you were a really good team worker.

Pb6:   Yeah, but I kept falling off.

Pb4:   Yeah, but you were pretty good.

Pg2:   I kept falling off. (She placed herself far away from the centre)

Lucy: But you did well?

Pb5:   In my view, Eve should be there (placing it close to the centre), 'cause she was really good, helping others.

Lucy: Does everyone agree?

Ps: Yeah!

Pb1:   I think we got better all the way.

Lucy: Right, does everyone think they've improved.

Ps: Yeah!

Lucy: All the time you're here, you need to think about team work.

(Fieldwork I, pp. 81–88)

Through dialogue and interactive practices, the children are encouraged to work together and build upon the answers of others (Alexander, 2004). In the examples above, learning is constructed between the children and the teacher, through dialogic talk. Reciprocity is essential, as the children and the teachers/facilitators listen to each other, share ideas and consider various points of view. The process is collective, but also cumulative with the teacher and the children building on their own and each other's ideas, creating coherent lines of enquiry. The discussions between the learners and the teacher are purposeful, as they have a specific educational goal. All this is done in a supportive atmosphere, where pupils can freely express themselves and help each other to reach a common understanding.

Future directions

In conclusion, it appears that simply providing well-planned outdoor activities for children is not enough, even if they are well embedded in the curriculum. The way these activities are delivered has a significant impact on the children's wellbeing, as 'well-planned' and 'inspiring' activities do not necessarily guarantee the desired outcome (Dickson, 2005). When teachers adopt a controlling approach in the outdoors, many of the benefits are lost, and consequently children's wellbeing is negatively impacted. Conversely, empowering approaches in the outdoors lead to personal growth and contribute to the children's holistic wellbeing, as they engage them in challenging physical and cognitive activities. This chapter has taken a critical view of outdoor learning, by making references to notions of power and control and how they impact on teaching in the outdoor classroom. More research is needed which provides an insight into the children's outdoor experience and enables the emergence of democratic and social understanding of the teaching process from a critical perspective. Children's perceptions also need to be considered, rather than assumed, and they need to be contextualised within the broader theoretical and social milieu.

Summary of key findings

- Research demonstrates the benefits of being in the outdoors for the mental and physical wellbeing of children and young people.
- The participants' perspectives on wellbeing support these research findings, but this chapter also provided the parents' and children's understanding of wellbeing and how outdoor learning can contribute to children's personal growth.
- A detailed analysis of the teaching approaches in the outdoor classroom revealed that controlling approaches suppress children's development and thus are detrimental to their wellbeing.
- Empowering approaches are better suited to engage children in outdoor learning and allow them to improve as human beings. This positively benefits their wellbeing.

Reflective tasks

- What would be the key aspects to consider when planning an outdoor activity that is linked to the school curriculum?
- How could the effectiveness of such an activity be evaluated?
- To what extent can the findings of this chapter influence your teaching practice in the outdoors?

Notes

1 P stands for pupil, g stands for girl, and b stands for boy. The numbers indicate that different pupils were talking.
2 All the names of the participants are pseudonyms.
3 P stands for pupil, g stands for girl and b stands for boy. The s indicates the plural. The numbers indicate the different pupils.
4 Comments in square brackets are my interpretation in the field.
5 Gary was one of the facilitators at the centre and Tm stands for male teacher.
6 John was a 15-year-old student doing his work experience at the outdoor centre.

Further readings

Alexander, R.J. (2004). *Towards Dialogic Teaching: Rethinking Classroom Talk*. Cambridge: Dialogus.

Rea, T., & Waite, S. (2009) International Perspectives on Outdoor and Experiential Learning, Editorial, *Education 3–13, Special edition*, 37 (1), 1–4.

Robinson, H.A. (1994) *The Ethnography of Empowerment: The Transformative Power of Classroom Interaction*. Washington, D.C.: The Falmer Press.

References

Alexander, R.J. (2004). *Towards Dialogic Teaching: Rethinking Classroom Talk*. Cambridge: Dialogus.

Bendaly, L. (2000). *The Facilitation Skills Training Kit*. New York: McGraw-Hill.

Brookes, A. (2004). Astride a Long-Dead Horse. Mainstream Outdoor Education Theory and the Central Curriculum Problem, *Australian Journal of Outdoor Education*, 8(2), 22–33.

Brown, M. (2001). *What does a close reading of interaction tell us about how we conduct facilitation sessions?* The 12th National Outdoor Education Conference: Education Outdoors – Our Sense of Place Proceedings (pp. 109–126). La Trobe University, Bendigo, Victoria.

Chapman, S. (1995). 'What is the question?' In K. Warren, M. Sakofs & J. Hunt, Jr. (Eds.), *The Theory of Experiential Education* (pp. 236–239). Dubuque: Kendall/Hunt.

Chawla, L., Keena, K., Pevec, I., & Stanley, E. (2014). Green Schoolyards as Havens from Stress and Resources for Resilience in Childhood and Adolescence, *Health and Place*, 28, 1–13.

Delamont, S. (1983). *Interaction in the Classroom: Contemporary Sociology of the School*. London: Methuen.

Dickson, T. (2005). "Deconstructing 'The five generations of facilitated learning from adventure experiences'". In T.J. Dickson, T. Gray & B. Hayllar (Eds.), *Outdoor and Experiential Learning: Views from the Top*, (pp. 230–239). Dunedin: Otago University Print.

Downer, J., Rimm-Kaufman, S., & Pianta, R. (2007). How Do Classroom Conditions and Children's Risk for School Problems Contribute to Children's Behavioral Engagement in Learning? *School Psychology Review*, 36(3), 413–432.

Ebberling, C., Pawlak, D., & Ludwig, D. (2002). Childhood Obesity; Public Health Crisis, Common Sense Cure, *Lancet*, 360, 473–482.

Eick, C.J. (2012). Use of the Outdoor Classroom and Nature-study to Support Science and Literacy Learning: A Narrative Case Study of a Third-grade Classroom, *Journal of Science Teacher Education*, 23, 789–803. Retrieved from http://www.tandfonline.com/doi/full/10.1007/s10972-011-9236-1

Ernst, J. (2014). Early Childhood Educators' Use of Natural Outdoor Settings As Learning Environments: An Exploratory Study of Beliefs, Practices, and Barriers, *Environmental Education Research*, 20(6), 735–752. Retrieved from http://www.tandfonline.com/doi/full/10.1080/13504622.2013.833596

Fjortoft, I. (2001). The Natural Environment as a Playground for Children: The Impact of Outdoor Play Activities in Pre-Primary School Children, *Early Childhood Education Journal*, 29(2), 111–117.

Fjortoft, I. (2004). Landscape as Playscape: The Effects of Natural Environments on Children's Play and Motor Development, *Children, Youth and Environments*, 14(9), 21–44.

Glasser, W. (1990). *Quality School*. New York: Harper and Row.

Hayllar, B. (2005). 'Leadership and facilitation'. In T.J. Dickson, T. Gray & B. Hayllar (Eds.), *Outdoor and Experiential Learning – Views from the Top* (pp. 179–183). Dunedin: Otago University Print.

Humberstone, B., & Stan, I. (2009). Well-being and Outdoor Pedagogies in Primary Schooling, *Australian Journal of Outdoor Education, 13*(2), 24–32.

Humberstone, B., & Stan, I. (2011). Outdoor Learning: Primary Pupils' Experiences and Teachers' Interaction in Outdoor Learning, *Education 3–13: International Journal of Primary, Elementary and Early Years Education,* Retrieved from http://www.tandfonline.com/doi/full/10.1080/03004279.2010.487837

Jacobi-Vessels, J. L. (2013). Discovering Nature: The Benefits of Teaching Outside of the Classroom, *Dimensions of Early Childhood, 41*(3), 4–10.

Korpela, K.M., & Hartig, T. (1996). Restorative Qualities of Favorite Places, *Journal of Environmental Psychology, 16,* 221–223.

Kreisberg, S. (1992). *Transforming Power: Domination, Empowerment and Education.* New York: State University of New York.

Muños, S. (2009). *Children in the Outdoors: A Literature Review.* Forres: Sustainable Development Research Centre.

O'Brien, L., & Murray, R. (2007). 'Forest School' in England: An Evaluation of Three Case Study Settings, *Environmental Education,* Spring, 8–9.

O'Brien, L., William, K., & Stewart, A. (2010). *Urban health and health inequalities and the role of urban forestry in Britain: A review.* Report to the Forestry Commission. Retrieved from http://www.forestry.gov.uk/pdf/urban_health_and_forestry_review_2010.pdf/$FILE/urban_health_and_forestry_review_2010.pdf

Ofsted. (2008). *Learning outside of the classroom: How far should you go?* Retrieved from http://www.lotc.org.uk/wp-content/uploads/2010/12/Ofsted-Report-Oct-2008.pdf

Pollard, A. (1985). *The Social World of the Primary School.* London: Holt, Rinehart & Winston.

Priest, S., & Gass, M.A. (1993). Five Generations of Facilitated Learning from Adventure Experiences, *Journal of Adventure Education and Outdoor Leadership, 10*(3), 23–25.

Rea, T., & Waite, S. (2009). International Perspectives on Outdoor and Experiential Learning, Editorial, *Education 3-13, Special edition, 37*(1), 1–4.

Rickinson, M., Dillon, J., Team, K., Morris, M., Young Choi, M., Sanders, D., & Benefield, P. (2004). *A Review of Research on Outdoor Learning.* London: National Foundation for Educational Research and King's College London.

Robinson, H.A. (1994). *The Ethnography of Empowerment: The Transformative Power of Classroom Interaction.* Washington, D.C.: The Falmer Press.

Sandseter, E.B.H. (2009). Characteristics of Risky Play, *Journal of Adventure Education and Outdoor Learning, 9*(1), 3–22.

Stan, I. (2009). Recontextualising the Role of the Facilitator in Group Interaction in the Outdoor Classroom, *Journal of Adventure Education and Outdoor Learning, 9*(1), 23–43.

Stan, I. (2010a). *Group Interaction in the 'Outdoor Classroom': The Process of Learning in Outdoor Education.* Saarbrücken: VDM Verlag.

Stan, I. (2010b). Control as an Educational Tool and Its Impact on the Outdoor Educational Process, *Australian Journal of Outdoor Education, 14*(2), 12–20.

Stan, I., & Humberstone, B. (2011). An Ethnography of the Outdoor Classroom – How Teachers Manage Risk in the Outdoors, *Ethnography and Education, 6*(2), 213–228.

Sustainable Development Commission. (2008). *Health, place and nature. How outdoor environments influence health and well-being: A knowledge base.* Retrieved from http://www.sdcommission.org.uk/data/files/publications/Outdoor environments_and_health.pdf

Tunnicliffe, S.D. (2008). Children's Understanding of the Natural World – Ponds, *Environmental Education,* Summer, 16–28.

USDA Forest Service. (2001). Trees for children: Helping inner city children get a better start in life', *Technology Bulletin 7*. Retrieved from http://www.sactree.com/assets/files/greenprint/benefits_of_trees/social_psychological_community/KidsTreesTechBulletin7.pdf

Waite, S., Davis, B., & Brown, K. (2006). *Final Report: Current Practice and Aspirations for Outdoor Learning for 2–11 Year Olds in Devon*. Plymouth: University of Plymouth.

Wells, N.M. (2000). At Home with Nature: Effects of 'Greenness' on Children's Cognitive Functioning, *Environment and Behavior, 32*(6), 775–795.

12

WELLBEING AND AESTHETIC IMAGINATION

Christine Doddington

Introduction

While some aspects of education have the appearance of being constant, much of what constitutes education in the form of schooling is subject to change. Over time, schooling has faced a wide range of political and social demands and what children and students actually experience as *their* education has often been dramatically steered and shaped in the face of these demands. In recent years, the demand for a country's economic stability and progress has dominated the changes faced by many education systems across the globe. Desirable characteristics for a future workforce have filtered into and adapted the educational experience of both students and educators alike. This, in part, explains current shifts in the perceived value of certain subjects, prioritising the sciences above the arts, for example, or increasing the presence of technology within the curriculum. Accountable measures to ensure that these kinds of demands are met and to confirm that changes are bedded into practice include legislation, inspection and increased assessment in schools.

While political and social demands can result in concrete changes to the experienced curriculum, visions of what is needed to maintain or increase the economic prowess of a nation can also generate more pervasive and subtle shifts in schooling. So calls for education to produce independent thinkers, resilient competitors or creative collaborators, might generate less explicit change. The effects are there but are often more generally felt on the values that dominate the experience of schooling. Since the character and experience of one's education can profoundly influence both the persons we become and the society that is formed, demands of this nature obviously touch upon but are less explicitly tied to, the world of work and economic progress. And it is here we might find demands that call for education to generate certain values, for example to enhance the inclusivity of society or increase the wellbeing of individuals.

Clarity about what is meant by any of these kinds of aspirations is then vital in order to determine in more detail how the very process and day-to-day educational experience can be designed responsively to any particular context, and thus help schools travel in the desired direction. But it is not just the change in educational activity or practice that matters; strong conviction and commitment of those directly involved – the main designers, actors and directors is also important to ensure daily practice reflects those values.[1] In other words, educators need to believe in the worth of these aspirations and learners themselves need to understand and become committed to them too. Aspirations of this nature need to be carefully conceptualised and, if they are to be fully embraced, supported by sound and persuasive argument.

Previous chapters have illustrated the complexity of conceptualising wellbeing but in this section of the book, we look to the future, beyond current international education systems that are fashioned around performativity and prescriptive patterns of learning. Just as wellbeing cannot be generated by, nor restricted to, what happens in schooling, what follows is based on arguing for a view of living well generally and will thus call on examples from everyday living as well as examples from education. This chapter then explores the idea of why an aesthetic and imaginative approach to life might lead towards increased wellbeing, and if this kind of approach to life can do this, asks what this might mean for education, and thus, schooling.

Much will hang on how we conceptualise the terms 'aesthetic' and 'imagination'. These are both rich and complex terms that offer a wide variety of interpretations. I intend to follow a pragmatist view and suggest why this view has particular pertinence for wellbeing, for education and for how we might move to change education in the future. Many of the previous chapters are able to draw on empirical forms of educational research to present their main findings in support of their claims concerning wellbeing. Rather than setting out findings in this sense, this chapter looks to the future through particular conceptualisation, supported by the scholarship of others whose work is largely philosophical. The following section therefore invites you, the reader, to follow the lines of thought as they are presented, to enlarge your understanding but also to actively, critically engage with the argument. This amounts to an invitation to read the next section less to gain new knowledge but more to engage in philosophical thinking as you consider and evaluate the worth and the strength of the claim and supporting argument, that the aesthetic imagination should be seen as a constituent of wellbeing.

Main argument

A Deweyan perspective on wellbeing – what constitutes a flourishing life?

In an earlier chapter, Claire Cassidy asks us to make the useful distinction between 'being' well and 'becoming' well. Her argument is that in education, we should avoid thinking that wellbeing is a desirable state only for a child's future, with school preparing the ground for generating that state. My metaphor of travelling in the light of aspirations may appear to fall into this assumption. But, since I also agree with Cassidy's suggestion that schooling should prioritise a child's current state of 'being', a closer look at how I am using the notion of wellbeing as a form of flourishing is necessary. My argument needs the idea of wellbeing or a flourishing life, to capture both living in the present and what it might mean to live well throughout life.

In much of his prolific philosophical writing, John Dewey was concerned to articulate the idea of human and societal flourishing. At the time his writing was first published, America was struggling with economic pressures and with holding together a society formed of many different cultures. Dewey identified an urgent need to find ways for individuals to live well together, in association with one another, despite differences. This was his meaning of what it was for a society to become democratic. Profoundly influenced by the idea of evolution, he observed that people, like all sentient beings, are never 'fixed' or finalised in their physical, cultural or psychological development but always continue to live by adaptation to their surroundings and situations. Because of this, he believed that communities and society as a whole, with all its multiplicity, are also capable of evolving. Thus he argued that it is desirable that change in both society and individuals should be progressive i.e. towards a better state. This is why he developed his strong focus on education, believing it to be the most central and powerful opportunity for supporting progressive growth in both individuals and society. Yet, as a pragmatist, Dewey is also focused strongly on the value of experience, and makes some important and careful distinctions: 'It is not enough to insist upon the necessity of experience, nor even of activity in experience. Everything depends upon the quality of experience which is had' (Dewey, 1938/1997, p. 27).

Experience is a constant feature of living but it is only in certain distinctive kinds of experience that progression, development or, as Dewey terms it, growth, can happen. While growth happens through and during experience with particular qualities, this kind of experience, with its opportunities for growth, can be a normal feature of life available in the present and is also something to aspire to. It is in this sense that 'growth' in experience functions simultaneously as both the 'means' and 'ends' in life and in education. Thus we can say that, for Dewey, continued 'growth' is a significant feature for existing 'well', it is the mark of a rich, ongoing, flourishing life that is worth aspiring to.

There have been many attempts to critically evaluate or excavate Dewey's complex and, some would say, vague idea of growth. The most salient questions from critics ask 'growth into what?' But despite the need for growth to be ongoing, Dewey is clear that the form of growth he is advocating cannot be prescriptive and is not pre-programmed in nature, as in the bulb that matures into the tulip. In humans, what constitutes progressive and beneficial growth in each individual cannot be precisely predetermined and standardised. If we are to judge whether educational experiences are valuable because they contribute towards growth Dewey suggests we have to ask: 'Does this form of growth create conditions for further growth or does it set up conditions that shut off the person … from the occasions, stimuli and opportunities for continuing growth in new directions' (Dewey, 1938/1997, p. 36).

The sense in which growth has to be open-ended fits well with a non-standardised view of wellbeing.

> Prescription of the ends of a conception of on-going human flourishing is highly problematic – how would we go about pre-determining the sensibilities necessary for someone … to engage, relish and pursue further experiences that deepen and expand their sense of their existence?
>
> *(Doddington, 2014, p. 45)*

Some educationalists have translated Dewey's notions of growth and experience into creating in children an open love for learning or a strengthened curiosity about the world. These readings capture a large part of what Dewey is after and are clearly related to the universal motivation in evolutionary thinking, often found in pragmatist views of learning, that attaches value to the seeking out and solving of problems. However, I am suggesting that wellbeing and satisfaction in life require a broader appetite than problem solving. Our experiences radically affect what we wish to continue to experience. Whether we want it or not, 'every experience lives on in further experiences' (Dewey, 1938/1997, p. 27). So in terms of education Dewey explains 'Every experience' (worthy of the title educative), 'should do something to prepare a person for later experiences of a deeper and more expansive quality. That is the very meaning of growth, continuity, reconstruction of experience' (Dewey, 1938/1997, p. 47).

Growth therefore occurs not simply through the hedonistic pleasure of enjoyable experiences but by experience that has continuity, drawing on previous experience and looking forward, thus creating a continuing desire to expand and deepen one's experience of life. If our aspiration is wellbeing and we follow Dewey, I suggest we are looking at qualities of experience that allow us to continue to expand our abilities and deepen our understanding and interests by giving us a zest for living in all aspects of life. As Kristjánsson (2016b, p. 713) remarks of Maslow's influential work: 'Maslow believed that in order to fully actualise their potential, human beings needed to activate their Dionysian side as well as their Apollonian one'. The very top of his pyramid thus includes ecstatic 'peak experiences'. So, for Dewey, the most precious thing we can gift to children through their education is to intensify this desire for continuity in growth through experience:

> If impetus in this direction is weakened instead of being intensified, we don't just fail in preparing someone for the future – we actually rob them of natural capacities that, if strengthened, would enable someone to become self-sufficient and resilient to cope with the circumstances that person might meet in the course of their life.
>
> *(Dewey, 1938/1997, p. 48)*

What part does aesthetics play in wellbeing?

If we accept that one conception of wellbeing could be having a life offering rich experience that generates an appetite for life and growing, we need to explain how the aesthetic dimension of our lives helps to distinguish those kinds of experiences. While the arts offer the most obvious examples of experiences that call strongly upon our aesthetic sense (and I will return to consideration of the arts at a later stage), the arts do not encompass the full extensive nature of living, nor are they, of course, the sole means of schooling. We need a broader perspective on how aesthetics might feature in wellbeing. We have aesthetic experience and make aesthetic judgements continually in our everyday lives quite apart from works of art. An exhilarating morning walk, a pleasurable meal with friends or appreciation of a modern building are all experiences that will involve some sense of the aesthetic. And beyond separate episodes or events, Peter Abbs makes the point that aesthetic sensibility is the primary feature of how we live and exist in the world:

> Nearly all the early shaping responses of human life are aesthetic in character, bringing through pleasure, pain or a diffuse sense of well-being, intimations of the nature of our common world. Long before we are rational beings, we are aesthetic beings; and we remain so, though often undeveloped and unsubtle, till ultimate insensibility defines the end of individual life. For death, in the precise words of Philip Larkin, administers 'the anaesthetic from which none come round'.
>
> *(Abbs, 1989, p. 4)*

Saito (2007) in her book entitled *Everyday Aesthetics* also discusses the limitations of art-centered aesthetics and her book as a whole tries to show how design and our everyday aesthetic tastes and judgements can have a powerful influence on the state of society, our quality of life and the world as a whole. And despite the title, if we return to Dewey's later work, *Art as Experience* (1934/2005) we find Dewey has begun to integrate the idea of the 'aesthetic' into the very heart of his notion of enriching experience. Indeed he states that: 'we might say that esthetic experience is pure experience' and he suggests it is 'To esthetic experience, then, the philosopher must go to understand what experience is' (Dewey, 1934/2005, p. 286).

As part of his argument for the value of seeing experience as based in our aesthetic nature, Dewey uses the term 'sense' in its full range of different meaning. This then includes use of the senses, general sensitivity to others and how we can seek out sense. In an attempt to point out the extent to which we can experience life in ways that do not require us to be fully present or fully engaged in finding meaning, Dewey cites how a mundane life or an over-crowded, rushed life *limits* our opportunities to grow through experience. This form of frantic or dull living signals that our aesthetic awareness is largely absent, with the results that 'We see without feeling; we hear, but only a second-hand report ... we touch, but the contact remains tangential because it does not fuse with qualities of senses that go below the surface' (Dewey, 1934/2005, p. 21).

It is a very small step to turn this statement into a comment on how some students presently experience schooling. The demands of pace, time limits, feelings of boredom and the purpose of learning reduced to passing tests, are all likely to rob schooling of opportunities where the aesthetic could characterise educational experience. However the worth of aesthetic experience needs a stronger account to persuade us that education needs to change to embrace it for wellbeing.

Scholars such as Thomas Alexander, Richard Shusterman and David Granger have recently returned to Deweyan aesthetics to offer fresh interpretations of the way in which life experience generally has significant aesthetic dimensions. To appreciate this we need a little more understanding from Dewey. Their arguments rest on Dewey's idea of both 'undergoing' and 'doing' as the significant features of experience. In his explanations of what constitutes experience, Dewey highlights the need for receptivity to our environment and any situation in which we find ourselves for it is this that simultaneously allows for our full entry, our active engagement or participation in that situation and therefore our sense of directly 'experiencing' that place, episode or event. The degree to which we are able to both be open and responsive is related to our general aesthetic awareness. And here it is important to remind ourselves of the emphasis on the body in Dewey and which Richard Shusterman has developed in his work in Somaesthetics (Shusterman, 2008). Unlike the dualism so prevalent in philosophies that assume a mind/body divide, when Dewey speaks of experience, he is always speaking of fully embodied experience. As well as physical sensation in terms of seeing, touching or hearing what is happening in experiences, we have sensibilities that are less literally sense-based, such as when we speak of 'reading' situations or 'sensing' the moods of others. The suggestion here is that beyond a mere passive 'undergoing' of an experience, by perhaps simply registering sensation, for example, we participate and create our own experience by action that helps us to make *sense* of what happens to us. Dewey is arguing that the motivation to create sense wherever we find ourselves is ultimately a drive to find or make *meaning* in what we experience. Wellbeing is a feature of a person's life where there is a desire to continue having experiences that are meaningful and have value for that person. Granger (2006, p. 3) explains this line of Dewey's thinking thus:

> In highlighting the many benefits of learning how to explore and appreciate the rich and variegated tapestry of everyday experience in all of its colours, contours and dimensions, Dewey's aesthetics actively nurtures what Alexander has fittingly dubbed 'the human *eros*': the native impulse to live life with an ever-expanding sense of meaning and value.

Dewey asks us to understand the nature of truly educational experience by looking more closely at what happens when we speak of 'an experience'. By this he means those occasions which have a pervasive, qualitative 'feel' that is discernable throughout the course of the experience and gives it coherence and a sense of unity. These are experiences that stand out for us and have a shape to them. We could think here of a powerful encounter with a work of art but also maybe, a sustained discussion with a friend or, in an educational context, a visit to a historically significant building, or even what Maslow described as 'peak experiences' (Kristjánsson, 2016b, p. 713). These may not always be positive experiences (Dewey cites a quarrel, for example) but they are consummatory experiences in which every part integrates and blends freely into what follows and they feel out of the ordinary run of experience. Furthermore, they leave a residue with us and can profoundly influence us into the future. The most dramatic of these kinds of special experiences will stand out because of their immediacy – striking qualities felt aesthetically and fully somatically, but also because they contribute to a new or restructured understanding of ourselves or our understanding of the world, including others. They are transformative. This transformational capacity therefore does not lie solely in the characteristics of the object, person or building but also in the 'work' that the encounter calls from us, internal activity that we might call work of the aesthetic imagination.

Wellbeing and the significance of the imagination

Dewey is clear that 'Esthetic experience is imaginative'. And 'all *conscious* experience has of necessity some degree of imaginative quality' (Dewey, 1934/2005, p. 283). Before we consider what all this might mean for schooling, a non-educative example might serve to explain how the aesthetic imagination comes to feature in real-life experience. We can manage this by thinking of an example of a memorable experience. If we find ourselves caught in the midst of a sudden storm it is easy to see how this might give us sensations, feelings and emotions, causing us to live in the moment and feel all the reality of being present. But as well as the immediate sensations of exposure and of emotion, maybe exhilaration or maybe fear, we might find thoughts entering our mind to help to give meaning to, or to reconcile our condition. These thoughts could be what we already know about how storms occur and could include the possibilities of what could happen imminently (to us, to the surrounding environment, to others). We might recall previous experience of turbulent weather and times when we found ourselves exposed to the elements, then of how we were able to return to safety. Or we might recall others' accounts of associated experiences, including tales, films or images we have seen. This entering of thought or things 'called to mind' in our conscious experience, are all the work of the imagination and they serve to make sense of this experience and give it meaning. Provoked by sensation but more fully experienced through imagination and the need to give meaning to what is happening, is what allows us to label this an *aesthetic* experience, according to Dewey. He stresses that, 'Imagination is the only gateway through which these meanings can find their way into a present interaction' (Dewey, 1934/2005, p. 283).

Educational implications

Let us now see what this account of an aesthetic experience might tell us about the qualities of educational experience that could help to cultivate wellbeing. If we start with Dewey's own account of what mitigates against the aesthetic there are clear parallels for school but we need to press further with a series of questions. What is it that teachers can actually do? What is it that students need? What could policy makers learn? I have split the next section under a number of headings to consider how aspects of aesthetic experience, including the imaginative dimension, might be supported in educational contexts. Under these headings I select features of experience that can help cultivate aesthetic experience in school contexts and finish with a brief consideration of literature and the arts.

Finding meaning

The role that Dewey gives imagination as the gateway for all meaning to enter into a situation is fundamental to our account of experience for wellbeing. A stress on the aesthetic, experiential aspects, with students asked to use their imagination within a history lesson for example, can help that lesson become more meaningful. Some schools already approach history in this way, by using the handling of artifacts or drama to re-enact historical events which help to bring that chosen episode and the study of history alive in the classroom. Similarly, some schools will arrange visits to actual locations to increase historical, geographical or scientific understanding, with the same ambition of making this knowledge come alive. Dewey argues that much of school subject knowledge is necessarily distant and remote from the present lives of students and we could agree that this is still the case, particularly to the extent that curriculum knowledge is seen as purposeful only in terms of exams. The research of William Damon, cited by Kristjánsson (2016a, 2016b) gives a perspective on students' views of school work and the extent to which they saw the work as meaningful. The research involved surveying over 1200 young people between the ages of 12 and 26 with a quarter of these being interviewed in depth. Of the cohort surveyed, only one-fifth of young people claimed that they felt their learning had clear meaning and purpose. Thus, the majority tried to find some meaning in what they were doing, while only a quarter of young people reported complete disengagement, or finding no meaning in the work undertaken.

To be meaningful, however, an education cannot just rely on what students can personally experience, for personal experience to be '*enlarged*' and '*deepened*' and '*widened*' (Dewey, 1916/1966, p. 232). This means that students need meaningful access to the rich areas of known experience of others and this requires a sophisticated form of mediation on the teachers' part if they are to encourage students to find meaning by imaginatively connecting their present experience with what is not *actually* present. The solution is not as straightforward as it may first appear, since it is not just achieved by introducing activities into a lesson or pointing out how knowledge is relevant to real-life situations. From our discussion of aesthetic sensibility we can argue that students have to be responsive to be able to participate in meaning-making and will need to feel safe to be truly open to experience in this way. Engaging responsively in any activity needs to be a regular and familiar way of how they experience being taught and students need to be encouraged and happy to work out connections from their own experience for themselves. If the teacher is focused primarily on the students finding new knowledge *meaningful*, she will need to plan for this. In practice, the teacher needs those sensitivities, capacity for judgement and even defined procedures to be able to ascertain the extent to which the students are alive to the activity and are finding it meaningful. So one criterion for whether teaching encourages wellbeing from this perspective would be to ask whether there are opportunities to hear what meanings the students have made of their experiences. This implies that the teacher is interested in students expressing the genuine meaning they have made rather than the trite re-iteration of a stipulated learning objective.

This kind of educational experience may be far removed from what students at present experience in schools. In his account of flourishing as an aim of education, Kristjánsson (2016a, p. 12) states 'It is almost a truism that for many students school work fails to become a flourishing-instantiating activity simply because it does not carry meaning for them. Instead, they become ensnared by anxiety, emptiness or apathy'. My suggestion here is that by focusing on expanding students' ability to make meaning throughout their school experience is crucial to wellbeing. However, as previously suggested, while 'finding meaning' is likely to be a precondition for wellbeing, we must see it as 'a necessary but not sufficient condition of flourishing' Kristjánsson (2016a, p. 9).

The place of knowledge

If personal, direct experiences are to be '*enlarged*' and '*deepened*' and '*widened*' (Dewey, 1916/1966, p. 232) by accessing established knowledge, this will add to the wellbeing of students to the extent that knowledge comes 'alive' to them and nourishes an appetite for seeking out further expansive and educative experience, including but not exclusively, acquiring knowledge. We have looked at examples from history teaching, but this enlivening need not only be with certain subjects or knowledge presented within strict discipline boundaries. We might want to suggest that in the search for meaning, the imagination knows no such subject boundaries. If the main focus is to find meaning, make sense or allow what is known to touch experience in the present, the role that knowledge can play needs further consideration and exemplification. In other words, how might students be active so that recognisable knowledge can enter their lived experience, helping to transform it beyond mere activity and therefore make it meaningful?

Let us consider a group of eager 5-year-old children with their helpers and teacher going outside their classroom and making an expedition to a local spinney. There are few observable signs of traditional teaching in this 'outing' and no specific learning objectives have been announced to the children. Instead, perhaps there is a general suggestion to 'see what you can find that's interesting'. Perhaps the children carry small empty bags, for previous experience tells them that they can look for and collect small items during their expedition. For an hour the children explore and play, sometimes together, sometimes alone and occasionally they initiate interaction with an adult. They come together for a warm drink, talk and rest, and then simply resume their independent and shared play and activity without further guidance. How could recognisable knowledge impinge on this form of experience for the children?

The location and the children's activities have obvious features that could resource traditional school knowledge. The physical environment, with its vegetation, trees or wildlife might call on natural scientific knowledge as the children find, observe and appreciate spiders and their webs, or test the strength of trees or examine the rotting habitat of leaves. Mathematics might happen, with the playful counting and arranging of stones, the discerning of shapes and patterns and stepped measurements between trees. Artistic experience is also possible, with the drawing of shapes in the mud, the dancing of steps and jumps to rhythms, the beating of sticks on a hollow trunk to make sound patterns. And finally there could be many linguistic and fictional opportunities, with conversations, questions and the imaginative telling of stories.

These then are valuable actions that might bring knowledge alive into the present. They require aesthetic discernment and awareness along with the imagination to go beyond the actual into the realm of possibility. Resources such as dried twigs are not just ignored and left lying. Once noticed, they can be handled and their possibilities imagined. They might be held and examined closely, collected as witch's fingers or lined up and counted. Each child will take different meanings away from this experience depending on what they sensed and imagined. In true pragmatic thought, we might add that some will want to enquire further – wanting to find out why twigs have gnarled bumps on them, for example. But others will make overall sense of their expedition through expression – narrating the story of what they are doing, as they do it, or telling of the crocodile that lives deep in the pond. Recapturing the experience back in the classroom the children might mould the clay that is available to look like footprints they made or begin to paint the tree they climbed. These expressive activities all help to make the experience meaningful through what children imagine and can bring to the experience.

There is obvious opportunity here for the teacher to introduce aspects of standardised knowledge through telling or showing, her questioning or structuring of the activity. However, if personal meaning for the children is the aim, involvement of the teacher as mediator needs sensitivity to ensure this is not done at the expense of the children's own aesthetic and imaginative experience. The stress on the direct aesthetic nature of their experiencing is equally as vital as the imagination that allows for reflection and the drawing-in of knowledge to that experience. Too much of the latter, at the expense of the former can easily reduce the possibility of meaning-making. The teacher in a situation with children such as this will, therefore, also need aesthetic awareness and her imagination to see all these possibilities and maintain the space for the children to make their own meaning out of the experience.

This 'expedition' drawn from early years' practice is designed to show how 'an' experience, requires knowledge to be available and its traditional boundaries to be flexible and porous for meaning-making. The principle of porous boundaries for the sake of meaning is, however, applicable to any age. XP, a South Yorkshire school recently reported in a British newspaper,[2] has abandoned a subject-based curriculum in favour of projects or, as they pertinently call them, 'expeditions'. The headteacher, claims that as a result, the curriculum is more 'engaging' and the school's prospectus speaks of aiming for an 'academically rigorous curriculum with deep, visceral experiences'. 'Purposeful fieldwork' and 'long, engaged learning expeditions' addressing 'real world issues and problems' that are mapped carefully to the National Curriculum to ensure that content is still covered.[3] The newspaper article sets this example in the context of moves by the Finnish Board of Education which has introduced a new school curriculum for secondary-aged pupils that emphasises 'the joy of learning'. The Finnish curriculum has reduced subject content and required coverage is replaced by 'competences' with the proposal that these might best be achieved through projects that draw on cross-curricular knowledge. These examples might all be seen as indicative of schooling still focused on attainment, progress and knowledge but with approaches that are aiming for the kind of engagement I have proposed is inherent to wellbeing.

Embodiment, expression and the experiential – the special place of literature and the arts

Earlier in the chapter, mention was made of how aesthetic experience concerns corporeality as we 'undergo' and respond in 'an' experience. The urge to making meaning for ourselves and to share this with others implies that growth and wellbeing is far from a solitary, individualistic characteristic. Indeed, it may be frequently the case that different ways of expressing what we think we have experienced to ourselves and others is the prime way of finding the meaning of our experiences. Living well in association with others is particularly vital in the social context of school, and in-depth understanding about others including the cultivation of empathy is generally seen as part of the rationale for the place of literature and the arts within the curriculum. Embodiment, expression and aesthetic experience in general appear to come to the fore through curriculum areas such as drama, music, poetry and art and therefore literature and the arts could offer extensive resources for deepening our aesthetic experience. The arts seem the most obvious of experiential activities with their stress on the body, the senses and the imagination and the study of poetry, plays and novels call surely upon the imagination and raise questions of meaning. However, educational approaches that are destructive rather than supportive of creating an appetite for seeking out value and meaning in experience can just as well characterise schooling in the arts and in literature as elsewhere within the curriculum.

Dewey cites chaotic experience as an enemy of the aesthetic and applied within the arts this argues against totally free activity and lack of structure. The suggestion instead is that confident intentions and careful mediation are needed on the part of teachers of art. For example, in spite of what might appear as total freedom in our spinney 'expedition', the powerful underlying educational purpose of allowing full aesthetic experience gives ongoing subtle and skillful structure to the episode. Alongside chaotic experience, the mundane and habitual can also discourage the aesthetic sensibility necessary for this view of wellbeing. Here, the tendency in schooling to give standardised patterns to all lessons, with explicit objectives, structured activities and timed plenaries, first advocated within the UK in literacy lessons,[4] is a tangible risk to the freshness required for responsiveness and sustained engagement.

The pressure to produce standardised, right answers for exam purposes and the notion of 'correct meaning' is likely to mitigate against openness and the authentic form of engagement that aesthetic experience calls for and this can be equally as true of the arts and literature as it is within other curriculum subjects. The reduction of arts experience in school to production of correct meanings risks a ruthless emphasis on the dissection of poetry and art with damage to the coherence, unity and richness of experience that a painting or a play, for example, can offer.

One pervasive dimension offering a particular threat to wellbeing through engaging with the arts and literature is the challenge of utility. The impetus to find meaning is sometimes replaced or reduced to the question of 'what use is this?' With the dominance of this view in life generally, we see the tree merely as a supply of wood and the meadow only as ripe for housing development. In education, artistic imagery is easily rationalised and reduced to mere illustration or passages from fiction become cut and extracted from complete texts for the purpose of teaching grammar.

There is no doubt that we could argue that schooling needs and will continue to need a wide range of approaches to teaching and learning including offering experiences that are routine and perhaps even devoid of meaning. The problem for wellbeing is when experiences that exclude the aesthetic imagination in the ways I have described, *dominate* school experience and there is little attention given to encouraging children or students to seek for meaning and value in their lives.

To conclude, I have tried to set out an argument for the future of schooling in terms of aesthetic experience and wellbeing, and in this section, a very brief suggestion of how literature and the arts might feature within this. Based on insights available from Dewey it is worth repeating that: 'For Dewey, the aesthetic is one of the basic moments of human experience, and the making of art is one of the most basic ways in which the meanings of human life are enriched' (Hickman, 1998, p. xii). It is the *totality* of aesthetic experience with its strong draw on our imagination that then feeds the desire for further experience in meaning making. Wellbeing can be theorised as aesthetic experience so that its features and emphasis can permeate throughout the curriculum at every stage of schooling. This view compliments the argument to carefully address *real* wellbeing, as opposed to superficial features of wellbeing or *pseudo* wellbeing as discussed in James MacAllister's chapter of this book.[5] It aligns with the widespread general view that education for flourishing is meant to permeate the whole curriculum and influence every salient educational decision taken within the school (Kristjánsson, 2016a).

Future directions

The chapter has argued that learning and teaching in schools that aims at wellbeing would benefit from a particular understanding of wellbeing that has deep roots in pragmatism. It has visited some neo-pragmatic ideas arising from the work of John Dewey, to explore what this might mean for current educational practice in particular circumstances. The main suggestion is that the role of the aesthetic imagination in encouraging wellbeing could be used to frame and conceptualise future educational research. Further exploration might strengthen explanations of the value of this approach and hopefully provide an ongoing evidential base for changes to educational policy and practice. It is acknowledged that research and guiding principles and values cannot dictate specific practices for every context. The hope is that greater understanding and the aspiration for education to enhance wellbeing in this sense will allow schools to determine practices that are highly responsive to their context and their students while still meeting those worthwhile social and political demands that schools should meet.

Summary of key points

This chapter has set out an argument for a particular view of what might constitute wellbeing in school and beyond.

- It presents a philosophical view that draws on a pragmatic approach to experience, suggesting that wellbeing requires school experiences to have special qualities.
- It advocates a distinctive form of 'growth' that depends on the continuous nature of all experience and gives an ongoing appetite for seeking out life experiences that are meaningful.
- The nature of aesthetic sensibility as it pervades much of human living is outlined, with a fuller exploration of the special qualities of aesthetic experience for growth, and thus, for wellbeing.
- The integral part that the imagination plays in episodes distinguishable as aesthetic experience is explained.
- The central value for wellbeing that emerges is an ongoing ability to seek meaning and value in one's living and one's experience.

The relevance of this argument for wellbeing and for schooling is exemplified with consideration of some explicit features such as:

- Approaching subject knowledge in ways that enhance growth and wellbeing, such as by being drawn into the present experience of students to help knowledge 'come alive' and meaningful.

- By considering cross-curricular activity, students may find meaning is more readily made through experience where knowledge is operationalised as, and when, it is needed. This suggests that in any one episode of learning, different kinds of knowledge can be available for making sense of that experience, as opposed to learning being restricted to knowledge within a single subject.
- Literature and the arts are considered as obvious curricular opportunities for the aesthetic imagination, but are used to illustrate how teaching and learning may still neglect important features that contribute to wellbeing.

Reflective tasks

- To what extent do you think this account of aesthetic experience is sufficient for achieving wellbeing?
- What are the main issues for schools that are raised with this account?
- Dewey's educational ideas stressed the importance of collaborative meaning-making. How might students working together help them derive meaning from present school experiences?
- Choose a single curriculum area that you think might benefit from an approach involving the aesthetic imagination and discuss the ways in which this could be achieved.
- Why is 'enjoyment' not sufficient for experience that encourages wellbeing?
- To what extent could teachers exemplify aesthetic imagination in their planning of the curriculum?

Notes

1 See the case made for a phronesis-based view of teaching in Doddington, C. (2013).
2 Abrams, Fran. 'The school that has projects, not subjects: "we're not hippies, we're punks"'. *Education Guardian*, (31 January 2017, p. 35).
3 http://www.xpschool.org/xp-school-prospectus/
4 This was the model of lessons advocated within the UK National Strategies for Literacy and Numeracy and was adopted by many primary and secondary schools as a template for other curriculum areas.
5 MacAllister, James. The Teacher Perspective: A Community Approach to Wellbeing in Schools.

Further reading

Doddington, C. (2014). Education in the Open: The Somaesthetic Value of Being Outside, *Other Education: The Journal of Educational Alternatives*, *3*(1), 41–59.

References

Abbs, P. (1989). *A is for Aesthetic: Essays on Creative and Aesthetic Education*. New York: Falmer.
Alexander, T. (1998). 'The art of life: Dewey's aesthetics'. In Hickman, L. (Ed.), *Reading Dewey: Interpretations for a Postmodern Generation* (pp. 1–22). Bloomington: Indiana University Press.

Alexander, T. (2013). *The Human Eros: Eco-Ontology and the Aesthetics of Existence*. New York: Fordham University Press.

Dewey, J. (1916/1966). *Democracy and Education*. Toronto: MacMillan.

Dewey, J. (1934/2005). *Art as Experience*. New York: The Berkeley Publishing Group.

Dewey, J. (1938/1997) *Experience & Education*. New York: Touchstone

Doddington, C. (2013). The Global Search for Better Teaching: How Should Teachers Think for Themselves? *Education 3–13, 41*(2), 218–232.

Granger, D. (2003). A Review of Richard Shusterman, Pragmatist Aesthetics: Living Beauty Rethinking Art, *Studies in Philosophy and Education, 22*(5), 381–402.

Granger, D. (2006). *John Dewey, Robert Pirsig, and the Art of Living: Revisioning Aesthetic Education*. New York: Palgrave Macmillan.

Hickman, L. (1998). *The Essential Dewey: Pragmatism, Education, Democracy*. Indiana: Indiana University Press.

Kristjánsson, K. (2016a). Recent Work on Flourishing as the Aim of Education: A Critical Review, *British Journal of Educational Studies*, Retrieved from: http://dx.doi.org/10.1080/00071005.2016.1182115

Kristjánsson, K. (2016b). Flourishing as the Aim of Education: Towards an Extended, 'Enchanted' Aristotelian Account, *Oxford Review of Education, 42*(6), 707–720.

Shusterman, R. (2008). *Body Consciousness: A Philosophy of Mindfulness and Somaesthetics*. Cambridge: Cambridge University Press.

PART VI

A personal perspective on wellbeing

13

A PERSONAL PERSPECTIVE ON WELLBEING

Lessons learned or insufficiently grasped?

George MacBride

Introduction

This chapter provides a perspective on the development over half a century of culture, concepts, systems, policy and practice related to wellbeing in Scottish schools which, it is hoped, can inform forward thinking. A number of assumptions underlie this perspective:

- While I recognise that wellbeing is a contested and often ill-defined concept, I accept as a working proposition Thorburn's (Chapter 2) definition of wellbeing: 'wellbeing is more than happiness and something which connects with flourishing as a person *and* with making a positive contribution to the community and wider society' (Shah and Marks, 2004).
- In this context, I accept McLellan and Steward's (2015) proposal that: 'eudemonic wellbeing depends on the fulfilment of three core needs, namely the need for competence, autonomy and relatedness, with humans possessing the capacity or "will" to choose how to do this' (p. 310). This capacity is partially determined by one's society, culture and context.
- 'Equifinality' (Ungar *et al.*, 2013, p. 348) is significant in recognising autonomy and agency: 'there are many proximal processes that can lead to many different, but equally viable, expressions of human development associated with well-being'.
- The systems and processes of education are complex: change may be easy to initiate but is often, for powerful reasons, difficult to sustain and expand.
- Education systems, schools and teachers should be, can be and are forces for good which help make young people's lives more fulfilling and meaningful; the aim is to transform children's lives (now and in the future) rather than reproduce social structures which limit wellbeing.

- For both principled and pragmatic reasons, children's voices must be heard in discussions of wellbeing.

I taught in Glasgow comprehensive secondary schools for thirty-seven years from 1969, for thirty of these years in pupil-support posts. When I started teaching, some learners in Scotland thrived in academic learning and enjoyed positive relationships with teachers. However, the type and status of secondary school which children attended was in some areas determined by the results of a promotion test at the end of primary school. This reflected the widely-held view that one's intelligence and future success were fixed by one's genetic inheritance. Disability was a set of medical labels; indeed, some children were labelled as unsuitable for education. Responsibility for failure to engage, attain or behave was the fault of the individual or, perhaps, their family. Gender equality was a rumour, homophobia common, corporal punishment legal. Teachers addressed and spoke about whole groups of pupils with contempt. Some schools provided part-time education and there was no limit on class sizes: the lower your status, the more likely you were to be educated part-time in a large class. The curriculum was largely a handed-down version of a traditional academic curriculum; pedagogy was to a large extent marked by teacher voice and learner silence; assessment was usually by simple tests of recall or limited skills; errors could lead to corporal punishment. Gow and McPherson (1980) provide extensive powerful evidence from young people of their continuing deep levels of dissatisfaction with their school experiences.

For some teachers, this was a satisfactory way of working: it guaranteed them status and respect; it absolved them from accountability; their word was rarely questioned and failure could be attributed to the learner or the social context; teachers could often run their classrooms with little interference. Life could be easy: teaching was textbook based and required little teacher reflection, hangovers could be addressed by setting undemanding written tasks to ensure silence. But for other teachers, this was not satisfying; while one might enjoy some freedom, curriculum, culture and the community of one's peers enforced uncongenial teaching methods. Support at critical times (e.g. on entry to a new school) was largely lacking (a set of class lists, a box of jotters and, if lucky, a note on how to access the store cupboard). Teaching was hierarchical and status status-ridden: a head teacher could make a teacher's life wretched or ensure rapid promotion for those he liked; 'he' because all secondary heads (apart from in the few all-girls schools) were men and men were disproportionately promoted in primary schools. Differences in qualifications status were reflected in eight different pay scales for unpromoted teachers. Teachers who found teaching difficult or were alcoholics or were mentally ill were moved without support from school to school.

Today, Curriculum for Excellence (CFE) makes clear (Education Scotland, 2009a, 2009b) that all practitioners share responsibility for every learner's wellbeing, mental and emotional, social and physical, through all stages of early years and school education. Education Scotland (2009b, p. 1) is categorical that all staff will support all learners *inter alia* to:

- build my resilience and confidence;
- understand and develop my physical, mental and spiritual wellbeing and social skills;
- understand how what I eat, how active I am and how decisions I make about my behaviour and relationships affect my physical and mental wellbeing;
- acknowledge diversity and understand that it is everyone's responsibility to challenge discrimination.

Teachers will contribute through their practice in their classrooms, through their contribution to the life and ethos of the school and through their relationships with learners to the development of a wide range of experiences and outcomes related to wellbeing – mental and emotional, social and physical. A typical example from each category:

- I understand that my feelings and reactions can change depending upon what is happening within and around me. This helps me to understand my own behaviour and the way others behave.
- Through contributing my views, time and talents, I play a part in bringing about positive change in my school and wider community.
- I am learning to assess and manage risk, to protect myself and others, and to reduce the potential for harm when possible (Education Scotland, 2009b, pp. 2–3)

It is evident that a broad and encompassing concept of wellbeing has been developed.

How have we reached this position? The answer is through a series of inter-linked, if sometimes inconsistent, processes which have enhanced pupils' compe-tence, autonomy and relatedness (McLellan and Steward, 2015), explicitly identified by McLean (2003) in his teacher handbook as learner autonomy, agency and attach-ment; we have not always planned carefully but our general direction of travel has promoted children's wellbeing.

Factors contributing to promoting wellbeing

The political context

While 'wellbeing' has rarely been clearly defined in Scottish education, the word has generally been understood in ways typical of a welfare regime in a social demo-cratic society (Khadka 2013, p. 620). CFE is based on the values that underpin our parliamentary democracy and society:

> Wisdom, justice, compassion and integrity: the words which are inscribed on the mace of the Scottish Parliament have helped to define values for our

> democracy. It is one of the prime purposes of education to make our young
> people aware of the values on which Scottish society is based and so help
> them to establish their own stances on matters of social justice.
>
> *(Scottish Executive, 2004, p. 11)*

A number of authors (e.g. Hofman *et al.*, 2008; Hall *et al.*, 2015) assume that there
is a common 'Anglo-Saxon' commitment to new public management in education.
However in Scotland, privatisation and competition remain peripheral features of
the education system: 96% of pupils attend schools provided by local councils;
parents are partners not consumers or managers; hostility to national testing and
rejection of school league tables are longstanding. This has upheld a concept of education as a public good, a broad definition of education and a focus on the interests
of the child. Many (e.g. EIS, 2010) would agree with ETUI and ETUC (2011) that
action limited to schools cannot fully compensate for the inequalities of society,
that the promotion of wellbeing must be addressed across social structures and that
wellbeing, social cohesion and solidarity are interdependent.

The promotion of wellbeing through education is consonant with the principles
underpinning other aspects of social policy. Children's Hearings (panels of trained
members of the local community) in 1971 took over from the courts almost all
responsibility for dealing with children and young people who commit offences
or who are in need of care and protection. Children's Hearings have the needs and
wellbeing of children at the heart of their work; society carries the responsibility for supporting children.[1] The statutory post of Children and Young People's
Commissioner Scotland (CYPCS), established in 2003, ensures that all policy making is pro-actively informed and monitored to ensure recognition of children's
rights.[2]

School culture

Progress and Proposals (Scottish Executive, 2006) emphasised the importance of a
positive school culture in promoting agency, autonomy and attachment:

> [t]eachers know that positive relationships and the climate for learning in a
> school – its values, its ethos and its life as a community – are essential start-
> ing points for successful learning. The wider life of the school – activities
> such as assemblies, community events and school projects – makes an impor-
> tant contribution to the development of the four capacities ... Schools also
> offer pupils opportunities to learn through such activities as peer mentoring,
> membership of school councils, undertaking responsibilities and playing a
> part in decision making.

Elovainio *et al.* (2011) reported that enjoyment by teachers of higher levels of procedural and relational justice was clearly associated with greater pupil satisfaction;
John-Akinola and Nic Gabhainn (2015) found that 'the school socio-ecological

environment is clearly related to general health and wellbeing outcomes for pupils' (p. 427). While the danger of generalising across all of Scotland's 2500 schools must be recognised, many teachers (and ultimately learners) benefit from higher levels of procedural and relational justice than in the past. This came from the contractual requirement for collegiality, negotiated working-time arrangements in each school, collaborative self-evaluation and improvement planning, and explicit recognition and extension of teachers' professional rights and responsibilities.

Legislation

In Scotland, parliamentary legislation has generally been accepted as an inappropriate vehicle for prescribing details of curriculum, assessment or pedagogy. Rather, legislation provides the structure and culture within which curriculum and pedagogy are developed. Since the introduction of universal compulsory primary education in 1872, legislation has erratically moved Scottish schools towards structures and culture likely to promote wellbeing. In 1945 secondary education was extended to all children and in 1974, legislation finally 'discontinu[ed] the ascertainment of mentally handicapped children as unsuitable for education at school' (HMSO, 1974). Conservative Government legislation in the 1980s sought to foster competition by treating parents as consumers of education, focusing on their rights and ignoring the rights of children; the impact was less than intended. Devolution in 1999 ensured a political climate largely sceptical of such views. The Standards in Scotland's Schools Act (Scottish Parliament, 2000) embedded wording from the United Nations Convention on the Rights of the Child (UNCRC): 'education is directed to the development of the personality, talents and mental and physical abilities of the child or young person to their fullest potential' (§2(1)); 'due regard [should be paid] to the views ... of the child or young person in decisions that significantly affect that child or young person' (§2(2)); §15 promoted inclusive education for children who required additional support. The Additional Support for Learning Act (Scottish Parliament, 2004) further promoted inclusion by adopting a social model of disability, recognising that support may be required not only to address traditionally recognised 'special needs' of a quasi-medical nature but also to ensure that children flourish in difficult social contexts (e.g. disrupted family life) or during challenging life experiences (e.g. bereavement). Recent major legislation (Scottish Parliament, 2014) requires public bodies to promote wellbeing of children (§9).

Comprehensive education

In 1945 the Labour Government legislated to establish universal secondary education in the form of a selective two-tier system, despite the arguments of the Educational Institute of Scotland (EIS – teachers union) and others for comprehensive schools. Twenty years later another Labour Government issued Circular 600 which ensured the implementation of comprehensive secondary education across Scotland:

> a system which segregates children into separate schools at the age of 12 is wrong … young people will greatly benefit in their personal and social development by spending the formative years of early adolescence in schools where the pupils represent a fuller cross section of the community.
>
> *(Scottish Education Department, 1965, §5)*

Ball (1981) identified three models underpinning the development of comprehensive schooling in England:

- meritocratic, which, to reduce the inefficiencies and injustices of selection, offered nominal equality of opportunity to all children, regardless of social background;
- integrative, which, to encourage a tolerant society, educated children of different social classes together;
- egalitarian, which, to make equality real, required changes in ethos and pedagogy and a review of the established academic aims of secondary education.

In Scotland, Circular 600 moved beyond the meritocratic model to the broader aims of the integrative and into the radical egalitarian models.

Analysis of the 2002 national debate on education which preceded and informed the development of CFE found that the 'vast majority of the people who responded to the Debate believe in the strength of the Scottish comprehensive system and want to build on that' (Scottish Executive, 2003, p. 4). The OECD (2007) review of national policy noted the success of Scotland's comprehensive schools in ensuring equity of provision across the country but the inability of the system on its own to address the effects of inequality outside the school:

> Who you are in Scotland is far more important than what school you attend, so far as achievement differences on international tests are concerned. Socio-economic status is the most important difference between individuals.
>
> *(OECD, 2007, p. 15)*

In their survey of the effects of Scotland's comprehensive schools over half a century, Murphy, Croxford, Howieson and Raffe (2015, p. 46) conclude:

> The values that guide the development of comprehensive schooling are thus no different from those of democratic life more generally: liberty, equality, fraternity – balanced in a fair process.

They summarise that Scotland's comprehensive schools have extended liberty, have enhanced equality of value and respect (but less so equality of outcomes) and, most significantly, have greatly strengthened fraternity. Relationships with concepts of autonomy, agency and autonomy may be tacit but positive implications for the development of wellbeing seem evident.

Social inclusion

There is agreement among key partners in Scotland of the value of inclusive education. During the half century since Circular 600 (Scottish Education Department, 1965), there has been a move from a focus on the vulnerable and their 'deficiencies' to inclusive universal provision which seeks to enhance the capacities of all. The national inspectorate (HMIE, 2002) defines an inclusive approach to education as involving:

- creating an ethos of achievement for all pupils within a climate of high expectation;
- valuing a broad range of talents, abilities and achievements;
- promoting success and self-esteem by taking action to remove barriers to learning;
- countering conscious and unconscious discrimination that may prevent individuals, or pupils from any particular groups, from thriving in the school; and
- actively promoting understanding and a positive appreciation of the diversity of individuals and groups within society. (p. 4)

Learning and Teaching Scotland (2006) identifies the important characteristics of an inclusive school as 'relationships, ethos, empowerment, engagement and esteem, collaborative support, promoting positive behaviour, mutual support among children' (pp. 5–6). The main teacher union considers (EIS, 2007, p. 8) that 'inclusive education ... is about the participation of students in key aspects of their schools; their cultures ... their curricula ... and their communities, that is the sets of relationships they sustain'. These approaches recognise that inclusive schooling which celebrates diversity and empowers learners can promote wellbeing, individual and social.

Wellbeing and rights

Getting it Right for Every Child (GIRFEC) (Scottish Government, 2012) establishes the principles which underpin all policy related to children. The wellbeing of all children, not only the vulnerable, lies at the heart of this policy which identifies (p. 9) 'eight areas of wellbeing in which children and young people need to progress in order to do well now and in the future': every child has the right to be safe, healthy, achieving, nurtured, active, respected and responsible. These indicators, often referred to by the acronym SHANARRI, are intended to support a common understanding of what wellbeing means. The eight indicators are now incorporated in legislation (Scottish Parliament, 2014, §96(2)):

> [a] person is to assess the wellbeing of the child or young person [this is to be done] by reference to the extent to which the child or young person is or, as the case may be, would be – Safe, Healthy, Achieving, Nurtured, Active, Respected, Responsible, and Included.

They are incorporated into education policy and practice through various channels (inspection, self-evaluation, standards for teacher registration).

The relationship of rights and welfare is often elided in official or NGO documentation. Thus, the Scottish Government (2009) restricts references to wellbeing to rights to health and to inclusion of those affected by disability. Together (2015), written on behalf of a number of Scottish children's charities, similarly assumes that rights and wellbeing are closely linked and that there is no need to define wellbeing. Tisdall (2015), referring to the Children and Young People Act (Scottish Parliament, 2014), argues that we should not casually equate rights and wellbeing (e.g. as in Scottish Government, 2013). The former are legally required, enjoy powerful political support, set only minimum standards and omit much that is of importance to children. The latter are 'aspirational and maximising, easily incorporating children's relationships and collective needs' (Tisdall, 2015, p. 807), but risk becoming apolitical and professionally determined. The Act provides no assistance on how children's wellbeing and rights can be related to each other in policy and practice.

A more fundamental critique of the use of rights (or at least UNCRC) as the basis for considering children's wellbeing comes from those who consider that these rights are determined by particular social or historical or cultural contexts. Khadka (2013) argues that UNCRC places much greater emphasis on political and civil rights than on social, economic and cultural rights; pursuit of political and civil rights may hinder development of other rights. This issue is relevant in a society, such as Scotland, which is marked by both diversity and inequality and by the complex interrelationships of these features. Debates on equality have recognised that legal equality of opportunity is no substitute for action directed at the reduction of inequality.

Teacher professionalism

Scotland was the first country in the world to establish by statute (HMSO, 1965) an independent national regulator (the General Teaching Council for Scotland (GTCS) and require that all teachers in public schools be professionally registered with it. The standards for registration (GTCS, 2012) identify 'social justice' as the first professional value and personal commitment at the core of being a teacher (p. 5). This commitment encompasses among other attributes:

- embracing locally and globally the educational and social values of sustainability, equality and justice;
- committing to the principles of democracy and social justice through fair, transparent, inclusive and sustainable policies and practices;
- valuing … social, cultural and ecological diversity;
- respecting the rights of all learners as outlined in … UNCRC and their entitlement to be included in decisions regarding their learning experiences and have all aspects of their well-being developed and supported (GTCS, 2012, p. 9).

The standards make further specific references to wellbeing, including requiring that all teachers 'know how to promote and support the cognitive, emotional, social and physical wellbeing of all learners' (§2.1.4).

In parallel to this the Scottish Negotiating Committee for Teachers (SNCT) which agrees the employment conditions of all teachers in public schools is committed to 'promoting core values of social justice, equality and diversity'; the basic national agreement (Scottish Executive, 2001, p. 4) explicitly states:

> [teachers'] work is, critically, carried out within the framework of social inclusion which seeks to engage every child in learning and personal development to secure achievement and the promotion of confidence and ambition in all our young people.

The curriculum

Scotland is notable for the very limited extent to which the curriculum is nationally prescribed (European Commission/EACEA/Eurydice, 2016); however, there is an expectation, promoted through a range of types of authority, that teachers will use and develop national guidelines to meet the needs of their pupils. The current CFE builds on previous curriculum models and papers.

The secondary curriculum was reformed after the school-leaving age was raised to 16 in 1972. The Standard Grade programme of the early 1980s was designed to ensure that all young people (rather than as previously a minority) would have their learning certificated at the age of 16; this would itself lead to increased pupil engagement; considerable attention was also paid to designing courses, the content and pedagogy of which would itself be engaging. Inclusion and attainment would thus be promoted and greater equality and opportunity fostered. The Higher Still programme of the late 1990s was based on similar aspirations in developing a common certification structure for all pupils at age 17 and 18; motivation, staying-on rates and achievement would all be enhanced. Wellbeing was not formally recognised in these developments but it was expected that young people would benefit particularly through an increased sense of agency.

For primary and younger secondary pupils, the 5–14 Curriculum of the late 1980s initially recognised wellbeing through Personal and Social Development (PSD). Learning and Teaching Scotland (1999) summarises PSD 'knowledge, skills and dispositions' (p. 7) as those required 'to live purposefully in society and contribute effectively to it': these refer to the individual (e.g. 'deal responsibly with their emotions'), interpersonal relations (e.g. 'being sensitive and responsive to the needs of others') and contributions to society (e.g. 'an informed, compassionate, responsible view of the world and its peoples') (p. 10).

In the later years of 5–14, National Guidelines on Health (Learning and Teaching Scotland, 2000, §1.2) recognised that health extended beyond physical health to encompass emotional and social health. Wellbeing and the importance of community for promoting this are explicitly recognised:

The wellbeing of both pupils and staff is promoted by taking a coherent approach to every aspect of school life. The health-promoting school ... recognises that responsibility for improving health does not lie solely with the individual. It is a responsibility shared among all members of the health-promoting community.

A number of Scottish Consultative Committee on the Curriculum (SCCC) papers (e.g. SCCC, 1994, 1995, 1999) argued for an education which extends beyond attainment to include promotion of wellbeing and personal and social development; this encompasses a sense of a rounded whole person, skills and dispositions required to live in a changing world and commitment to tolerance, interpersonal concern and sustainability. These papers stress the importance of the school as a community with a supportive and challenging ethos which promotes respect and caring for self and others, social responsibility and a sense of belonging to a just society. Learning includes developing values and dispositions as well as knowledge and understanding.

The Scottish Executive (2004) report of the Curriculum Review Group sets out the bases for CFE for all learners aged 3–18. The curriculum organisers include: four capacities – successful learners, confident individuals, effective contributors, responsible citizens – accompanied by illustrative 'attributes and capabilities'; seven curricular principles (notably, from the learner's viewpoint, 'challenge and enjoyment','personalisation and choice','relevance','coherence'); curricular areas including *health and wellbeing*.

Progress and Proposals (Scottish Executive, 2006) stressed the need to think about the curriculum in CFE in a different way: '[a]ctivities such as enterprise, citizenship, sustainable development, health and creativity, which are often seen as add-ons, can be built into the curriculum framework'. The curriculum is:

> more than curriculum areas and subjects: it is the totality of experiences which are planned for children and young people ... the curriculum will include learning through:
> - the ethos and life of the school as a community;
> - curriculum areas and subjects;
> - interdisciplinary projects and studies;
> - opportunities for personal achievement.

CFE requires learning that extends beyond conventional bodies of knowledge and skills to include a wide range of attributes and capabilities, many clearly related to concepts of wellbeing (personal, interpersonal and social, affective dimensions, skills in monitoring one's own thinking and learning). The associated pedagogical principles require the active engagement and autonomy of learners.

As noted in the Introduction, the Scottish Government and Education Scotland expect that all practitioners share responsibility for all learners' mental and emotional, social and physical wellbeing and will contribute to providing particular experiences and ensuring particular outcomes. There are more general expectations of their contribution to school ethos and life.

Much has been done to embed wellbeing in Scottish education. Education Scotland (2013) provides an evaluation of practice in the aspects of health and wellbeing that are the responsibility of all. While Thorburn and Dey (Chapter 4) question the more extended approach towards policy guidance which this represents, a range of practice informs its conclusions:

> Three key elements contribute to the effective delivery of health and wellbeing:
> - the **culture** which is necessary to build and sustain a supportive ethos and high-quality relationships;
> - the **systems** which are in place to develop and sustain a strong and shared focus on creating a supportive and nurturing ethos;
> - in **practice**, productive partnerships, and a sense of teamwork which creates positive and productive environments for learning and teaching.
>
> (Education Scotland, 2013, pp. 4–5)

Assessment

Significant developments in assessment preceded and accompanied CFE. The Assessment is for Learning Programme (Condie, Livingston and Seagraves, 2005) noted the value of formative assessment which included the learner's perceptions and judgements: self- and peer-assessment are both necessary. CFE guidance on assessment developed the value of learner agency and autonomy in guidance documentation: Scottish Government (2010a) recommends that 'Learners should be encouraged and supported to contribute to decisions on what evidence is to be drawn upon, irrespective of where learning takes place' (p. 14).

Through the recognition that learning takes place outside the formal structures of the classroom, learners can draw on evidence of achievement from other areas, including the recognition of achievement beyond school (Scottish Government, 2010a, p. 8):

> Gaining recognition for a range of achievement … benefits all children and young people … Achievement covers learning within curriculum areas and interdisciplinary learning, including recognition through qualifications, but it is much wider than that. It includes achievement in other areas within the life of the school and outside the school – sometimes referred to as wider achievement.

Other strands

Specific relevant strands of policy development, which may not have had an impact on all schools but which have contributed to an ethos supportive of learner autonomy, agency and attachment, have included the promotion of positive school cultures (most relevantly, McLean, 2003), the promotion of positive behaviour (Black, Chamberlain, Murray, Sewel and Skelton, 2012), the introduction of restorative justice (Kane *et al.*, 2009) and the establishment of rights-respecting schools (Sebba and Robinson, 2010). As Scotland has become a more diverse nation through immigration, this has been recognised in practice, e.g. Learning and Teaching Scotland (2005) which stressed an inclusive approach and recognition of individual capacities:

> Inclusion, race equality, cultural diversity, bilingualism and effective additional language provision must be considered by all educational establishments, regardless of their current ethnic composition.
>
> (p. 1)

> The home language is vitally important – the school needs to provide the parents/carers with every encouragement to maintain and develop it.
>
> (p. 5)

Pastoral care

Major strands in policy and practice have included the introduction of promoted posts in secondary schools with responsibility for pupil support, operating in parallel to the traditional subject structures of secondary schools. The most inclusive of these is the guidance system; more specific support includes support for learning, for English for bilingual learners and for behaviour. It is notable that in all of these categories support has moved from a focus on individuals seen as vulnerable to more inclusive forms of support which addressed structural issues. 'More than Feelings of Concern' (Scottish Central Committee on Guidance, 1986, §2.04) established principles for the development of guidance including the need to:

- consider children's personal, social and intellectual development;
- enable children to be aware of own development and responsible for it;
- foster the development of good relations between teachers and children;
- work well with the home in all aspects of pupil development;
- liaise with and supports welfare services.

The report emphasises (§1.03) that it shares the philosophy of the Pack Committee (Scottish Education Department, 1977): 'the organisation, curriculum and staffing structure of a school should be designed to accord with the ideas of a caring society and should meet its requirements for all pupils'. The school is a caring community and pastoral care is a whole-school responsibility.

The findings of a National Review of Guidance (Scottish Executive, 2005, p. iii) include:

> Scottish schools have at their heart a vision of enabling all children and young people to thrive and achieve their full potential as learners and as members

of society. Supporting pupils' personal, social and emotional development in school has been a focus of professional commitment and growing expertise for many years.

The fundamental aims of the Report were to establish common principles to underpin personal support for all pupils in Scottish schools and set out a standard of support, informed by the GIRFEC principles, which would meet the needs of all, while recognising that some face particularly stressful situations, temporary or long-lasting, which will require more intense support. The report identifies ten standards which should be available to all learners which include ensuring:

- opportunities for developing the knowledge, skills and attitudes children and young people need to enable them to seek information and support throughout life;
- opportunities for children's citizenship and participation;
- all children and young people, and their parents, feel confident that the school will support them;
- access to staff by children and parents who want support;
- [co-ordinated] support between agencies and schools, wherever learning takes place (Scottish Education Department, 1977, pp. 10–11).

There is a clear commitment to an inclusive philosophy, the recognition of diversity and the need for schools to address the effects of social inequality. Similar developments have taken place in support for learning and behaviour, moving from a focus on 'deficient' individuals to planning curricula, pedagogies and assessments which can meet the needs of a diverse school community.

Defining and evaluating wellbeing

These developments have taken place without a clear definition of wellbeing based on theory or research. Over the past half-century there has been a move, largely tacit, from understanding 'wellbeing' as limited to developing for individual vulnerable children their currently defective personal qualities to an understanding that wellbeing includes developing for all children opportunities for meaningful empowered participation in our society, now and in the future. Tisdall (2015) notes that the Children and Young People Act does not provide a definition of children's wellbeing; the GIRFEC indicators act as a substitute. Thus the interpretation of the word 'wellbeing' in the Act is dependent on current (and open to change) policy. While the SHANARRI indicators are promoted in policy documents and widely used in practice, it is arguable that this discourse has closed down discussion of what we mean by 'wellbeing' and of the possible negative side effects of our approach.

It is difficult to measure wellbeing without a clear conceptual understanding. Attempts to measure the wellbeing of Scottish children have produced mixed results. A number of surveys, such as McLaren (2007) or UNICEF (2013), whatever questions there may be about definitions, methodologies employed and inconsistencies among their findings, suggest that the UK in general and Scotland in particular have far to go in promoting children's wellbeing. On the other hand, pupil responses to questionnaires, reported in the 2009 Scottish Survey of Achievement (Scottish Government, 2010b) indicate high levels of pupil agency and attachment. Behaviour in Scottish schools continues to improve (Black *et al.*, 2012). These positive views are confirmed by research (SCRE Centre University of Glasgow, 2005, p. vii):

> Primary pupils presented a very positive picture of their schools: 82% were happy, 98% liked their teacher and 91% liked themselves ... Three-quarters (75%) of secondary school pupil respondents were happy; almost eight out of ten (79%) thought that their school promoted an inclusive ethos; 89% regarded their school as either friendly or very friendly.

Challenges and future directions

It is evident from the Education Scotland (2013) impact study that there is much good practice in this area in Scotland's schools. Ethos, systems and practice are all important in ensuring that promoting and sustaining the wellbeing of children through enhancing their autonomy, sense of agency and engagement is effective. It is essential that development is informed by research, by consequent enriched understandings of wellbeing and by synergy and consistency across all educational policies. We need to move beyond 'the effective delivery of health and wellbeing' which suggests teachers are technicians, to recognising that fostering wellbeing is complex and requires common principles to operate in ways that reflect cultures, contexts and individual needs. Ungar *et al.* (2013) introduced a concept of equifinality, requiring the active professional engagement of teachers. To support this, we need more explicit discussion, including teachers and pupils, about what we mean by wellbeing. This discussion is unlikely to be fruitful if teachers, as currently, remain affected by high workload and stress. Within this discussion there is a need to consider the relationship between rights and wellbeing to avoid clashes which lead to litigation.

We need to critique views which continue to portray inclusion and wellbeing as therapeutic control. Watson (2010) argues that 'only those who are 'included' in a control society can be managed by it and made productive for it ... the society of control becomes inclusive through extending to all the therapeutic net of what formerly led to exclusion' (pp. 97–98). Similarly, Williamson (2012) concludes: 'education is encouraged to manage children's emotional state in order to ensure the well-being of the future workforce and, therefore, the overall wellbeing of the competitive economy' (p. 437). Rather we need to develop models of wellbeing which enhance qualities such as flourishing and virtue and which celebrate empowerment, resilience, challenge and critical thinking.

Policy developments may not lead to their promoters' intended outcomes (Cuban, 1984). Hayward *et al.* (2005) and Hayward and Spencer (2010) conclude that sustainable innovations were based on three aspects of integrity:

- Educational integrity: any innovation must have educational value based on recognised principles and be likely to give young people better experiences and outcomes.
- Personal and professional integrity: all involved must be treated with respect while their knowledge and expertise contribute to the planning, implementation and evaluation of the innovation.
- Systemic integrity: All elements of the education system must work together to ensure alignment with the principles of the innovation.

While few may doubt the value of wellbeing, teachers have not always been fully engaged in the development of policy and practice related to wellbeing and there has been inconsistency in policy formation. Health and wellbeing has been distinguished from all other aspects of the CFE. For all of these, Education Scotland has published teacher support materials related to progression: broad statements of experiences and outcomes specified for five levels of progression; progression frameworks; annotated examples of learners' work to illustrate progression. The health and wellbeing experiences and outcomes are common to all stages and the other materials have not been published. Washback from examination systems is powerful; this has ensured that, despite explicit aspirations, the senior phase of secondary schooling focuses largely on attainment of the knowledge and skills required for National Qualifications and remains semi-detached from the wider aims of CFE. And there is always the possibility of interpreting policy (e.g. GIRFEC) in reactive bureaucratic ways rather than in pro-active informed ways.

OECD (2015), reviewing implementation of CFE, concludes that Scottish education is currently at a watershed moment. Schools are inclusive, learners are generally engaged and positive about their schools and levels of risk-taking behaviour are declining. But there is evidence at some points of declining achievement, of disaffection with school, and the gap in achievement associated with socio-economic status remains difficult to reduce. Addressing this last point through introducing standardised assessment as currently suggested runs counter to experience in other jurisdictions, which suggests this is likely to have negative consequences for children's wellbeing. Arnott and Ozga (2010) note that Scottish Government policy discourse has moved to stressing the contribution of education to the economic wellbeing of the country; it will be important not to remove the learner from the centre of our concerns.

Issues of teacher professionalism have not been fully addressed in the development of policy and practice. Some secondary teachers have resisted the introduction of pastoral care systems where each teacher had a first-line responsibility; others felt themselves to be inadequately prepared to take on such a role; in some cases those in promoted posts considered that the work they had put into developing effective systems was put at risk by such developments. This raises questions about how well prepared the school system is to ensure that aspirations of a 'responsibility for all' approach can be put into practice. Many teachers are uncertain about the practicalities of how they can assess wellbeing, about ethical issues and about possible impacts on more traditional aspects of achievement.

Bradshaw, Martorano, Natali and de Neubourg (2013) point out the often considerable differences between children's perceptions and adult views on what makes for wellbeing. Fattore, Mason and Watson (2007) argue for the importance of involving children in any process of defining and measuring wellbeing. Murphy *et al.* (2015) argue that a comprehensive system should evaluate itself with reference to all its intended outcomes and aspirations for individuals and for society. These three arguments should be borne in mind as we try to evaluate the success of our wellbeing policy and practice.

Summary of key findings

- Over half a century, promotion of wellbeing has become a central feature of Scotland's education system.
- Much of this development has been supported by developments in policy and practice which were not explicitly related to wellbeing.
- The direction of travel has been slow, at times halting.
- Enhancing wellbeing has tacitly been affected through enhancing the agency, autonomy and engagement of children in school.
- There is a need for wider and fuller and inclusive discussions about our understandings of wellbeing.
- Teacher engagement is essential.
- The engagement of children and young people is essential.
- The effects of inequality may be mitigated by action in schools but schools alone cannot address the causes of inequality.

Reflective tasks

- To what extent and in what ways are lessons related to the development of wellbeing in Scotland's schools transferable to other jurisdictions?
- How valuable is the use of 'agency, autonomy and attachment' ('competence, autonomy and relatedness') as proxies or characteristics of wellbeing?
- How can schools and teachers promote wellbeing by extending the curriculum to recognise learning that takes place outside the school?
- How can we recognise individualisation, diversity and equifinality without risking labelling and discrimination?
- In what ways can schools and teachers contribute to countering the sources of inequality as well as mitigating the effects of inequality?

Notes

1 Further information on Children's Hearing can be found at http://www.chscotland.gov. uk/
2 Further information on the Children and Young People's Commissioner Scotland can be found at http://www.cypcs.org.uk/

Further readings

Anderson Moore, K., Lippman, L. H., & Ryberg, R. (2015). Improving Outcome Measures Other Than Achievement, *AERA (Open)*, *1*(2), 1–25.
Bradshaw, J., Hoelscher, P., & Richardson, D. (2007). An Index of Child Well-being in the European Union, *Social Indicators Research*, *80*, 133–177.

References

Arnott, M. & Ozga, J. (2010). Education and nationalism: the discourse of education policy, *Discourse*, 31(3), 335–350.
Arnott, M. & Ozga, J. (2010). Nationalism, governance and policymaking in Scotland: The Scottish National Party (SNP) in power, *Public Management and Money*, 30(2) 91–96.
Ball, S.J. (1981). *Beachside Comprehensive: A Case-Study of Secondary Schooling*. Cambridge: Cambridge University Press.
Black, C., Chamberlain, V., Murray, L., Sewel, K., & Skelton J. (2012). *Behaviour in Scottish Schools 2012*. Edinburgh: Scottish Government.
Bradshaw, J., Martorano, B., Natali, L. & de Neubourg, C. (2013). Children's Subjective Wellbeing in Rich Countries, *Working Paper 2013-03*. Florence: UNICEF Office of Research.
Condie, R., Livingston, K., & Seagraves, L. (2005). *Evaluation of the Assessment is for Learning Programme*. Glasgow: Quality in Education Centre, University of Strathclyde.
Cuban, L. (1984). *How Teachers Taught: Constancy and Change in American Classrooms 1890–1980*. New York: Teachers College Press.
Education Scotland. (2009a). *Health and Wellbeing Across Learning: Responsibilities of All – Principles and Practice*. Glasgow: Education Scotland.
Education Scotland. (2009b). *Health and Wellbeing Across Learning: Responsibilities of All – Experiences and Outcomes*. Glasgow: Education Scotland.
Education Scotland. (2013). *Health and Wellbeing: The Responsibility of All 3–18*. Glasgow: Education Scotland.
Educational Institute of Scotland. (2007). *Inclusive Education*. Edinburgh: EIS.
Educational Institute of Scotland. (2010). *Poverty and Education*. Edinburgh: EIS.
Elovainio, M., Pietikäinen, M., Luopa, P., Kivimäki, M., Ferrie, J.E., Jokela, J., Suominen, S., Vahtera, J., & Virtanen, M. (2011). Organizational Justice at School and Its Associations with Pupils' Psychosocial School Environment, Health, and Wellbeing, *Social Science and Medicine*, 73, 1675–1682.
ETUI and ETUC. (2011). *Trade Unions and the Fight Against Poverty and Social Exclusion*. Brussels: ETUI.
European Commission/EACEA/Eurydice. (2016). *Recommended Annual Instruction Time in Full-time Compulsory Education in Europe 2015/16*. Luxembourg: Publications Office of the European Union.
Fattore, T., Mason, J., & Watson, E. (2007). Children's Conceptualisation(s) of Their Wellbeing, *Social Indicators Research*, 80, 5–29.

General Teaching Council for Scotland. (2012). *The Standards for Registration: Mandatory Requirements for Registration with the General Teaching Council for Scotland*. Edinburgh: GTCS.

Gow, L., & McPherson, A. (1980). *Tell Them from Me*. Aberdeen: Aberdeen University Press.

Hall, D., Grimaldi, E., Gunter, H. M., Møller, J., Serpieri, R., & Skedsmo, G. (2015). Educational Reform and Modernisation in Europe: The Role of National Contexts in Mediating the New Public Management, *European Educational Research Journal, 14*(6), 487–507.

Hayward, L., Simpson, M., & Spencer, E. (2005). *Assessment is for Learning: Exploring Programme Success*. Edinburgh: Scottish Executive Education Department.

Hayward, L., & Spencer, E. (2010). The Complexities of Change: Formative Assessment in Scotland, *Curriculum Journal, 21*(2), 161–177.

HMIE. (2002). *Count Us In: Achieving Inclusion in Scottish Schools*. Edinburgh: Scottish Government.

HMSO. (1965). Teaching Council (Scotland) Act 1965.

HMSO. (1974). Education (Mentally Handicapped Children) (Scotland) Act 1974.

Hofman, R.H., Hofman, W.H.A., & Gray, J.M. (2008). Comparing Key Dimensions of Schooling: Towards a Typology of European School Systems, *Comparative Education, 44*(1), 93–110.

John-Akinola, Y.O., & Nic Gabhainn, S. (2015). Socio-Ecological School Environments and Children's Health and Wellbeing Outcomes, *Health Education, 115(3/4)*, 420–434.

Kane, J., Lloyd, G., McCluskey, G., Maguire, R., Riddell, S., Stead, J., & Weedon, E. (2009). Generating an Inclusive Ethos? Exploring the Impact of Restorative Practices in Scottish Schools, *International Journal of Inclusive Education, 13*(3), 231–251.

Khadka, S. (2013). Social Rights and the United Nations Child Rights Convention (UN-CRC): Is the CRC a Help or Hindrance for Developing Universal and Egalitarian Social Policies for Children's Wellbeing in the 'Developing World? *International Journal of Children's Rights, 21*, 616–628.

Learning and Teaching Scotland. (1999). *Curriculum for the Secondary Stages: Guidelines for Schools*. Dundee: Learning and Teaching Scotland.

Learning and Teaching Scotland. (2000). *Health Education; National Guidelines*. Dundee: Learning and Teaching Scotland.

Learning and Teaching Scotland. (2005). *Learning in 2(+) Languages: Ensuring Effective Inclusion for Bilingual Learners*. Glasgow: Learning and Teaching Scotland.

Learning and Teaching Scotland. (2006). *Focusing on Inclusion*. Glasgow: Learning and Teaching Scotland.

McLaren, J. (2007). *Index of Wellbeing for Children in Scotland*. Edinburgh: Barnardo's Scotland.

McLean, A. (2003). *The Motivated School*. London: Sage.

McLellan, R., & Steward, S. (2015). Measuring Children and Young People's Wellbeing in the School Context, *Cambridge Journal of Education, 45*(3), 307–332.

Murphy, D., Croxford, L., Howieson, C., & Raffe, D. (2015). *Everyone's Future: Lessons from Fifty Years of Scottish Comprehensive Schooling*. London: Trentham, Institute of Education.

OECD. (2007). *Quality and Equity of Schooling in Scotland*. Paris: OECD.

OECD. (2015). *Improving Schools in Scotland: An OECD Perspective*. Paris: OECD.

Scottish Central Committee on Guidance. (1986). *More than Feelings of Concern*. Dundee: Consultative Committee on the Curriculum.

Scottish Consultative Council on the Curriculum. (1994). *A Sense of Belonging*. Dundee: SCCC.

Scottish Consultative Council on the Curriculum. (1995). *The Heart of the Matter*. Dundee: SCCC.

Scottish Consultative Council on the Curriculum. (1999). *The School Curriculum and the Culture of Scotland*. Dundee: SCCC.

Scottish Education Department. (1965). *Circular 600: The Reorganisation of Secondary Schools on Comprehensive Lines*. HMSO.

Scottish Education Department. (1977). *Truancy and Indiscipline in Schools in Scotland*. HMSO.

Scottish Executive. (2001). *A Teaching Profession for the 21st Century*. Edinburgh: Scottish Executive.

Scottish Executive. (2003). *Educating for Excellence: Choice and Opportunity: The Executive's Response to the National Debate*. Edinburgh: Scottish Executive.

Scottish Executive. (2004). *A Curriculum for Excellence: The Curriculum Review Group*. Edinburgh: Scottish Executive.

Scottish Executive. (2005). *Happy, Safe and Achieving their Potential: A Standard of Support for Children and Young People in Scottish Schools*. Edinburgh: Scottish Executive.

Scottish Executive. (2006). *A Curriculum for Excellence: Progress and Proposals: A Paper from the Curriculum Review Programme Board*. Edinburgh: Scottish Executive.

Scottish Government. (2009). *UN Convention on the Rights of the Child: UK Concluding Observations 2008*. Edinburgh: Scottish Government.

Scottish Government. (2010a). *Building the Curriculum 5: A Framework for Assessment: Recognising Achievement, Profiling and Reporting*. Edinburgh: Scottish Government.

Scottish Government. (2010b). *Programme for International Student Assessment (PISA) 2009 Highlights from Scotland's Results*. Edinburgh: Scottish Government.

Scottish Government. (2012). *A Guide to Getting It Right for Every Child*. Edinburgh: Scottish Government.

Scottish Government. (2013). *UNCRC: The Foundation of Getting It Right for Every Child*. Edinburgh: Scottish Government.

Scottish Parliament. (2000). Standards in Scotland's Schools etc. Act 2000.

Scottish Parliament. (2004). Education (Additional Support for Learning) (Scotland) Act 2004.

Scottish Parliament. (2014). Children and Young People (Scotland) Act 2014.

SCRE Centre University of Glasgow (2005) Supporting pupils: A study of guidance and pupil support in Scottish schools. Available online at: http://www.gov.scot/Resource/Doc/36496/0023573.pdf.

Sebba, J., & Robinson, C. (2010). *Evaluation of UNICEF UK's Rights Respecting Schools Award*. Brighton: Universities of Sussex and Brighton.

Shah, H., & Marks, N. (2004). *A Well-Being Manifesto for a Flourishing Society*. London: The New Economics Foundation.

Tisdall, E.K.M. (2015). Children's Rights and Children's Wellbeing: Equivalent Policy Concepts? *Journal of Social Policy, 44*, 807–823.

Together. (2015). *NGO Alternative Report to the Committee on the Rights of the Child Implementation of the UN Convention on the Rights of the Child*. Edinburgh: Together (Scottish Alliance for Children's Rights).

Ungar, M., Ghazinour, M., & Richter, J. (2013). Annual Research Review: What is Resilience Within the Social Ecology of Human Development? *Journal of Child Psychology and Psychiatry, 54*(4), 348–366.

UNICEF. (2013). *Child Well-being in Rich Countries: A Comparative Overview, Innocenti Report Card 11*. Florence: UNICEF Office of Research.

Watson, C. (2010). Educational Policy in Scotland: Inclusion and the Control Society, *Discourse: Studies in the Cultural Politics of Education, 31*(1), 93–104.

Williamson, B. (2012). Effective or Affective Schools? Technological and Emotional Discourses of Educational Change, *Discourse: Studies in the Cultural Politics of Education, 33*(3), 425–441.

INDEX